Dayton's
MINNEAPOLIS

MODERN HOUSEWARES

Spring and Summer 1953

Schuneman's

The Young-Quinlan Co.
MINNEAPOLIS

Jandel's
ST. CLOUD

suits on the
American Plan
blouses included !

THE
Golden Age
of MINNESOTA
DEPARTMENT
STORES

Kristal Leebrick

The publication of this book was supported through a generous grant from the Atherton and Winifred (Wollaeger) Bean Fund for Business History.

www.mnhspress.org

The Minnesota Historical Society Press is a member of the Association of University Presses.

Manufactured in Canada

10 9 8 7 6 5 4 3 2 1

∞ The paper used in this publication meets the minimum requirements of the American National Standard for Information Sciences — Permanence for Printed Library Materials, ANSI Z39.48–1984.

International Standard Book Number
ISBN: 978-1-68134-097-5 (cloth)

Library of Congress Cataloging-in-Publication Data
Names: Leebrick, Kristal, 1958– author.
Title: Thank you for shopping : the golden age of Minnesota department stores / Kristal Leebrick.
Description: St. Paul, MN : Minnesota Historical Society Press, [2018] | Includes bibliographical references and index.
Identifiers: LCCN 2018022613 | ISBN 9781681340975 (hardcover : alk. paper)
Subjects: LCSH: Department stores—Minnesota—History.
Classification: LCC HF5465.U55 M554 2018 | DDC 381/.14109776—dc23
LC record available at https://lccn.loc.gov/2018022613

FRONTISPIECE, CLOCKWISE FROM UPPER RIGHT: *Minnesota Historical Society Collections. Christine Johnson. Peter Fandel. Via's Vintage, Minneapolis. Author's collection. Hennepin County Library.* FACING TITLE PAGE: Women's clothing window display, 1962. *Minnesota Historical Society Collections.* OPPOSITE: Dayton's fashion show, 1959. *Minnesota Historical Society Collections.* PAGE V: Appliance and television department at Donaldson's, circa 1965. *Minnesota Historical Society Collections.*

Contents

ENJOY THE ADVANTAGES OF A
DONALDSON'S – GOLDEN RULE
ABC CHARGE ACCOUNT...
Ask any sales person
FRIGIDAIR

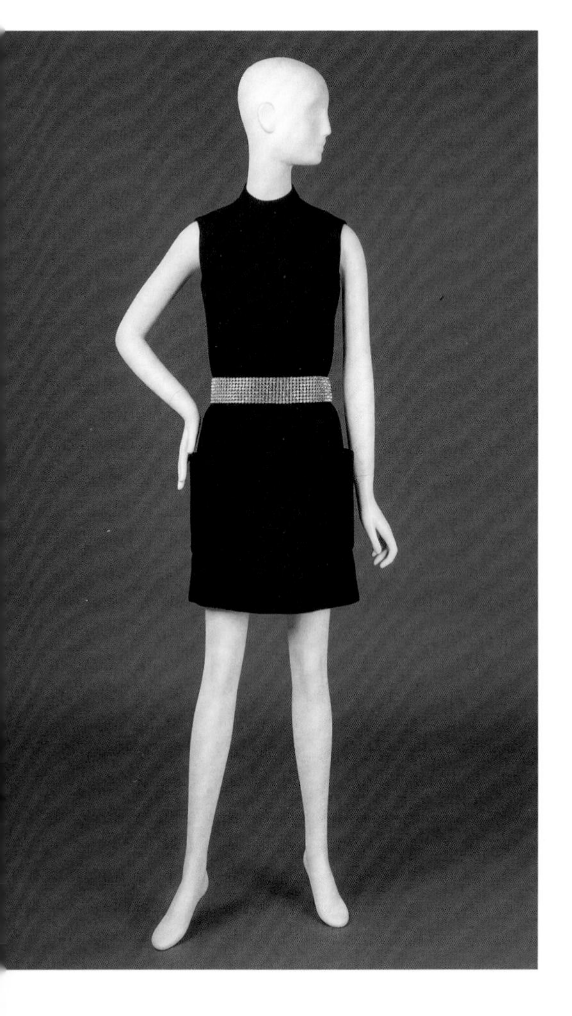

Dolores DeFore's top-three favorite items from her wardrobe: a black, high-neck dress with rhinestone belt by Norman Norell; a black jumpsuit by Oscar de la Renta; and a black wool crêpe dress with a brown-and-white feather trim by Geoffrey Beene. DeFore said she wore this latter dress on a number of occasions from 1970 to the 1990s. *Goldstein Museum of Design.*

Foreword

by Dolores DeFore

Back When We Touched the Merchandise before We Bought It

It is three in the afternoon, and I am leaving campus and friends to go to work at Dayton's. I have a part-time job selling at the hat bar. I hate leaving in the afternoon but need money, and it is a job. Once I get there, however, I love it. No longer is it a job; it is a challenge to see how much I can sell this day.

I sold hats behind a counter in the late 1940s. The hats were set on the counters amid many mirrors. A customer would try them on and could instantly tell whether she liked the way she looked. It was a time when many women wore hats, and often the customer would leave with more than one—an easy sell. It was fun to dialogue with the customer, as most wanted some affirmation that the hat looked great on her. I sold lots of hats, the managers liked me, and how lucky could I be to have such a fun job?

How different it is today. Hats are seldom worn, and selection is limited and available in only a few stores. Cold-weather headwear is available, but again, styles are limited and often lack fashion newness or direction. Fashion does dictate trends, but rarely do you see hats as a fashion "must-have."

Shopping changed when the suburban centers began to dominate consumer shopping in the 1950s and 1960s. It was much easier for the consumer to shop indoors and walk to many stores, both department stores and specialty stores. But now, as the days of shopping in downtown department stores has come to an end in the Twin Cities, suburban mall shopping is seeing a decline as internet shopping gains in importance. Shopping in front of your laptop is far less time consuming and often requires just a short wait for delivery, which in most cases is free.

Many consumers like this shopping method, as it works well for basic items, it saves the consumer time and energy, and the merchandise often can be returned by mail with no charge. Yet, internet shopping has its limits. Fashion apparel usually needs to be tried on, and success can be limited.

This is so different than what it was like when I started my college job at Dayton's. I have always felt that seeing and touching was important in a fashion merchandise sale.

I suppose the hat bar job was what sold me on retailing, and it has been a fun and exciting career. But I also had a few very lucky job assignments. There is an old adage about how important it is to be in the right place at the right time, and that certainly was true for me. Retailing was a great professional choice—lots of hard work, but it was so challenging and rewarding.

Dolores DeFore began her career at Dayton's and worked her way from the hat bar to buyer of junior dresses and sportswear to divisional manager of the Oval Room, then divisional manager of Juniors and Dresses before leaving to join Bob Dayton at Harold, a boutique clothier specializing in women's designer clothing. She retired from Harold in 1990 as president and co-owner.

Window displays at Christmastime were a popular attraction for shoppers of all ages. Here, Cinderella flees from the prince in a Dayton's window display in 1947. *Minnesota Historical Society Collections.*

Introduction

They Had (Almost) Everything You Needed

Sarah Massey's two older sisters often took the bus from their home in south Minneapolis to downtown in the late 1950s, baby dolls in hand, and headed to Dayton's, where the ten-year-old twins would take the escalator up to the furniture department and play house in the display rooms—until they were asked to leave. Then they'd wander to the fur department and play in the racks—until, again, they were asked to leave.

And every now and then, the sisters brought young Sarah on their excursions, which included popping in on their mom's best friend, Maude Peterson, who was secretary to Donald Dayton, president of the company at the time. Would she like to take them to lunch in the Sky Room? Of course she did, and those impromptu meals on the twelfth floor continued—until their mother found out and put a stop to it.

Years later, Massey showed up in Dayton's Oval Room to look for a dress to wear in her upcoming wedding. An art major at the University of Minnesota at the time, and a self-described hippie, she came to the store in her paint-and-plaster-splotched clothes and with the hundred dollars her mother gave her for the occasion. Despite her attire, "the salesperson was just wonderful," Massey said. "She treated me like anybody else, was polite and patient, and I ended up buying a beautiful navy blue Italian wool knit dress"—just like the Crissa Linea Italiana dress Mary Tyler Moore wore in an episode of her early-1970s show *The Mary Tyler Moore Show.*

Sarah Massey's wool wedding dress, by Crissa Linea Italiana. *Sarah Massey.*

Picture Panorama of the Store
ADJUSTMENTS
7th OFFICES · CREDIT DEPARTMENT · ADJUSTMENTS
5th NORTHWEST'S BIG ONE-FLOOR CHILDREN'S STORE
TAVERN SHOP
4th TEA ROOMS · SEA-FOOD GRILL · LOUNGE · CHINA · HOUSEFURNISHINGS
3rd DONALDSON VILLAGE · ORIENTAL and DOMESTIC RUGS · FURNITURE · DRAPERIES
BEAUTY SALON
2nd WOMEN'S & MISSES APPAREL · BEAUTY SALON · MILLINERY · SHOES · RIDING SHOP
PRESCRIPTIONS
Street ACCESSORIES · PRESCRIPTIONS · RENTAL LIBRARY · FLOWERS · FOOD · FOUNTAINETTE
Basement A COMPLETE STORE ON ONE FLOOR · SHOE SHINING · BEAUTY SHOP · LUNCHROOM

Richard Stryker sold women's shoes at the Powers branch store in Knollwood Plaza in the 1970s, as he worked his way through college. He was paid straight commission selling designer shoes by Garolini, Etienne Aigner, and Anne Klein, a job that turned out to be quite lucrative. He wasn't one of the "shoe dogs," the name the part-time salespeople called those who sold shoes full time during the week, and that was a good thing. "As part-timers, we had the best hours to sell—evenings and weekends," he said. "We made the most money on Saturdays." Each week, Stryker received his pay envelope containing his commission—in cash.

Mary Scanlon knew the downtown Minneapolis Dayton's phone number by heart as she raised her seven children through the early 1990s, and she used it often. The store's delivery service was "so prompt and daily," she said. "I had a bunch of kids at home. I don't know what I would have done without Dayton's."

For Attila Ray Dabasi's family, which emigrated from Winnipeg, Manitoba, to Minneapolis in 1969, when Dabasi was eleven years

OPPOSITE: Department stores were a place for one-stop shopping for all your needs, as shown on this Donaldson's menu cover from the 1930s. *Hennepin County Library.* THIS PAGE, TOP: A Donaldson's saleswoman helps a customer pick out a fur coat, 1951. ABOVE: Luxurious dining could be had at Dayton's Sky Room restaurant. *Both Minnesota Historical Society Collections.*

old, the downtown department stores played an important role in their new lives in the Twin Cities. They didn't have a car and relied on city buses. It was easier to take public transportation downtown than to the shopping centers in the suburbs. And those downtown stores had everything they needed. For Dabasi's boyhood appetite, that included Powers's "amazing" basement cafeteria.

Once upon a time, Minnesota's downtowns had *department stores,* where people shopped, worked, and gathered. Most began as dry goods stores in the late 1880s, offering yard goods and notions, boots and shoes, crocks and silverware, hardware, clocks, furniture, and often groceries. These businesses grew with their respective cities and offered floors and floors of merchandise. By the early twentieth century, department stores had become

shopping and cultural destinations. They were our village squares, our community institutions.

That began to change in the 1950s with what the late University of Minnesota historian Hy Berman called the "malling of Minnesota." As enclosed shopping centers took center stage in suburban communities and big box stores moved in, downtowns in small communities became smaller, and some disappeared. People shifted away from shopping at ma-and-pa shops, and the enclosed malls, which began with the opening of Southdale in the Minneapolis suburb of Edina in 1956, became the new village centers. "Soon it became clear there wasn't room for both," Berman said in an interview on Twin Cities Public Television's *Almanac* in late 1999. "What was gained at the mall was lost downtown."[1]

OPPOSITE, TOP: The shoe department at Powers Mercantile Company, 1922. *Minnesota Historical Society Collections.* BOTTOM: Department stores were an institution in cities and towns throughout Minnesota. Fandel's catered to St. Cloud shoppers for more than a century. *Peter Fandel.* THIS PAGE: The holidays were a particularly joyous time at Minnesota's department stores. Young-Quinlan is decorated for that festive time of year. Dayton's gift box. *Both Minnesota Historical Society Collections.*

Toiletries
Leather
Goods

Then came Amazon and online purchasing.

When Macy's announced in 2017 that it would close its downtown Minneapolis store—the last department store in Minnesota's largest city—no one was surprised. But it marked the end of an era. These large, multifloor establishments had been more than just places to buy a new suit or a set of dishes. They were the spots where you could hear a symphony concert, attend a lecture by a current author, buy a canoe for a trip to the Boundary Waters, see a foreign film, or just wander the aisles to catch up on fashion trends. They were the places people worked to get through college or held the career job that took them to retirement. Many of the families that established Minnesota's major department stores were the philanthropists who gave back to the communities

OPPOSITE: Dayton's transformed the main floor of its Minneapolis store into "Boulevard International," featuring a group of small shops made to replicate a European village, October 1958. THIS PAGE, TOP: The silk department at St. Paul's Emporium department store, 1915. *Both Minnesota Historical Society Collections.* ABOVE: Special events, like Dayton's Paris Flea Market, enhanced Minnesotans' shopping experience. *Hennepin County Library.*

by helping establish the orchestras, theaters, and beloved museums we still enjoy today.

Talk to anyone who shopped in Minnesota in the twentieth century, and they'll likely have a department store story that marks some rite of passage: the first prom dress, the first date, the airline ticket for that first trip to Europe, the first charge card.

There was a time when you could get almost anything you wanted at just one place: the department store. *Thank You for Shopping* is a little bit history, a little bit anecdote, a little bit scrapbook of that golden age of Minnesota-bred retail. Let's go shopping through some of these legendary stores.

OPPOSITE: High fashion was on display at this Young-Quinlan show in 1947. *Hennepin County Library.* THIS PAGE: The opening of Southdale shopping center in suburban Edina forever changed the face of retail. *Author's collection.*

DONALDSON'S
GLASS BLOCK

1

The Granddaddy of Minneapolis Retail: Donaldson's Glass Block

Al Boyce lists three takeaways from his post–high school job at Donaldson's in downtown Minneapolis: meeting chef Steve Wetoska, who made "the greatest walleye in the world" and would play a pivotal role in Boyce's career; learning the recipe for "one hell of a dessert"—an exquisite coconut-pineapple mousse; and meeting Maxine Engman.

Boyce was hired at Donaldson's in 1954 to work in the commissary, the top-floor kitchen where food was prepared for the store's restaurants: the North Shore Grill, the Garden Room, and the basement lunch counter. Working with him was Martha Engman, a quick-witted older woman he enjoyed visiting with when he took a break. Engman enjoyed Boyce, too, and invited him to stop by her south Minneapolis home anytime he was nearby. One day he did. Did she tell him she had a pretty daughter just a year younger than him? He can't recall, but the day he dropped in at the Engman home after a doctor's appointment in the neighborhood, he met Martha's daughter, Maxine.

Two years later, Al and Maxine were married. Eight years later, they had four children. And after nine years of working in the kitchens at Minneapolis's oldest department store at that time, Boyce would leave Donaldson's to work with Wetoska at Jax Café in Minneapolis and continue his career as a chef at several other notable Twin Cities restaurants.

Lynne Hartert's time at Donaldson's–Golden Rule wasn't as life changing as Boyce's, but landing a job in the hosiery department in downtown St. Paul in the late 1960s was a dream come true for her. She was a sixteen-year-old high school girl from suburban Cottage Grove, and she loved wandering through the capital city's downtown on her hour-long lunch breaks. And she remembers the crowds and the thrill of meeting actor and bridge champion Omar Sharif in 1970, when he came to the store to promote his book *How to Play the Blue Team Club*.

Donaldson's has been gone from the Twin Cities' downtowns and shopping malls since the mid-1980s, but for nearly a century, it was a major part of Minnesota's retail and cultural landscape. It all began when a couple of Scottish brothers came to town near the end of the nineteenth century.

OPPOSITE: Donaldson's Glass Block illuminated at night. THIS PAGE: Postcard view of Donaldson's Glass Block. *Both Minnesota Historical Society Collections.*

When William S. Donaldson's new Glass Block store opened in 1889, it was called "a marvel of construction" and a "revelation to Minneapolis." The five floors, elaborate stairways, elevators, and electric illumination of the new building were "a wonder." With its glass dome

Newspaper photo of the original Glass Block building, late 1800s. *Hennepin County Library.*

and vast stretch of plate-glass windows, the store was an elegant addition to Minneapolis when it opened at Sixth Street and Nicollet Avenue. The new store included an open interior courtyard lit by the rooftop dome that would make the 164-foot structure a tourist landmark. The store remained an anchor in Minneapolis retail for a century.[1]

A former draper's apprentice from Milnathort, Scotland, William Donaldson left his home country in 1878 for New York. His younger brother, Lawrence Stedman Donaldson, soon followed. By 1880, they had made their way to Minnesota, a part of the country then known as the Northwest. The brothers took jobs at Auerbach, Finch & Van Slyke, a St. Paul dry goods company, but within a year William opened his own business on Nicollet Avenue in Minneapolis. It was short-lived, however. After his lease ended, he found work at Colton and Company at Sixth Street and Nicollet, an area of the city that was still mostly residential. The Colton dry goods store was housed in a unique-looking one-and-a-half-story building named for its large number of plate glass windows: "the Glass Block Store." There weren't many other businesses in the area, and the lack of foot traffic eventually caused the store to close. Donaldson stayed on as a manager after another dry goods firm, Samuel Groucock and Sons, purchased it. When that store went out of business, the Donaldson brothers pooled their resources and bought it.

Gunpowder explosions burst from the rooftop at Sixth Street and Nicollet Avenue throughout the day on April 26, 1884, and free trolley rides brought the curious to the grand opening of the Donaldson brothers' new store.

An advertisement ran the next day in the *Minneapolis Sunday Tribune* thanking the public "for coming in such great numbers to our Grand Opening" and for "the very liberal way you spent your money on the many bargains we were offering." Those bargains included "fine double-width cashmeres" at twenty-three cents a yard, taffeta silk gloves at fifty-nine cents a pair, twenty-five-cent short dresses for infants, and a promise to have more slat-body baby buggies by the next Tuesday or Wednesday—a bargain at $10.50 apiece. Boots, fabrics, rattan rockers, dinner sets, and tea sets were all in the offering.

Within four years of the grand opening, the Donaldson brothers demolished the small Glass Block and in its place built a five-story "skyscraper" that included a basement. The store was expanded in 1891 with the addition of a 79-by-165-foot annex on Sixth Street. The new Glass Block employed 475 people, had 150,000 mail-order customers, and

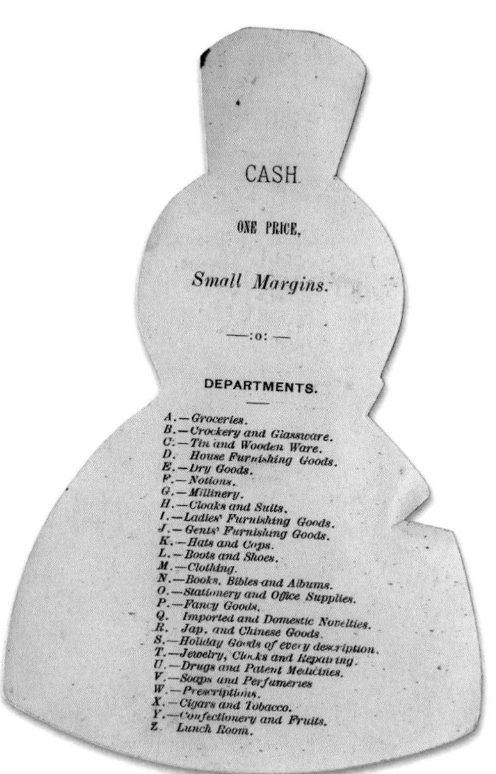

Trading card for Colton's. *Hennepin County Library.* SIDEBAR: Two long-term employees, Anna Cyphers (left) and Jack McCormick (right), are honored by Donaldson's managing director Ralph Waltz at the store's fifty-sixth anniversary party at the Nicollet Hotel. Cyphers joined the store in 1881 and McCormick had worked there forty-seven years when the *Minneapolis Tribune* took this undated photo. *Hennepin County Library.*

HELP WANTED

What was it like to work in a dry goods store in those early days? Following are the store rules at L. S. Donaldson Company from 1882, as reprinted in the store's employee newsletter, *Looking Thru,* in June 1930.

1. *This store must be opened at Sunrise. No mistake. Open 6 o'clock A. M. Summer and Winter. Close about 8:30 or 9:00 P. M. the year around.*
2. *Store must be swept, dusted, doors and windows opened, lamps filled, trimmed, and chimneys cleaned. Counters, base shelves and show cases dusted, pens made, a pail of water also the coal must be brought in before breakfast, if there is time to do it and attend to all the customers who call.*
3. *The store is not opened on the Sabbath day unless absolutely necessary, and then only for a few minutes.*
4. *Should the store be opened on Sunday the clerks must go in alone and get tobacco for customers in need.*
5. *The clerk who is in the habit of smoking Spanish Cigars, being shaved at the barbers, going to dancing parties and other places of amusement and being out late at night, will assuredly give his employer reason to be ever suspicious of his integrity and honesty.*

Men clerks are given one evening a week off for courting

6. *Clerks are allowed to smoke in the store provided they do not wait on women with a stogie in the mouth.*
7. *Each clerk must pay not less than $5.00 per year to the Church and must attend Sunday School regularly.*
8. *Men clerks are given one evening a week off for courting, and two if he goes to Prayer Meeting.*
9. *After the 14 hours in the store the leisure hours should be spent mostly in reading.*

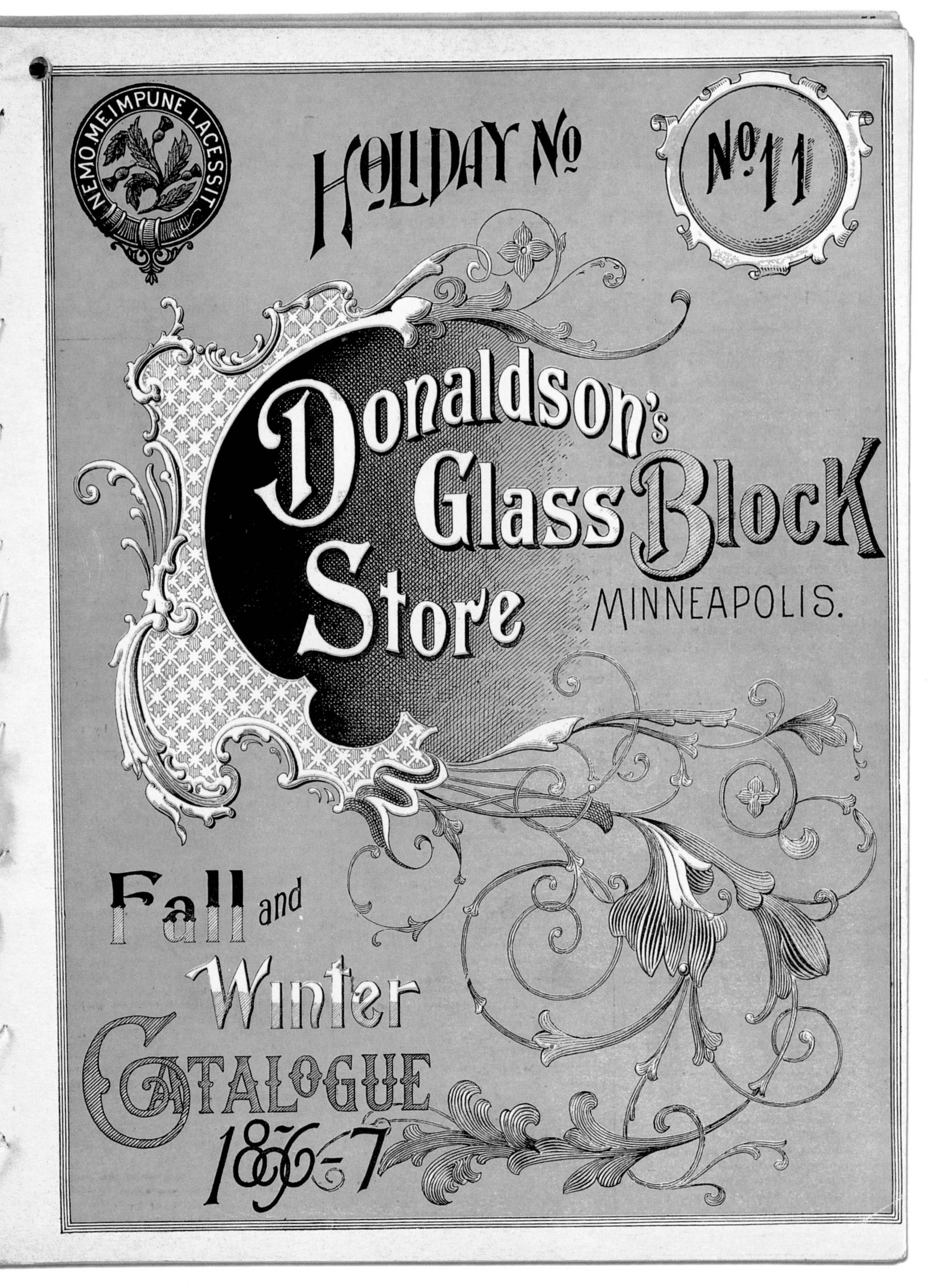
NEMO ME IMPUNE LACESSIT
HOLIDAY No
No. 11
Donaldson's
Glass Block
Store
MINNEAPOLIS.
Fall and
Winter
CATALOGUE
1896-7

6 WM. DONALDSON & CO., MINNEAPOLIS, MINN.

NO MATTER WHERE YOU RESIDE, North, East, West or South, wherever postage stamps are used or express goes, you will find it easy to buy of us.

CLOAK AND SUIT DEPARTMENT---Continued.

BETTER VALUES HAVE NEVER BEEN OFFERED THAN THESE.

48 Ladies' Close Fitting Jacket, made of two toned boucle cloth, storm collar, new shaped leeves, plaited back, shield front, trimmed with loop ornaments and buttons, fronts silk lined. Price, $15.00.

43 Ladies' Cape, made of fine seal plush, edged all around with fine quality thibet fur, lined throughout with silk serge, deep storm collar, very wide sweep. Price, $12.50.

51 Ladies' Double Cape, made of seal plush, edged with fine thibet fur, lined with fine serge, deep storm collar, very wide sweep. Price, $15.00.

52 Ladies' Jacket, made of fine kersey cloth, in black, navy, tan or havana, lined with best quality taffeta silk, front, collar and cuffs trimmed with strap trimming and silk velvet, plaited back, new shaped sleeves. Price, $25.00.

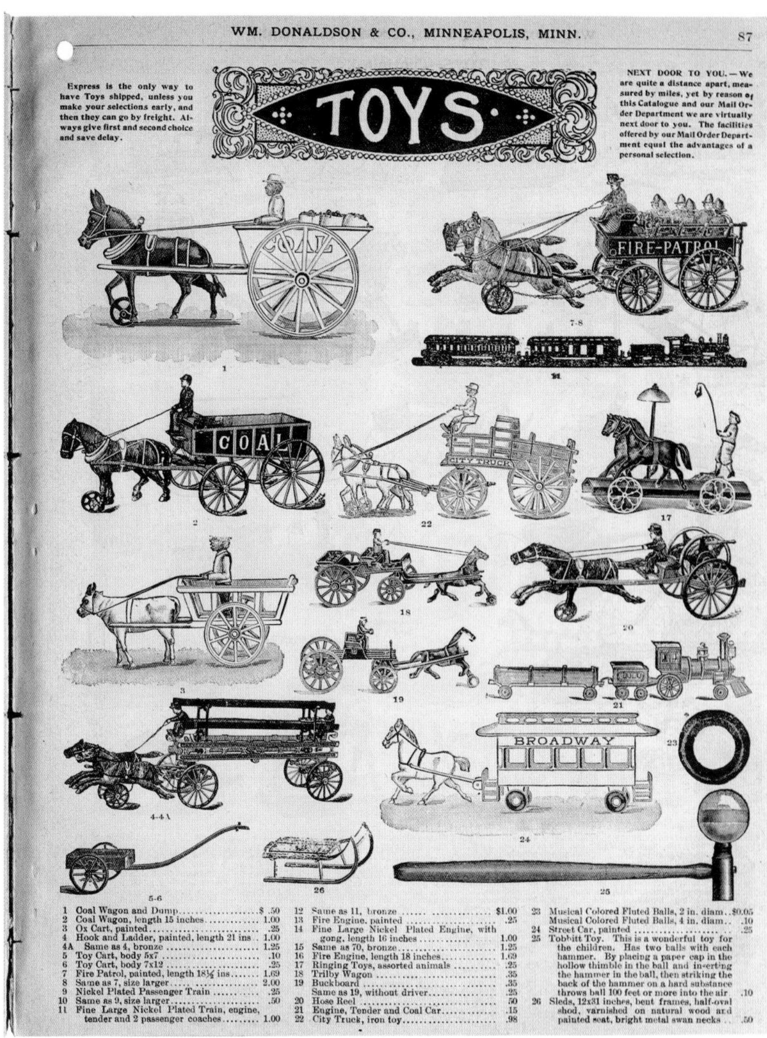

WM. DONALDSON & CO., MINNEAPOLIS, MINN. 87

Express is the only way to have Toys shipped, unless you make your selections early, and then they can go by freight. Always give first and second choice and save delay.

TOYS

NEXT DOOR TO YOU.—We are quite a distance apart, measured by miles, yet by reason of this Catalogue and our Mail Order Department we are virtually next door to you. The facilities offered by our Mail Order Department equal the advantages of a personal selection.

No.	Item	Price
1	Coal Wagon and Dump	$ .50
2	Coal Wagon, length 15 inches	1.00
3	Ox Cart, painted	.25
4	Hook and Ladder, painted, length 21 ins	1.00
4A	Same as 4, bronze	1.25
5	Toy Cart, body 5x7	.10
6	Toy Cart, body 7x12	.25
7	Fire Patrol, painted, length 18½ ins	1.69
8	Same as 7, size larger	2.00
9	Nickel Plated Passenger Train	.25
10	Same as 9, size larger	.50
11	Fine Large Nickel Plated Train, engine, tender and 2 passenger coaches	1.00
12	Same as 11, bronze	$1.00
13	Fire Engine, painted	.25
14	Fine Large Nickel Plated Engine, with gong, length 16 inches	1.00
15	Same as 70, bronze	1.25
16	Fire Engine, length 18 inches	1.69
17	Ringing Toys, assorted animals	.25
18	Trilby Wagon	.35
19	Buckboard	.35
	Same as 19, without driver	.25
20	Hose Reel	.50
21	Engine, Tender and Coal Car	.15
22	City Truck, iron toy	.98
23	Musical Colored Fluted Balls, 2 in. diam.	$0.05
	Musical Colored Fluted Balls, 4 in. diam.	.10
24	Street Car, painted	.25
25	Tobbitt Toy. This is a wonderful toy for the children. Has two balls with each hammer. By placing a paper cap in the hollow thimble in the ball and inserting the hammer in the ball, then striking the back of the hammer on a hard substance throws ball 100 feet or more into the air	.10
26	Sleds, 12x31 inches, bent frames, half-oval shod, varnished on natural wood and painted seat, bright metal swan necks	.50

had buying offices in New York, London, and Paris. By 1895, annual sales had reached $2 million.

While the brothers attributed their profitable business to their hard work and retail expertise, the fact that Nicollet Avenue was becoming the city's retail center contributed to their success.

The front-page headline in the *Minneapolis Tribune* on January 30, 1899, announced the death of fifty-year-old William Donaldson with the words "Death's Icy Touch." Donaldson died from heart failure while on vacation to California with his wife, Mary, and two of their five children. "In his death the community sustains a great loss," the newspaper read. "No man stood higher in

OPPOSITE: Donaldson's 1896–97 holiday catalog listed more than thirty departments and noted, "every department owned and controlled by us solely—none are sublet or farmed out to anyone." THIS PAGE, ABOVE: Donaldson's catalog pages from the 1890s. LEFT: Donaldson's, circa 1900. *All Hennepin County Library.*

L. S. Donaldson Company
Minneapolis

From the Customers Viewpoint

There can be no greater success for an institution than to win the confidence of the communities which it serves. It is the sum total of all other successes, great and small. It testifies to the long proven trustworthiness of the spoken and printed word; to an unswerving policy of upright and just dealing from the customer's viewpoint, and to the truism that no transaction is of benefit to the institution unless it is profitable to the customer. This is the aim and achievement of the L. S. Donaldson Company.

Free Check Rooms

may be found on the lower floor — (basement) here your packages or grips may be left without cost to you while you are shopping or going about your various missions.

The Mail Order Department

A special shopping service for out-of-town patrons—a branch of our service organization which keeps the Donaldson Store within easy reach of the suburban shopper—it literally brings this great store to the door, for a corps of experienced shoppers personally carry out the customer's bidding in a most conscientious and careful way. A reliable Fashion Style catalog is issued Semi-annually for the convenience of out-of-town patrons.

Register your name for a catalog with the Mail Order Department or with any clerk and let this great institution serve you when your home dealer cannot supply your needs.

L. S. Donaldson Company
Minneapolis

The Donaldson Beauty Shop

Scientific, Electric

Turkis
Swe
Marcel

Resting Rooms are Sp
Perfect

After a long auto
ing as a bath and s
these may be indulgec
his separate business.

One of the many e
able features is the ind
ual rest rooms in v
patients may rest for
length of time after t
ments.

Store brochure, 1917. *Hennepin County Library.*

public esteem or commanded greater respect in the commercial and social world in which he has for many years been a commanding figure."

Lawrence Donaldson, age forty-four, took the lead of the company through the next quarter century. He oversaw another store expansion in 1903, during which the Sixth Street annex was replaced with a taller building that matched the architectural style of the main building. In 1907, the company name was changed to L. S. Donaldson Company. By 1913, the store commanded the entire Nicollet Avenue block between Sixth and Seventh Streets.

The Glass Block was a Minneapolis tourist attraction, and the company published maps

displaying the best roads to the store and a guide to the store's departments and services. Such services included a US post office, a branch of the local telegraph company, the "Ask Mr. Foster Travel Service," a circulation library, a playroom supervised by a trained attendant where parents could leave their children while they shopped, a cold room for summer fur storage, the largest private telephone switchboard in Minneapolis open twenty-four hours a day, a greenhouse nearby on Portland Avenue that supplied fresh flowers and plants, a 772-foot-deep artesian well that supplied water for the store and all the Minneapolis public schools, and in summer, the Lake Minnetonka Motor Boat Express Delivery service for patrons who spent the warm months on the lake.

The store took care of its employees by offering a savings department, much like a bank, with 4 percent interest posted twice a year, and

A view of Donaldson's at the corner of Seventh Street and Nicollet Avenue, kitty-corner from Dayton's, 1922. *Photo by J. Kammerdiener, Hennepin County Library.*

Beauty shop at Donaldson's, 1915. *Minnesota Historical Society Collections.*

SEPARATION OF CHURCH AND BUSINESS

During the second decade of the twentieth century, the L. S. Donaldson Company was at the center of rumors alleging that the thirty-year-old store was firing employees who were members of the Masonic Order or Protestants and was hiring only Catholics.

The *Masonic Observer* investigated and found that one member of the local order of Masons had been discharged in January 1914, but thirty-two Masons were still employed at the store, and many of them were department managers. Three members of the Donaldson Company's board of directors also belonged to the fraternal order.

One year later, Mrs. S. W. Jacobs of Motley, Minnesota, sent a letter to L. S. Donaldson himself to clear up the rumor that had been swirling in her town: "L. S. Donaldson of Minneapolis, being a Catholic, will employ no one but Catholics to work for him." Mrs. Jacobs also asked if Donaldson would give her the numbers of Catholic and non-Catholic employees. Here is his response:

Dear Madam:
I am in receipt of your letter of May 4th, and am very glad to be able to reply that at no time in the history of this store, which I have been connected with and been manager of for practically thirty-two years, have we allowed a religious question to enter into our business affairs. I may state that we have nearly four Protestants to every Catholic in the house. We have never employed anyone or discharged anyone on account of their religious belief—we never ask an applicant their religion or their politics—it is a matter of pure business. All of the Directors of our company are Protestants—all the heads of departments except three are Protestants. It is absurd for anyone to think that an institution of this kind, as large as we are, would so far forget itself as to allow religion to enter into the business affairs.
—Yours truly, L.S.D.

in 1911, a profit-sharing plan was instituted for department heads. In 1913, the L. S. Donaldson Company launched a plan to buy homes to house single working women to draw more employees from rural Minnesota. The company cited the "lack of competent city girls to supply the needs of the large department stores," according to the June 7, 1913, *Minneapolis Morning Tribune*. "It is very difficult to get enough girls in the city just now, and this condition has existed for several months," Lawrence Donaldson told the paper. "It is also hard to hire girls from the country because when they come here they have no place to go and a big city is not desirable for a girl without friends or relatives with whom she may live." The company purchased a house at 233 Oak Grove Street that year, and it was ready for twenty occupants by September. The young women paid room and board, and a matron was in charge of the home at all times.[2]

The company's concern for the welfare of its employees extended to the community at large. Lawrence and his wife, Isabelle, who were devout Catholics, donated money and property to a number of church projects, including the building of a cathedral overlooking Minneapolis's Loring Park. In 1905, Donaldson presented the deed to the property at Sixteenth Street and Hennepin Avenue to Archbishop John Ireland, and three years later, the Cathedral of St. Mary was built. In 1926, the cathedral was designated by the church as a basilica (a Catholic church granted special ecclesiastical privileges), the first in the United States.

The store underscored its broader community role as a social center, as well as a business center, with a full-page advertisement in the *Morning Tribune* on Thanksgiving Day 1920 titled "Thankfulness," marking the store's thirty-eighth Thanksgiving: "The growth of this institution has always been steady and sure. From the small

Donaldson's *Looking Thru* employee newsletters. *Hennepin County Library.*

A PRACTICAL FAITH IN MINNEAPOLIS

On December 31, 1923, an editorial in the *Minneapolis Tribune* praised L. S. Donaldson and his department store company for its commitment to the city and its forward-thinking approach to business.

The plans of the L. S. Donaldson company looking to the rearing of a statelier and more commodious mercantile establishment on the site now occupied by the firm are significant of something more than growth of a private business enterprise from small to great and then to still greater proportions. They denote a vibrant and unshakeable faith in the future of Minneapolis and the Northwest.

Mr. Donaldson, who has been in business in Minneapolis for longer than two score years, has looked at close range as the city grew from 50,000 inhabitants to nearly nine times that number. The expansion has not been of the "boom" type, but steady, consistent and proportioned nicely to the demands of this great northwestern country for an adequate mercantile, commercial, industrial and financial center. Minneapolis has been fortunate in having men of vision, force and constructive ideals to shape its destinies and give direction to its physical development, and these men have been able to do great things in big ways because their dreams were given substance not merely by their own efforts, but by the nurturing economic forces of the country tributary to the city.

As Minneapolis has taken on stature in the past, it will continue to do in the future—steadily, sanely and in keeping with the agricultural and industrial development of the Northwest. In his plans, which are to be set in motion next month, Mr. Donaldson comprehends both the pearls of the present and the demands of the tomorrows in this community. This faith in the larger Minneapolis that is yet to be, and in the fixity and stability of its retail mercantile districts is to be expressed in deeds and visualized in towering structure of stone and steel. That there will be a widespread reflex of this faith in the general life and in the future casting of the city there can be no question.

The foresight of Mr. Donaldson is, we believe, the foresight of all who think of Minneapolis in adequate terms. There is much reason to believe the city and the far-flung country roundabout are entering upon a new period of expansion. Farming is to be placed on a firmer basis. There will be a steadier and surer flow of rural wealth. Industry will spread out to match agricultural and commercial development. Merchandising will take on greater scope. Minneapolis will wax as a receiving and distributing market. The stage for these larger activities must widen for the drama as it unfolds. That, we take it is the vision Mr. Donaldson has caught, and upon which he predicates his plans.

Catalog pages, 1922.
Hennepin County Library.

corner room of the Glass Block thirty-eight years ago to the city block of today is a story of building and expanding in response to the requirements of our patrons. Year after year we have grown; in reality one store after another has been added, for each of the stores that would ordinarily be called a department is a complete mercantile establishment, a division of a business center. . . . It is not only a business center, it is a social center—a meeting place, an institution."

In January 1924, L. S. Donaldson and Company announced plans for a new $6 million Glass Block building, but Lawrence did not live to see it come to fruition. On July 14, 1924, the *Minneapolis Daily Star* announced, "Death Takes L. S. Donaldson." The sixty-eight-year-old civic leader died from a heart attack after a two-month illness, leaving behind his wife and son, Lawrence. The *Star* ran a number of tributes from other leaders in the community, including remarks from his competitors: Elizabeth C. Quinlan, president of the Young-Quinlan Company; R. B. Gage, president of the Powers Mercantile Company; and George Draper Dayton, president of the Dayton Company.

"He was a progressive citizen whom the Northwest cannot well spare," Dayton wrote. "Mr. Donaldson's life was another illustration of what a boy can do and become. He became one of the foremost merchants of America by dint of hard work, patient industry and severe economy in his early years. In later life, he was able to give freely for many civic enterprises because he had learned the pleasure of giving. To him, it was no hardship to pass over his check when he knew the funds would help build up Minneapolis or enrich it in any appropriate way."

Four months after Donaldson's death, the new eight-story building was completed. The store was designed by the same architects who planned Marshall Field and Company in Chicago, Gimbels in New York, and Selfridges of London. Sitting atop the new building was the same glass dome that lit the interior court in 1889.

A three-day celebration was held in November to introduce the public to the "most attractive and best-arranged retail structure in the West." Festivities included an elaborate style show, a Minneapolis Symphony concert, tea served on several floors, and an Armistice Day program presented by the Donaldson Choral Club. A miniature German village complete with tiny people moving about its streets was displayed in the new toy department through Christmas. Another novelty was a duplicate in miniature of the Pillsbury flour mill that was operated by electricity. The radio department on the fifth floor hosted live broadcasts from WCCO.[3]

The new store boasted six elevators serving the eight floors and basement. Walnut woodwork, wainscoting, and paneling; mahogany floors; marble staircases; carpeted aisles; and "corridors and waiting rooms soft in luxurious colorings, mirrors reflecting the beauty of each department—all make the Donaldson store a joy to the visitor," reported the *Daily Star* on November 10.

L. S. Donaldson and Company joined Hahn Department Stores (the precursor to Allied Stores Corporation) in 1928. Donaldson's was one of twenty-two US department stores that would form a nationwide chain that included the

PEGGY WRITES ABOUT DONALDSON'S

In the 1920s, the *Minneapolis Sunday Tribune*'s Society section carried the column "Peggy Writes About Town Doings." In the November 16, 1924, edition, "Peggy" wrote about shopping in the "wonderful new building of the L. S. Donaldson Store."

I wonder if you were all as thrilled as I was at the opening of the new section of Donaldson's.

I know that I was one of the very first arrivals, and that every day this past week I have found something new to see and admire. . . . [W]hen one thinks of the completed Donaldson's a few years hence—well, it's breathtaking and makes you want to do a tremendous lot of bragging about your own hometown.

this is going to be one of the most popular places in town

I'm sure that the entrance of the new Arcade is the best place to meet friends for downtown appointments. I'll just wager that already many of you have used this for a meeting place. The aisles are so spacious here, and the crowds going through from one section to the other are so interesting, and the gorgeous wall displays offer fascinating diversions. And, by the way, aren't those wall cases works of art? I still stand and admire those beautiful matched woods.

And I was so impressed with the black display tables of the china department. Did you ever see anything so effective for the displaying of stunning table ware and artistic novelties of glass and pottery?

I can plainly see that this is going to be one of the most popular places in town to choose gifts for Christmas giving. It is such a spacious bright shop, so that making selections even in the midst of the Christmas rush will not be at all difficult.

On the entrance floor of the new section I was delighted with the fascinating displays of the new ideas of Costume Jewelry. Have you shopped here yet?

I suppose I'll see you one day this week, oh, say 'bout two-thirty o'clock on the entrance floor of Donaldson's Arcade—and we'll go shopping 'round.

DONALDSON'S DRESS CODE

The dress requirements for the Donaldson store's female employees in 1926 were listed in the company newsletter as "navy blue or black dresses of plain material, in a business-like style with conservative trimmings of white, gray, beige, flesh, or self-color. Dresses must have sleeves." Women were not to wear red fingernail polish, "excessive makeup," or long earrings, and hair was to be "neatly arranged." Coming to work in pin curlers was discouraged. Men had to have their hair neatly trimmed and their faces freshly shaven.

ABOVE: Street view, 1920s.
RIGHT: Women's dress department, circa 1925.
Both Minnesota Historical Society Collections.

ABOVE: Donaldson's fiftieth anniversary, 1931. OPPOSITE, CLOCKWISE FROM TOP RIGHT: Magazine advertisement, 1936. *Both Hennepin County Library.* Advertisement. *Minnesota Historical Society Collections.* Catalog, ca. 1920. *Hennepin County Library.*

Golden Rule, one of the leading stores in St. Paul at that time. Donaldson head Joseph Chapman told the press that the business had not been sold. Rather, the owners had acquired a large block of stock in the Hahn company and would retain the ownership of all the Donaldson's real estate. The merger enhanced the ability of Donaldson's to buy goods at lower prices and sell them at lower prices to the consumer. Each store in the Hahn group would operate under its own name and maintain its own management.

Three years later, Donaldson's celebrated its fiftieth anniversary with "an exterior lighting system that turned the entire building into a vivid and dramatic color pattern," according to the August 28, 1931, *Minneapolis Tribune.* Spectators packed Nicollet Avenue for several blocks, bringing motor traffic to a standstill. Mayor William Anderson had the honors of pressing the gold button that ignited "the most complete outdoor lighting composition ever attempted west of New York." Streetlights on Nicollet Avenue were dimmed and "more than a hundred floodlights poured alternating shafts of amber and green color onto the sides of the building. From the roof, seven searchlights cut through the night, their beams visible for miles. The glass dome on the Sixth Street corner of the building became luminous with amber and red lights, and over the main marquee a jeweled panel of incandescent bulbs flashed into color."

The "art composition in light" was designed by Edward Tilson, who was chair of the lighting committee for the 1933 Chicago World's Fair. Signs over the main marquee and at the Seventh Street corner of the store read "Fifty Golden Years."

"When all the lights were on enough electrical current was being consumed to light 182,500 homes, or enough for the needs of 730,000 people," the *Tribune* reported.

"Tonight," explained Donaldson president S. V. Silverthorne, "we look into the future to

(continued on page 16)

“MAKING HOME LIFE MORE ATTRACTIVE TO THOSE OF MODEST MEANS”

William A. French’s masterpieces were installed in homes in Cuba, South America, the Philippines, Canada, throughout the United States, and in Minnesota, where he started a small furniture shop in St. Paul in the late 1800s. His work was exhibited at the Metropolitan Museum of Art in New York City, and he worked with Thomas Edison in building furniture cabinets for Edison’s new phonograph. He was known for his reproductions of centuries-old carvings made from plaster casts of pieces in London museums and the Metropolitan Museum of Art. But the work W. A. French valued the most was “providing better things to modest homes.”

“Making home life more attractive has been a recognized social necessity for years,” French told the *Minneapolis Journal* upon his retirement in June 1932. “I have tried to do my part to provide furniture of such character as to contribute to the physical beauty of the home. The owner of a small home today may choose furniture of the sort which a few years ago was enjoyed only by the person of considerable means. It was my idea to build furniture of true heirloom character at prices well within the reach of the modest purse.”

When he retired, French sold his retail furniture and decorating store, along with its five floors of art treasures, rugs, lamps, mirrors, and draperies, to the L. S. Donaldson Company. All of it was transferred from French’s store at Marquette Avenue and Eighth Street to Donaldson’s, and French played the part of host to friends and customers during the sale of his stock by Donaldson’s.

French died at age seventy-eight in February 1942. Though he had sold his stock to Donaldson’s ten years before, he continued to design interiors and furnishings for dwellings. He and his wife, Fannie, lived at the Leamington Hotel in downtown Minneapolis but kept a summer home at Marine on St. Croix.

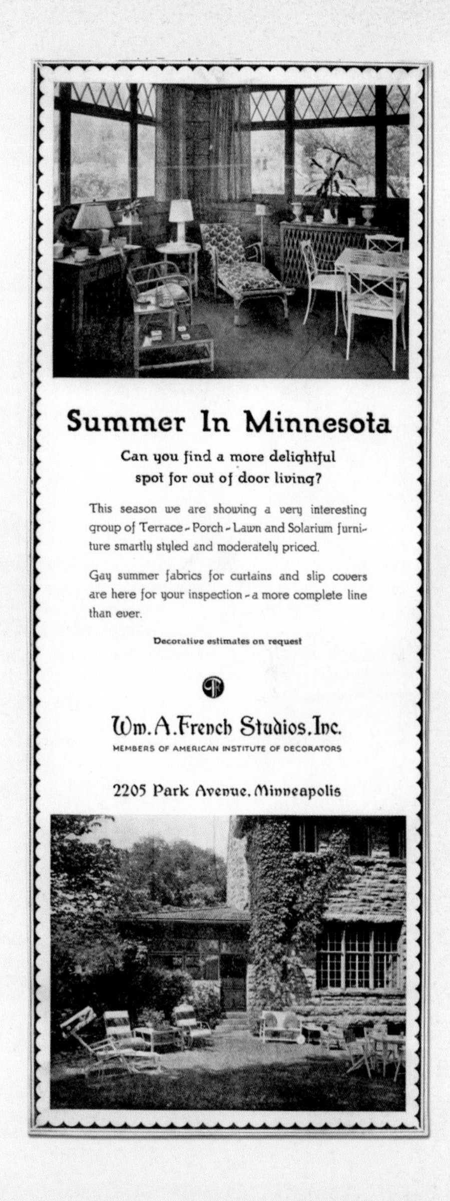

SHE HAD TO HAVE THAT HAT

On November 15, 1940, the *Minneapolis Star* reported that a woman, who caught a ride in an ambulance, made a quick trip into Donaldson’s to buy a hat:

“The clerks were in their places, but customers were few this morning when an ambulance drew up outside Donaldson’s store and a young woman alighted,” the news clip said. “She strode rapidly to the millinery department, hurriedly selected a $7.50 felt hat and presented a $100 check for payment. The transaction completed, she quickly left the store, after she explained, ‘I just had to have this hat for tonight.’”

CLOCKWISE FROM UPPER LEFT: Donaldson's cosmetic counter, 1957. *Minnesota Historical Society Collections.* Women modeling Donaldson's fashions, 1947; Catalog page, 1960s; A boy gets a haircut at Donaldson's barbershop, 1940s—*all Hennepin County Library.* Main floor of Donaldson's Minneapolis store, 1965. *Minnesota Historical Society Collections.* Donaldson's Basement Food Shop; Children's department at Donaldson's, circa 1940—*both Hennepin County Library.*

At heart every man's a stay-at-home . . . keep him there

77 — All Wool Plaid Robe by Wise. Handsome muted block laid in Springfield's fine quality wool. Full cut. Choose ine, blue, brown. Sizes S, M, L, XL. **$16.95**

B77 — Our exclusive Hardwick Terrycloth Robe. Rich, absorbent, thick-'n-thirsty washable terry that's generously full cut for easy fit. White, blue, maize. S, M, L, XL. **$9.98**

77 — Finely Tailored Vicara Tartan triped Robe by Wise. Ideal weight for ear round wear. Cashmere-like Vicara ashes like a dream. In authentic regiental stripes — Macqueen (red) or ampbell Dress (blue), shown above. izes S, M, L, XL. **$15.95**

D77 — Vicara Tartan Plaid Robe by Wise. Luxurious Vicara is completely washable. In handsome authentic tartan plaids. Campbell Dress (blue), MacDonald (green), Macqueen (red), shown above. Comes in sizes S, M, L, XL. **$15.95**

E77 — Fine Quality, Imported Tartan Plaid Terrycloth Robe by State-O-Maine. Handsome, comfortable, heavy-weight imported terry. Full cut, expertly tailored. Choose from popular colors of blue, red and gold. Comes in sizes S, M, L, XL. **$20.00**

77

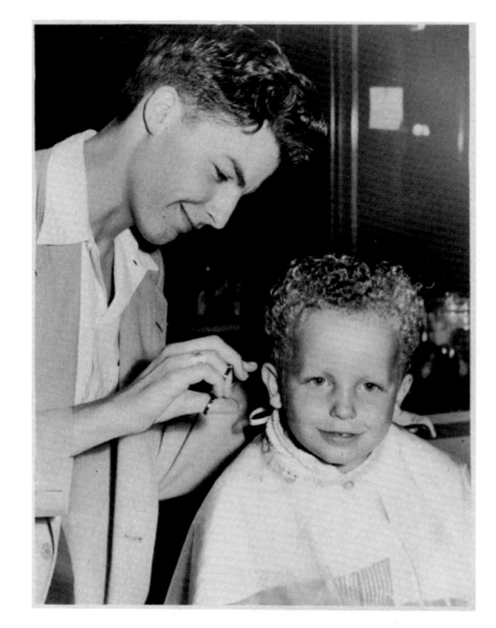

ABOVE LEFT TO RIGHT: The iconic Donaldson's dome comes down in spring 1942. *Minnesota Historical Society Collections.* "Patriotic Concert" at Donaldson's in support of the war effort, 1942. *Hennepin County Library.*

celebrate the past by using one of the greatest forward steps in the progress of civilization—light. Light is our theme in celebrating the progress of the past and the progress to come." The lights were kept in action until eleven o'clock each night through the week. The anniversary celebration also included a display of five full-size model homes erected on the third floor of the store. Each house represented a distinct type of architecture and was filled with furnishings.

In spring 1942, the country was in the throes of World War II, and on March 30, the *Minneapolis Star Journal*'s top three headlines announced: "Nazis Claim Ship Carrying U.S. Arms to Russia Sunk in Battle," "Chinese Units Capture Two Burma Towns," and "Donaldson Store Dome Is Doomed." A decade after Donaldson's illuminated its iconic steel dome to celebrate a half century of business, the Minneapolis landmark came down to be turned into war materials.

The war officially ended on September 2, 1945, and the next day, the L. S. Donaldson Company announced a three- to four-year "complete modernization plan" that would include "a huge motor ramp running through the entire store." In other words, the company was installing an escalator, along with new elevators and air conditioning throughout the store. A new façade was also in the plans, and when it was finished, most of the windows that gave the Glass Block its name were covered with Bedford limestone.

Donaldson's began expanding to other locations in the 1950s. Its first branch was in Rapid City, South Dakota, and it opened its second branch in the Miracle Mile shopping center in Rochester, Minnesota, in 1953. Donaldson's opened a third branch in 1956 in Southdale, the Edina shopping center that made history as the

nation's first indoor mall.

In July 1961, Allied announced the merger of Donaldson's and the Golden Rule, St. Paul's oldest department store, located at Seventh and Robert Streets. Donaldson's stores in downtown Minneapolis, Southdale, Rochester, and Rapid City, as well as the Golden Rule in St. Paul, were all renamed Donaldson's–Golden Rule. T. R. Brouillette, a Tower, Minnesota, native and University of Minnesota graduate who had been president at Donaldson's before being called to New York to work as vice president of Allied, came back to Minnesota to lead Allied Stores' new regional office in Minneapolis.

This store combination was following a retailing trend toward strong multiunit operations, Brouillette told the *Minneapolis Tribune* on July 27, 1961. Allied kept the Donaldson's–Golden Rule name until 1970.

TOP: Donaldson's at Southdale shopping center. ABOVE: Exterior view of the remodeled Donaldson's building, 1940s. *Both Hennepin County Library.*

Do you try harder when you're No. 2? That's the question a Donaldson's customer posed to store management in December 1968. Donaldson's was placing a new emphasis on fashion in all of its retail lines, adding new merchandise, creating a more interesting advertising campaign, going after the teen market, and increasing children's programs. After attending a store breakfast with Santa and a special holiday play put on by Minneapolis high school students with help from the Guthrie Theater—a smash hit according to local papers—one mom wrote to John Butterfield, who had been named president of the company in May: "Tell me Donaldson's, are you like Avis? Do you try harder because you are No. 2?"

No. 1, of course, was the store across the intersection of Nicollet and Seventh: the trend-savvy Dayton's, which had been ramping up its marketing and special events dollars through the 1950s and 1960s, opening an eighth-floor auditorium for dances, concerts, and fashion shows in 1963, and making headlines by being the first store in the country to carry the London "Youthquake" fashions in 1965 and hosting a visit from British fashion sensation Twiggy in 1967.

OPPOSITE: Pages from Donaldson's 1976 catalog. "Courtesy Days" promotion, early 1970s. *Both Hennepin County Library.*

The competition apparently didn't faze Butterfield. "There are many things Donaldson's can do that Dayton's can't because they're so big," Butterfield told the *Minneapolis Star* on December 23, 1968. A highly competitive situation was healthy for both stores, he said and emphasized that Donaldson's was not trying to be another Dayton's. He wanted each Donaldson's store to have a distinct personality that reflected the community that shopped there.

Donaldson's did one-up Dayton's in 1968, when it landed a partnership with New York teen magazine *Charlie*, which was issued through key stores around the country and used those stores' advertising. *Charlie* had a Twin Cities circulation list of twenty-five thousand, and a subscription included a record that had a popular song on one side and local teen information on the other with each issue. The *Charlie* contract was a coup for Donaldson's, as Dayton's tried to get the contract and failed.

Donaldson's opened stores at Rosedale shopping center in Roseville in 1969 and at Ridgedale in Minnetonka in 1975. In 1979, James Black Company stores in Waterloo and Cedar Falls, Iowa, were added to the Allied brand and gave Donaldson's a total of nine stores. In 1980, Donaldson's moved its St. Paul store from Seventh

DONALDSON'S BLOOMS

Dayton's wasn't the only department store to put on a flower show. In 1957, Donaldson's presented "Fantasy of Flowers," drawing thousands to the fifth floor of its Minneapolis store. Members of the American Carnation Society, along with the Twin City Florists and Donaldson's, created fairy-tale and holiday displays composed mainly of carnations, including scenes from Hansel and Gretel, Cinderella, and Red Riding Hood. Table settings, holiday decorations, wedding backgrounds, and corsages were all part of the show, which used some forty-five thousand carnations in more than fifty varieties.

THOUSANDS SEE FANTASY OF FLOWERS

The Digest has been delayed this month so that we can publish the story on this page.

The exhibit, "Fantasy of Flowers" drew thousands of people in the three-day period (February 28 – March 2) it was shown on our Fifth floor. "Hansel and Gretel" (left) was one of the many framed fairy-tale scenes composed mainly of carnations. Table settings representing social events, such as the bridal tea, (left, below) flanked the center lane. Farther down the lane were scenes depicting holidays. The Easter scene is shown below, right.

All of this was accomplished through the combined efforts of the American Carnation Society, the Twin City Florists and Donaldsons. Pictured below is the activity on fifth floor the night before the show opened.

4

RIGHT: Article about the Donaldson's "Fantasy of Flowers" exhibit in the employee newsletter, 1957. *Hennepin County Library.*

OUT OF THE BLUE AND INTO THE BLACK

At the stroke of noon Sunday, March 24, 1968, the doors to Dayton's and Donaldson's at Southdale and Brookdale shopping centers opened to thousands of shoppers and to a new chapter in retailing history in Minnesota.

The Minnesota Supreme Court had just ruled that a Sunday closing law passed by the state legislature in 1967 was unconstitutional. That brought an end to a long-held "blue law"—despite protests by area clergy, many of whom said they were more worried about "the rights of the working man" than whether or not it would hinder church attendance.

The parking lots at the two Dales were overflowing that Sunday in March, and the stores saw twice the number of shoppers

The parking lots at the two Dales were overflowing that Sunday in March, and the stores saw twice the number of shoppers than most saw on a normal shopping day. One woman at the Brookdale Dayton's told a *Minneapolis Tribune* reporter that the crowds made it feel "like a country fair."

Reporters spoke with shoppers who had driven in from as far away as Rochester, and many of those strolling the aisles with their families said that shopping on Sunday was convenient.

The JCPenney stores at both centers were closed that day, but a young man sat in the darkened store window at the Southdale store tallying figures on a clipboard as customers wandered past on their way to the competition. Stores were also shuttered in downtown Minneapolis, except for Walgreens drugstore and Arts International, a Nicollet Avenue store that sold "works by talented young artists from all parts of the world."

Leo Weisberg, who had sold papers downtown since 1918, told *Minneapolis Tribune* columnist George Grim that all stores should be open on Sunday. "I think they will," he said. "I remember when old man Dayton wouldn't have a light in his display windows on Sundays. So times change, don't they?"

Grim wrote that he table-hopped in Walgreens, which was doing a big Sunday noon budget meal business. "Unscientifically, I concluded that if you were under 25, you wanted all the stores open. If you were over that, the Sunday selling split of hawk and dove turned up. And as you approached the 60s, you wanted to amble, look, but not be able to buy."

ABOVE: Artist's rendering of the Donaldson's Rosedale store. *Hennepin County Library.* OPPOSITE: Donaldson's charge card. *Minnesota Historical Society Collections.* Christmas catalog, 1985. *Hennepin County Library.*

and Robert Streets to the Town Square complex on Cedar and Sixth Streets.

Donaldson's marked its centennial in September 1981 with a twelve-foot-high cake served to all comers in the IDS Center Crystal Court in downtown Minneapolis, a "100 years of Style" fashion show in the downtown store, and an appearance from *Today Show* weatherman Willard Scott at the store in Rosedale.

One year later, in August, Donaldson's opened its new flagship store in Minneapolis's City Center. Minnesota governor Al Quie cut the ribbon and Radio City Music Hall's Rockettes entertained the crowd. Donaldson's celebrated for twelve days with fashion shows, cooking demonstrations, live zoo animals in the children's department, and an appearance by Olympic medalist Bruce Jenner in Men's Activewear.

Just three months after the new store opened, the now-empty "Glass Bock" at Sixth Street and Nicollet Avenue was destroyed by a fire on Thanksgiving Day. The fire started in the evening on the Sixth Street side of the building. Demolition to the old store had begun a week earlier. The fire also destroyed the Northwestern National Bank building, where Charles Lindbergh's 1920s Curtiss JN-4 "Jenny" biplane hung in an exhibit on the skyway level. The plane was saved, and the bank made plans to build the 774-foot tower, now called the Wells Fargo Center.

It took 130 firefighters nearly twelve hours to stop the flames from spreading, according to the *Star Tribune*. Damage was estimated at $75 million. One month later, two boys, ages twelve and thirteen, were charged with starting the fire. Police said the boys crawled through a hole in a snow fence that surrounded the demolition site, climbed up a pile of rubble, and reached the second floor of the building, breaking through a plywood door to get inside. The boys used an acetylene torch they found at the demolition site to start the fire.

In June 1985, Allied Stores Inc., Donaldson's parent company, announced that it would buy the six suburban Twin Cities Powers stores, a move that would create a merged chain that included twelve Twin Cities department stores. Donaldson's acquisition of the Powers stores would give a powerful boost to the company and put Donaldson's stores in six additional Twin Cities shopping centers: Northtown Center in Blaine, Knollwood Mall in St. Louis Park, Highland Park in St. Paul, Burnsville Center, Eden Prairie Center, and Maplewood Mall.

Despite that acquisition, Donaldson's one-hundred-year run came to an end just a year later. Campeau Corporation of Canada bought Allied, and in 1986, Carson Pirie Scott and Company of Chicago bought Donaldson's from Allied–Campeau Corporation for $163.5 million. Carson Pirie Scott, itself a century-old operation, came into the Minnesota and Iowa stores hoping to bring more than just a new name to Donaldson's. The company added more eye-catching mannequins, more designer names, and more fashion in the moderate to upper-moderate price area. Those stores never performed well, however. In 1995, Carson's sold eight of its nine Twin Cities stores to the Dayton Hudson Corporation, which converted them to the mid-level Mervyn's. The store at Ridgedale was used to expand the existing Dayton's store. One shopper accused Dayton's of "trying to monopolize the marketplace."[4]

Nine years later, the former Dayton Hudson Corporation, now the Target Corporation, closed its Twin Cities Mervyn's stores and sold the chain.

DONALDSONS
17 783 07
MR D M CODDINGTON
A unit of Allied Stores Corporation

POWERS
POWERS

2

Always No. 3: Powers Dry Goods Company

In 1972, Powers Dry Goods Company—long the third-largest department store operation in Minneapolis—announced its plans to more than double its floor space and its hopes of doubling its sales volume by 1976.

The eighty-year-old store's ambitions were "not primarily concerned with challenging Donaldson's for the No. 2 spot," wrote *Minneapolis Tribune* reporter Charles B. McFadden.

"Anybody would rather be No. 2 than No. 3," said Powers president Alden R. Berman in an interview with McFadden, "but that's not our driving ambition." What the company really wanted, Berman said, was to be "the best damn store of our type and size in the area" and to add four branch stores by 1976.

At the time, retail insiders claimed Powers's annual volume was nearly $25 million, compared to Donaldson's at $50 million and Dayton's at $180 million.[1]

Powers was No. 2—once. In 1881, the same year William Donaldson and Company began advertising its bargain prices in Minneapolis newspapers, a man named M. D. Ingram opened the store that would later be known as Powers at 215 Nicollet Avenue, in the heart of the Minneapolis shopping district.

Norwegian immigrant Seaver E. Olson joined Ingram the next year, and the business was named Ingram-Olson Company. In 1887, Ingram died and the company name was changed to S. E. Olson Company.

After a decade of successful business, a new three-floor store opened in September 1893 at the corner of Fifth Street and First Avenue South (which later became Marquette Avenue). The September 24, 1893, *Sunday Tribune* ran a three-column-wide sketch of the new "dry goods emporium," and the headlines announced, "Epoch in the Business World: All Day a Stream of People Passed Within the Spacious Portals Pleased With All They Saw."

> *The whole building is equipped with every modern appliance, and from the roomy cage elevators, run by electricity, which ply between the department floors, to spacious mailing rooms in the upper story, there is nothing lacking for the comfort of patrons or employees. . . . Long lines of tables are weighted with the finest of china and crockery and an endless assortment of the best in the market is displayed in attractive fashion. . . . Lamps and house furnishings occupy a prominent position, and a picture department contains choice and interesting works of art, together with all necessary appliances for framing and hanging an etching or engraving.*

Installed next to the grand staircase were two large electric elevators, a novelty that was recently introduced in Chicago at the World's Fair. The main floor featured a boot and shoe corner that displayed footwear "in all conceivable styles"; a confectionery counter, with plans to add a soda fountain later; and laces, ribbons, "black goods," silks, hosiery, and underwear. Halfway up the staircase to the second floor, a gallery opened to a nursery with an attendant in charge, another innovative service introduced earlier that year at the Children's Building at the

OPPOSITE: Powers Department Store in Minneapolis, 1937. *Minnesota Historical Society Collections.*

A BRILLIANT SHOW OF SPRING HATS

MARCH 22, 1906, MINNEAPOLIS JOURNAL— The Powers Mercantile Company held its opening of spring millinery yesterday, and even the disagreeable March wind did not prevent hundreds of feminine shoppers from visiting the handsome department.

Hats of every description and for every occasion were shown, and the styles are so many and varied that there can be no excuse for any woman wearing an unbecoming hat this season.

One of the charming modes shown by Powers is the "Shepherdess," an exact reproduction of the quaint drooping hats, with garlands of flowers, seen in old engravings of fifty years ago.

The most distinctive feature of the new hats is the crown and the extreme tilt the wide bandeau at the back gives. Some of the popular crowns are the low, round derby, the mushroom, similar to the derby but larger; the large tam and the high square crown which was worn several years ago. The brims are mostly short in front and the backs both broad and long.

Another fetching mode shown yesterday is called the Marie Antoinette, copied from the headgear always worn by the ill-fated queen. Nearly all the mourning bonnets will be made in this design.

Never before has the millinery had so wide a scope in trimmings, nor have the materials used been so beautiful in weave and texture. Flowers, lace tulle, handsome ribbons, wings and even the birds which have heretofore been left to winter millinery are used in both the street and dress hats; nor need the bird-lover protest, for they are all made birds.

A handsome imported hat shown yesterday was made of white horsehair braid and folds of soft white silk. The broad back turned up with a mass of pink and white roses and fluffy bow of pink ribbon. . . . One imported model was of lavender chip, completely covered with lilacs of various tints of lavender. Underneath the brim was a wide bow of the lavender maline, a fluffy bow of brown maline, adding a touch of daring and originality. . . . A number of jaunty sailors and the ever-popular turbans were shown for the women who prefer the simple hat for street wear.

Minnesota Historical Society Collections.

World's Fair. One of the main attractions to the second floor: "a muslin underwear department," according to the *Tribune* writer.

"The dawn of a new era of prosperity is fitly ushered into the portals of the Olson emporium," concluded the *Tribune* reporter.

The Olson emporium did prosper. By 1898, the company had absorbed the stock of a half dozen Nicollet Avenue stores that went out of business. Just four years later, on New Year's Day 1902, Minneapolis newspapers announced that Seaver Olson had retired, and the S. E. Olson Company was now the Powers Mercantile Company.

The New York firm H. B. Claflin Company had bought the company and named Alonzo J. Powers president. Powers started his career at Field-Leiter Dry Goods in Chicago, the precursor to Marshall Field's, and then came to St. Paul, where he operated the Powers Dry Goods Company for nearly two decades. He sold his

ABOVE: Card for S. E. Olson Company, "the bargain house of the Northwest." Postcard view of Powers Mercantile Company. *Both Hennepin County Library.*

TOP: Olson's interior, 1897. ABOVE: Powers interior, 1905. LEFT: Exterior view of Powers Mercantile, 1906.
All Minnesota Historical Society Collections.

interests in St. Paul before joining the new Minneapolis venture. His son, Fred E. Powers, was named vice president of Powers Mercantile and assumed active management.

Downtown Minneapolis saw record growth in 1906. Prominent among the new buildings was the four-story Powers Mercantile building at the northeast corner of Nicollet Avenue and Fifth Street. The cost of construction was estimated at $130,000.

The H. B. Claflin Company collapsed in 1914, and the New York–based Associated Dry Goods Corporation took control of the store. The Powers name stayed, even after both Alonzo and Fred Powers left the company by the end of 1915.

In 1929, Powers Mercantile purchased a ninety-nine-year lease on the property at Nicollet Avenue and Fifth Street. The store launched a $500,000 remodel that included removing the twenty-seven-year-old food departments in the basement of the building to make room for a $75,000 luncheonette that would have the capacity to serve eight hundred people an hour. The luncheonette was built with Italian marble and Monel steel, a forerunner to stainless steel.

The first "moving stairway" in Minneapolis

POWERS

Nicollet Avenue at Fifth street to First Avenue south, Minneapolis

"Tussorah" rough silk.

Exclusive agents for the genuine.

WHEN "Tussorah" was first put on the market it was promptly imitated—but unsuccessfully. It is in a class by itself, and is the best and most satisfactory "rough" silk in America today.

We are exclusive sale agents in Minneapolis, and the genuine has the name "Tussorah" stamped on selvage. We have it in white, ivory, cream, light blue, pink, lavender, old rose, gray, Copenhagen, Alice, reseda, tan, natural, sapphire, five shades of brown, dark green, four shades of navy, and in black.

Use "Tussorah" Silks for walking suits, evening and afternoon gowns, children's frocks, separate skirts and waists. Here only--at per yard....... **$1**

OUR SILK DEPARTMENT—HEADQUARTERS FOR SILKS

Powers Mercantile Co.

Powers advertisement, 1908. *Hennepin History Museum.*

ONE SWEET-SMELLING ADVERTISING CAMPAIGN

Minneapolis residents received a bonus with their copy of the Minneapolis Sunday Tribune *on December 6, 1903, and Powers Mercantile Company pulled off a fragrant advertising trick: the newspapers had been sprayed with perfume as they rolled through the presses. That Sunday morning, readers were treated to the smell of "Gyp," a new perfume supplied by Powers Mercantile Company. Powers's advertising manager, O. G. Shoenert, arranged to have machines spray a constant mist of the perfume on the newsprint as it went through the presses. "It is a safe guess that Minneapolis never was as sweet a city as it was yesterday morning," the paper wrote in its Monday edition.*

LABOR RAG GIVES POWERS HIGH MARKS

The *Minneapolis Labor Review* reported on August 30, 1918, that Powers management and its relations with employees were "reported to be very agreeable, and productive of institutions and organizations which are of decided mutual benefit, deepening and strengthening a cordial interest in the welfare of the enterprise as a whole to the end of individual progress and benefit throughout.

very agreeable, and productive

"The store employed a Welfare Director to look after the welfare of the employees, a School of Salesmanship, that held classes every morning to educate employees of limited means with limited educations. Through the instructions and training received here, employees are fitted for higher positions and better wages, and this adds just so much to the collective enlightenment and business education of the city as a whole."

The United States was involved in World War I at that time, and the publication reported that all one thousand people employed at Powers were members of the Powers Loyalty League, an association "organized to help the government in the present war crisis in every way possible."

"All the women in this store have formed Red Cross Units, and are working hard and steadily for the government, holding their weekly meetings devoted to work on hospital supplies for use at the front. . . . As for the men employees, they have organized the Powers' Men's Club, a social club devoted entirely to good fellowship, giving point and interest to life and making it brighter for all, both on and off duty."

The store also got good marks for its employee restaurant, where meals were served at the actual cost of goods. The reviewer recommended Powers for its "material and progressive features."

Shoe department, 1922. *Minnesota Historical Society Collections.*

and the Northwest was installed at Powers in August 1930. Costing $60,000, the escalators were capable of transporting four thousand people an hour from the first to the second floor. Escalators had been in use for a number of years in stores in New York, Chicago, and some West Coast cities.

Seven years later, Powers management launched an extensive upgrade to the building. The store was refaced with cream-colored Kasota stone, new display windows were installed, and the whole exterior of the store was redecorated. Inside, departments such as china and glassware, house furnishings, and a few others were remodeled and equipped with new fixtures. President George F. Williams said in the August 18, 1937, *Morning Tribune* that the improvements were made because of the company's confidence "in the sound prosperity and prospects of Minneapolis and the northwest. We believe the northwest farmer is coming back into his own and that the

Hours at Powers

Vol. 2. No. 29 Powers Mercantile Co., Minneapolis, Minn. JULY 31, 1920

The Value of a Smile

The thing that goes the farthest
Towards making life worth while,
That costs the least and does the most
Is just a pleasant smile.

The smile that bubbles from the heart
That loves his fellow men
Will drive away the clouds of gloom
And coax the sun again.

It's full of worth and goodness too,
With genial kindness blent.
It's worth a million dollars
And it doesn't cost a cent.

—Walter D. Nesbit.

ABOVE: *Hours at Powers* employee newsletter, 1920. *Hennepin County Library.* LEFT: Powers baby department, 1922. *Minnesota Historical Society Collections.* BELOW: Identical twin sisters Doris and Mary Seign in their matching snowsuits, purchased at Powers in the early 1940s. *Mary Scanlon.*

buying power of Minneapolis and its territory is increasing and will continue to increase."

Minneapolis's "territory" extended throughout the state, and Powers used newspaper advertising and mailings to draw Minnesotans to "the cities" to shop. A postcard announcing the store's Milestone Day sale in 1939 carried the banner "All Minnesota Comes to Milestone Day" and a map outlining the mileage from various points in northern Minnesota (International Falls, 350 miles), along the North Dakota border (Fargo, 250 miles), and even towns in Iowa and Wisconsin (Des Moines, 286 miles; Milwaukee, 350 miles).

Mary (Seign) Scanlon grew up in the 1940s in Moorhead, Minnesota, across the border from Fargo, and at least twice a year, she and her identical twin sister, Doris, climbed into the back seat of their father's Lincoln for a daylong drive to Minneapolis to visit relatives, attend the Ice Follies in February, and shop for matching clothing for the twins. "Powers had the best children's shop in town, according to my mother," Scanlon recalled. The stores in Moorhead and Fargo didn't carry duplicates, something Scanlon's mother wanted for her twin daughters. If the family got into Minneapolis

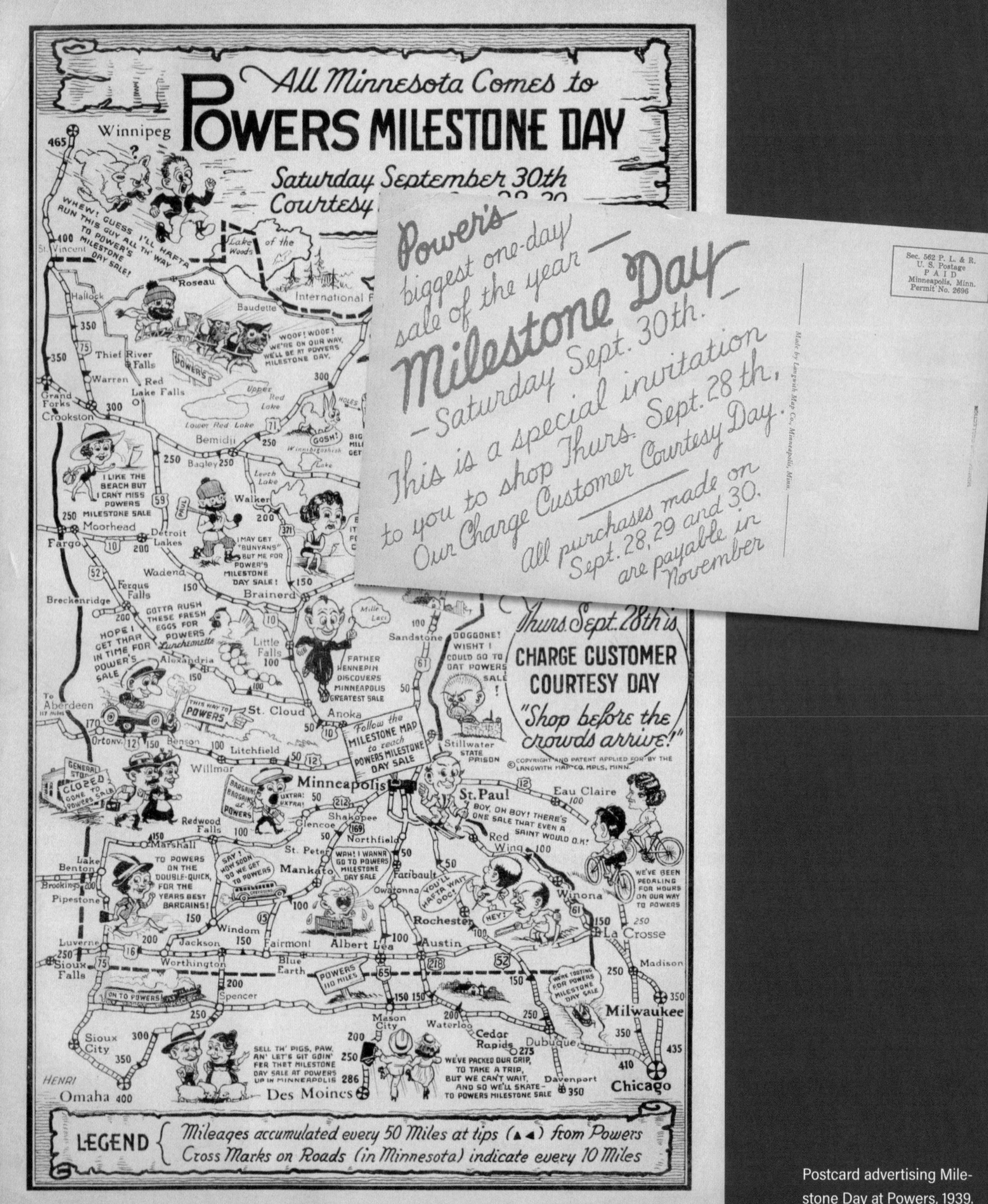

Postcard advertising Milestone Day at Powers, 1939. *Hennepin County Library.*

before closing time, Scanlon's dad would drop off his wife and daughters at the stores, and he'd head to the Sheraton Hotel, where they stayed. The shoppers wandered over to the hotel with their finds after the stores closed.

Powers was the first Minneapolis department store to expand to the suburbs. It opened a branch at Knollwood Plaza, at Highway 7 and Texas Avenue in St. Louis Park, on August 24, 1955. A second branch opened March 16, 1960, at Highland Village on Ford Parkway and Cleveland Avenue in St. Paul. The third branch opened at Northtown Center in Blaine in October 1972, the fourth at Maplewood Mall on White Bear Avenue in July 1974, the fifth in Eden Prairie in March 1976, and the sixth in Burnsville in July 1977.

Those branch locations were a primary problem in Powers's bid to compete with Donaldson's

(continued on page 34)

The Powers float for the Aquatennial Parade, 1942. *Minnesota Historical Society Collections.*

THE BEST BOOKSTORE

Powers was known for the expansive selection in its bookstore, which included the year's best sellers as well as rare antiques. In November 1966, book buyer Alice Carlson returned from a trip to Europe and unveiled her finds just before Christmas. The books included a first edition of *Aesop's Fables,* an 1832 copy titled *Foreign Cathedrals,* and a tome from the eighteenth century devoted to foreign field sports.

Minneapolis Star columnist Barbara Flanagan took a tour of the sale and found a leather-bound memoir of Lady Hamilton "with illustrated anecdotes" published in 1815 in London. The book bore the nameplate "Lord Birkenhead."

"One of the anecdotes offered concerned a party at Lord Nelson's house when Lady Hamilton disappeared, apparently with 'the vapors.' Nelson was outraged because his wife didn't whip out the smelling salts fast enough to please him," Flanagan wrote in her November 24, 1966, column.

ABOVE: Powers book department, 1915. *Minnesota Historical Society Collections.* RIGHT: Christmas book catalogs, 1936 and 1956. *Hennepin County Library.*

FIRE!

All three of the major Minneapolis department stores were hit by fire at some point in their time downtown. In February 1963, three of 125 firefighters who answered the five-alarm fire at the downtown Powers Department Store were injured.

It was a Sunday morning when a watchman saw flames spurt from a ground-floor wall in the store and sounded the first alarm at 9:11 AM. The fire was brought under control by 10:45 AM, but damage was estimated at $500,000. It was most severe on the first floor in the needlework, gift wrap, and photo sections. Flames also shot up a stairway into the women's lingerie section.

Smoke damage was so extensive that much of the merchandise was ruined. "We apparently will not be having a fire sale," quipped Powers president Edwin C. Moore.

A DOWNTOWN DEPARTMENT STORE ON FORD PARKWAY

Powers's roots were in Minneapolis, but a neighborhood in St. Paul claimed it as its own after the company opened a huge, elegant stand-alone store in the Highland Park neighborhood in 1960.

The three-story, ninety-two-thousand-square-foot store at Cleveland Avenue and Ford Parkway sold hosiery and linens, furniture and rugs, notions, housewares, jewelry, and more. Known for its selection of women's shoes and cosmetics, it stayed open for twenty-five years, offering easy and elegant shopping that didn't require a trip either to downtown or to the Dales.

The store's interior was designed by "the Father of Industrial Design" Raymond Loewy, whose work included Coca-Cola vending machines, the Lucky Strike cigarette package, the Studebaker Avanti, and the Coldspot refrigerator for Sears, Roebuck.

The outside of the store included a tile mosaic that ringed the first floor, entitled "Festival of Holidays." The mosaic highlights included Christmas, Hanukkah, Halloween, and the St. Paul Winter Carnival.

The Highland Park branch of Powers, 1960. *Minnesota Historical Society Collections.*

Shortly after Powers opened in Highland, St. Paul department store pioneers the Emporium and Field-Schlick opened branches nearby. For a brief time, Highland Park residents didn't need to head downtown or to a mall to shop at well-known department stores. The Emporium's time in Highland was short-lived, ending in 1967. Field-Schlick closed in 1979, and Powers closed in 1985. In 1994, the Powers building, with its festive mosaic, was demolished.

Onlookers survey the damage after a car crashed into a Powers window, August 1940. *Hennepin County Library.*

and Dayton's, said Barbara Armajani, CEO and president of the company from 1980 to 1983. Powers wasn't invited into the Dales (Southdale, Rosedale, Brookdale, and Ridgedale) with its two major competitors. Most of the Powers branches were in perimeter suburbs. When the Eden Prairie store opened, there was no freeway off-ramp nearby, Armajani explained. "[Competing] was difficult," she said.

Armajani was hired at Powers after two years as president of J. B. Hudson Jewelers, part of the Dayton Hudson Corporation. She began her retailing career at Dayton's in 1963, after graduating from Macalester College with a bachelor's degree in history and English. She answered a "sophisticated, upscale" blind employment agency ad and found herself interviewing for a position in Dayton's executive training program. She was hired and spent the next seventeen years learning about retail as a buyer, a group manager, and a division merchandise manager. She landed the job at Powers at age thirty-seven, "all because of Dayton's good training," she said.

She signed a three-year contract as CEO at Powers, a position she describes as "the most difficult job I ever had." When Armajani stepped in, interest rates were very high, making it the "most terrifically awful business period," she said. Despite the adverse economy, Powers's parent company, Associated Dry Goods, planned

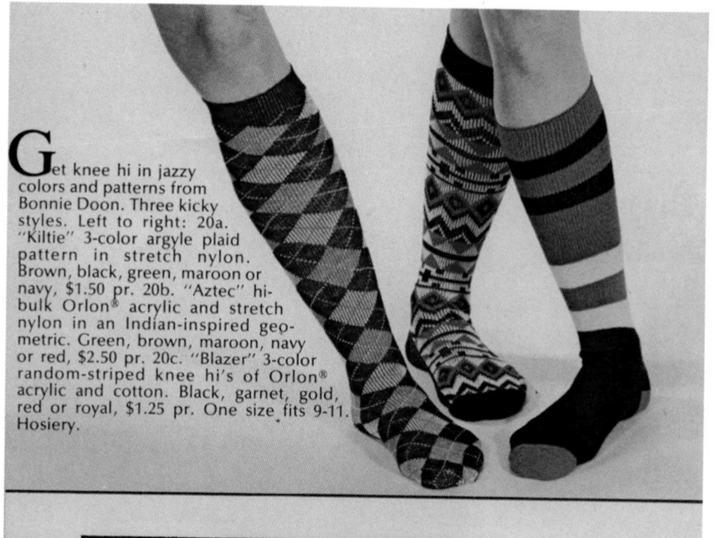

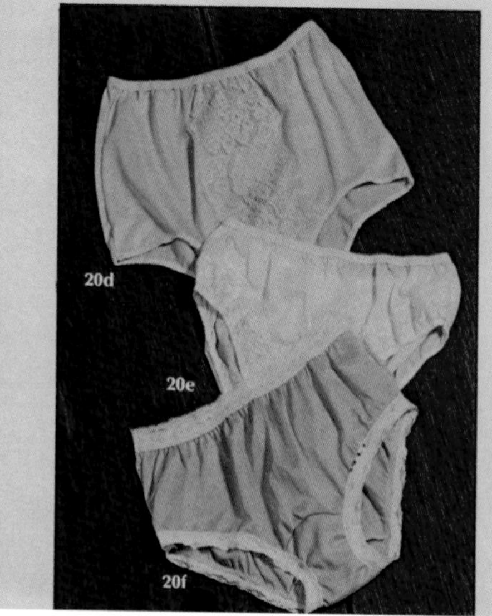

to put more capital into the Twin Cities market.

When Powers celebrated its centennial in 1981, "the dry goods chain was revamping for battle in a very competitive retail market," Walter T. Middlebrook wrote in the *Pioneer Press* on February 8, 1981, adding, "Officials say they're giving the stores more personality. Consumers, so far, have really had to extend themselves to make this discovery. But that's the way Powers is—quiet and subtle." Middlebrook went on to credit the company's new president as driving the new attitude: "Armajani, who joined the company last March as president and added the chief executive title in August, is bringing life back to Powers Dry Goods Co. Once an institution in the Twin Cities, the seven-store chain lost its stature as aggressive young competitors like Donaldson's and Dayton's took over. Now Powers, with Armajani at the helm, is planning a comeback."

Part of that comeback strategy included a focus on the upwardly mobile, professional consumer, Armajani said. The company started adding boutiques in the stores featuring the fashions of such American designers as Stanley Blacker, IZOD, Evan-Picone, Etienne Aigner, and Pappagallo. New brand identification, new point-of-sales displays, and new merchandise were all part of the store's new philosophy.

A month after Middlebrook's article, Dick Youngblood wrote about Powers's new

Powers catalog, 1976.
Hennepin County Library.

THE MODEL NEXT DOOR

In the mid-1980s, Powers used nonprofessional models in their print and television advertising. Ellen Share, Powers's director of special events in 1984, told *Skyway News* that the concept was "you don't have to be a model to look good in our clothes."

Local nonmodels included newspaper columnist Barbara Flanagan, restaurateur Rose Totino, lieutenant governor Marlene Johnson, and Marilyn Nelson, owner of Carlson Companies. Powers didn't just use public personalities. The store held tryouts for the television ads, and twenty-two people were chosen for the ads out of more than one hundred who applied.

philosophy in the *Minneapolis Tribune:* "Powers Dry Goods Co., the poor relation among big Twin Cities retailers for most of its 100-year history, is no longer the third largest department store chain in the metropolitan area. In fact, if there's one message that Barbara Armajani has been laboring to get across in her first year as Powers president and chief executive officer, it is that Powers *is no longer a department-store chain at all.*"

Powers was, in effect, giving up the traditional department store role of catering to all consumer needs, tastes, and incomes, Youngblood wrote. The store was repositioning itself to be the "largest specialty retailer" in the Twin Cities, with its focus on the higher-end market.

"In another ten years, all you'll have in retailing will be the Targets and the Lord and Taylors."

Barbara Armajani, Powers CEO and president, 1980–83

Retailing was becoming a game of trading up into higher-margin merchandise, trading down to lower price points, or becoming extinct, Armajani said. "In another ten years, all you'll have in retailing will be the Targets and the Lord and Taylors," she said in the March 22, 1981, article.

Powers's Knollwood Mall branch (Knollwood's name was changed from "Plaza" to "Mall" in 1980) was very profitable, and its women's shoes department was extremely competitive locally, according to Armajani, but the branch locations in second- and third-ring suburbs were hindrances, as was its core customer. Powers was built to be "elegant and glittery" and to cater to the mature woman, Armajani explained. The core customer was between ages fifty and seventy—a valuable demographic today—but in the 1980s that age group meant "blue-haired ladies," she said. Powers could not capture the youth market.

Armajani left Powers in 1983 and went on to open Pinstripe Petites, a twenty-five-store chain that focused on professional women five feet four and under "who didn't want to wear a dress to work."

Three years later, Associated Dry Goods Corporation sold the downtown Minneapolis store to Opus Corporation, a Minnetonka development company. The six branch stores were sold to the Twin Cities granddaddy of department stores, Donaldson's. On July 6, 1985, the Powers stores located in St. Louis Park, Highland Park in St. Paul, Blaine, Maplewood, Eden Prairie, and Burnsville closed at five thirty PM. When the stores reopened at noon the next day, they were Donaldson's.

Powers, circa 1980s. *Hennepin County Library.*

LANDING A JOB IN THE POWERS ADVERTISING DEPARTMENT

BY VALERIE ATKINSON

My first job straight out of college was working in the advertising department at Powers in downtown Minneapolis. The college, Minnesota College of Art and Design, had several job postings in the dean's office, and he suggested I apply for the "layout" position at the store. I didn't have a clue what that meant, since I was graduating with a bachelor's degree in fine arts, majoring in painting. I had serious doubts that I'd even get an interview, but I did.

I didn't have a résumé, and all I had to show the art directors (a husband-and-wife team held the art director's position then) was a portfolio full of nude model charcoal drawings. As they flipped through the drawings, I sat, red-faced, imagining what they thought as they looked at naked ladies in various positions. Much to my surprise, they liked what they saw and told me I had a natural talent for drawing the figure. "You'll get the hang of the job in no time," they said and hired me.

Shortly thereafter, I was assigned a drafting table with a

wonderful view of Nicollet Mall from one of the advertising department's top-floor windows. The directors were right; I caught on to drawing layouts for whatever product they placed in front of me: dresses, cosmetics, men's clothes, and shoes. Shoes gradually became one of my specialties. I don't know how many layouts I did featuring shoes plus ads for Powers advertising sale flyers featuring shoes.

Gradually, I was given more and more complicated projects: the cover for a white sale catalog and full-page ads for important product events. One of the fun projects was working on a British silverware sale with England's flag in the background. This was the time for "mod" clothes, "big" hair, fishnet stockings, and anything to do with Britain's pop Beatles culture.

No sooner would I get a layout done than off it would go to the next people in line to complete the ad: the copywriters, paste-up staff, and artists who would complete the finished artwork for the ad. Everyone worked like crazy, every day, meeting printing press and newspaper deadlines. In spite of how fast and furiously we worked, our little department bonded like a family, each of us helping whenever we needed to get done whatever job was running late.

The woman who shared the art director duties with her husband took me under her wing when she heard I aspired to go to New York to seek my fame and fortune. With her generous guidance, she helped me organize a professional portfolio. I, like so many other people in the Twin Cities currently reminiscing about the end of the department store era, have this couple to thank for having faith in me, giving me my first professional job, and then going above and beyond to help me launch my career in New York City at Gimbels Department Store (and yes, that store, too, is now history).

Valerie Atkinson, now retired, lives in West St. Paul. She and her husband, David Atkinson, are the authors of Snowplow Polka *(Romanesque Press, 2016), a humorous work of fiction describing the exploits of two energetic polka-loving senior citizens who decide to go into the snowplowing business.*

SHOWN HERE AND AT LEFT: Sampling of Valerie Atkinson's graphic design work for Powers, circa 1960s. *Valerie Atkinson.*

The Young-Quinlan Co

3

A Gem in the Crown of Minneapolis: Young-Quinlan

Jim Crego was a student at Patrick Henry High School in Minneapolis when he was hired to bus tables and wash dishes in the fourth-floor Fountain Room at Young-Quinlan in 1980. With its crystal chandeliers, walnut and brass trimmings, elegant merchandise, and sophisticated clientele, the opulently designed store "was a world of wonder" for this north Minneapolis boy. "It was magical," he said in a 2017 interview. "We don't have places like that anymore: beautiful, a restaurant with fashion shows every Tuesday."

Sarah Massey's Aunt Mildred often took her to lunch at the Fountain Room in the 1960s. Massey recalls the big, beautiful green room with its high ceilings and mirrored walls, the fountain, the egg sandwich she always ordered, and the two martinis her aunt enjoyed before whisking the teenager off to Dayton's for a little shopping. "By the time we left Quinlan's, she was pretty demonstrative and dramatic. We'd walk over to Dayton's to the Oval Room, where I would try on outfits until I found one I liked, and then she'd buy it"—an occasional indulgence that Massey's older sisters would not take part in. "They thought it was too demeaning and wouldn't do it. I thought it was worth the outfit," she said.

But that's another story.

Young-Quinlan closed its doors in 1985, but its flagship building on Nicollet Avenue and Ninth Street remains a landmark in downtown Minneapolis.

Elizabeth Quinlan was the first women's merchandise buyer in the United States and the only woman to serve in the National Recovery Administration, established in 1933 as part of President Franklin D. Roosevelt's New Deal program. She received lucrative offers from New York but turned them down to stay in Minneapolis, where she and Fred Young opened one of the first women's ready-to-wear shops in the United States in 1894. The only other shop like it was in New York.

"Her store would have embellished Fifth Avenue or the Rue de la Paix, but she built it instead on Nicollet Avenue," wrote Brenda Ueland in the *Minneapolis Times* in 1947.

The blue-eyed Irish American grew up in the Seven Corners neighborhood of Minneapolis, near the banks of the Mississippi River. Her father was a merchant, and she helped sell notions and penny candy in his store as a child. At age sixteen, Quinlan went to work at Goodfellow

OPPOSITE: Window display at Young-Quinlan, 1940. *Minnesota Historical Society Collections.*
THIS PAGE: Postcard view of Young-Quinlan, 1960s. *Hennepin County Library.*

Dry Goods store, where she met Young, a clerk who had higher ambitions in the retail world. Quinlan was paid $10 a week at Goodfellow's. According to Ueland's 1947 account, Mr. Goodfellow told Quinlan she would never make more than that "because that is all women are worth."

He was wrong. That $10-a-week job paved the way for a much more lucrative salary and her spot as a successful and celebrated businesswoman. Young persuaded Quinlan to leave Goodfellow's and help him in a new venture: a tiny shop in the back of Vrooman's Glove Company at 514 Nicollet Avenue. She signed on for a three-month trial.

Minneapolis was a town of 190,000 people on the edge of the prairie in 1894. Nicollet Avenue was lit with gaslights at night, and the streets were paved with red cedar blocks. Ready-to-wear was a daring concept at a time when women made their own clothing at home or paid a dressmaker to make their cloaks and suits. The new shop was just half a floor; one corner was devoted to dresses, another to hats, one for shoes, and the fourth, odds and ends. At a luncheon more than four decades later, Quinlan recounted that memorable first day in business: "In a few hours we were practically sold out. For a while, we thought we might have to close because of too much success."[1]

Quinlan also recalled her first buying trip to New York, when she was the only woman merchandise buyer in the country. "I climbed steps into dingy lofts to buy clothing for the women of Minneapolis," she said. "The wholesalers seemed suspicious at first. Some were not too pleasant as they talked with the woman from the sticks, silk hats on backs of their heads and cigars cocked in the corners of mouths.

"Minneapolis up to then had been my world. Incidentally, I then thought Minneapolis women were the best dressed in America. I still think they are."[2]

WHY CAN'T WE HAVE FRENCH CLOTHES?

This article was the third in a series of "little known human interest stories" about Young-Quinlan, run as advertisements during the store's fiftieth anniversary in 1944.

It was at a high tea in a palatial Lowry Hill home in 1899. A woman put down her Haviland teacup and flipped the train on her eight-yards-around tea gown as she whirled in half-anger.

"But I went to Europe on a pleasure trip!" Elizabeth Quinlan didn't admit the truth—that she was so intimidated by the extravagance of the French clothes and by the francs and the exchange and the duty that she didn't dare buy!

sell only what is in good taste, of good quality, in good fashion

She was soon back on the boat, though, making the first of her sixty-nine buying trips to Europe to bring back originals from the renowned couturieres of Paris, the fashion center of the world.

This time, there was nothing too good for her customers. She bought gowns of fabulous elegance, fashioned of Venetian Point lace, Chantilly lace, Irish lace. Or the sheerest softest batiste made heavy with hand-embroidery from the shoulder to the hem of the twelve-inch train. Gowns lined with taffeta and so exquisitely finished with pinking and feather-stitching that they might have been worn inside out!

Paris-made evening coats matched the dresses in magnificence. A deep Chinchilla cape worth a king's ransom, on a red velvet coat lined with pale pink chiffon, Sable cuffs reaching to the elbow of a white broadcloth coat.

Luxurious and beautiful and extravagant. But entirely in keeping with the formal balls, receptions, and teas that formed the social life of the "first families" of the Northwest.

Season after season Miss Quinlan traveled to Paris, Berlin, Vienna, London. William Lahiff usually accompanied her so that he might learn foreign buying and eventually take most of the responsibility of it. As the Young-Quinlan business grew, Miss Quinlan and Mr. Lahiff took their buyers with them. The gown buyer, the millinery buyer, the lingerie buyer, the handkerchief buyer.

Always Miss Quinlan was reiterating to her people her first principle in Merchandising: "Minneapolis and the Northwest rely upon us to sell only what is in good taste, of good quality, in good fashion. Our customers have faith in us. So with every purchase we make, we must deserve that faith."

Elizabeth Quinlan, circa 1910s. *Hennepin County Library.*

WHO IS THE YOUNG-QUINLAN CUSTOMER?

This article was the eighth in a series of "little known human interest stories" about Young-Quinlan, run as advertisements during the store's fiftieth anniversary in 1944.

"We theatrical women like good clothes. Shopping is a problem here in Europe, but when we're on tour in America, we just wait until we make Minneapolis and buy at Young-Quinlan."

Not such an unusual remark, except that the speaker was in a private buying room at Gerson's, an importing shop in Berlin—and Elizabeth Quinlan in an adjoining buying room heard it!

Theatrical people have always felt at home in Young-Quinlan. When we were still in our infancy, housed in the back half of the first floor of 113 Nicollet, the entire cast playing at the Met often dropped in after matinees and had tea, served informally behind a big screen. The Chauncey Olcotts would as readily have missed a performance as to miss that tea!

We theatrical women like good clothes.

Many famous persons have shopped at Young-Quinlan. Lillian Russell, Julia Marlowe, Mrs. Leslie Carter, Minnie Maddern Fiske, Maude Adams, Mrs. Patrick Campbell, Jane Cowl, Geraldine Farrar, Katherine Cornell, Lynn Fontanne, Helen Hayes, Nazimova, Princess Matchabelli, Ethel Barrymore, Grace Moore, Greer Garson, the Andrews Sisters. Oh, the list could go on and on!

But interesting as these customers are, they are not our pride and joy. We much prefer our "regulars."

The business girl who budgets her salary down to a split penny in order to buy war bonds, buys her frocks in our Silhouette Shop . . . "Because Young-Quinlan is so accustomed to choosing exclusive clothes that even their budget-priced dresses are bound to be 'right' than others."

The social leader, who now does her own housework besides being a nurse's aide and a frequent hostess, buys her clothes here because now, more than ever, she needs dresses of quality and right fashion to look her best under all circumstances.

The beautifully gowned matron who has been a Y-Q customer since the day the store opened, shops now with her daughter and granddaughter. Why, Young-Quinlan fairly brought those children up—starting them in the Bambino Shop with their christening dresses!

There's the co-ed who rushes in for a blue sweater and plaid skirt. The defense plant girl who just has to have a Y-Q glamour dress for Saturday night. The mail order customer who is considered a personal friend.

Oh yes—and the man customer. He regards Young-Quinlan as his special gift store. "When my girl sees that Y-Q box, she just naturally loves whatever's in it."

But the more we consider it, the more we know there isn't such a person in the Young-Quinlan customer. There are as many types as there are persons. But you all have this in common—you appreciate quality; you appreciate fashion.

And we appreciate you. *Don't think we don't!*

Quinlan's three months at the new store turned into a half century of innovation in women's fashion merchandising. By 1903, she had saved enough money to buy an equal partnership in the shop, and the name of the store became Young-Quinlan Company. As she helped women with their shopping at the store that bore her name, she was often asked, "Who is Mr. Quinlan?"

Young retired due to medical issues in 1904, and after he died in 1911, Quinlan bought his interest in the business and became the sole owner and president of Young-Quinlan Company. As the store's principal buyer, she traveled the world to keep current with fashions.

In 1926, the store moved into a new $1.25 million five-story home at 901–915 Nicollet Avenue. The architect, Fred Ackerman of New York, described the building as a pioneer in a new phase of architecture. Designed with Renaissance Revival and Chicago Commercial architectural details, the building reflected Quinlan's appreciation of Italian art and her vision of modern merchandising: elegance, luxury, and convenience. Finished in tan brick and Kasota limestone, the building featured four identical sides, each one carrying the same arched windows, columns, and decorative elements that made all four façades appear to be the entrance. It was one of the first buildings in the country to have an underground parking garage with an elevator that took patrons directly from the garage to the sales floors. Inside, a marble staircase swept up to a mezzanine wrapped in wrought-iron balustrades.

An estimated twenty thousand people attended the preliminary showing of the new store on June 15. Many were turned away or forced to wait outside until other patrons had left. Guests included the owners of virtually every Nicollet Avenue

TOP LEFT: The Young-Quinlan Company, 1908. *Minnesota Historical Society Collections.*
ABOVE: Program for the Spring Fashion Fete at Young-Quinlan, March 1925. *Hennepin County Library.*

ABOVE LEFT AND RIGHT: Construction of the Young-Quinlan building, 1925. RIGHT: Elizabeth Quinlan, circa 1940. *All Hennepin County Library.*

retail store. Joseph Chapman, president of the L. S. Donaldson Company, led the ceremonies.

Minneapolis mayor George Leach called the store a "gem in the crown of Minneapolis." "Miss Quinlan will always be remembered as one of the real builders of the city," he added.[3]

A booklet printed by the company to honor the grand opening described Quinlan as "the first, not merely in Minneapolis, or in the United States, but in the world, to foresee the possibilities of what has since become one of the greatest industries of two continents—women's ready-to-wear. . . . It was to the Minneapolis woman of 1894—gentle, formal, and demure, that the Young-Quinlan Company made its bow thirty-two years ago; it is to the Minneapolis woman of 1926—eager, adventurous, and subtly poised, that the same company does honor today."

One year after the new store opened, a team of moviemakers from the University of Minnesota's visual education department took over the first floor of the Young-Quinlan Company to film a feature on Quinlan for *The Most Distinguished Business Women of the United States*, part of *The March of Time* documentary series by Time Inc. that was broadcast at movie theaters around the United States.

During the Great Depression in the 1930s, Quinlan was the only woman to serve on the advisory board for the National Recovery Administration, a New Deal agency established by President Franklin D. Roosevelt in 1933 to aid businesses by creating "fair competition" and to

(continued on page 50)

TOP: Street view, November 1926. *Minnesota Historical Society Collections.* ABOVE: Postcard advertising the Young-Quinlan Company, "the Northwest's newest and finest specialty shop devoted to the correct appareling of gentle women and their daughters." RIGHT: Pamphlet advertising Young-Quinlan's new parking garage. *Both Hennepin County Library.*

BOYS' SHOP
MEN'S FURNISHINGS
HATS SHOES
SPORTSWEAR
ROBES

OPPOSITE, TOP: Millinery department at Young-Quinlan, 1930. Fur department, 1947. BOTTOM: Young-Quinlan interior, 1963. *All Minnesota Historical Society Collections.* THIS PAGE, ABOVE: Young-Quinlan display window, 1920s. *Hennepin County Library.* RIGHT: Display window at Young-Quinlan Rothschild, 1964. *Minnesota Historical Society Collections.*

set prices, minimum wages, and maximum work hours. In 1935, she was described by *Fortune* magazine as the "foremost women's specialty executive" in the United States and "among the top 16 businesswomen in the country."

In 1937, Quinlan told a *Washington Post* reporter that her success was "largely a matter of luck." "The collective forces from the first have been in my favor," she said. "I dreamed of having a woman's specialty shop at the very time there was a need for such shops. It was luck I had the encouragement, the help and the energy to carry out my dream. That's all there is to it."

When asked how a woman can be successful in the modern world, she said, "My own experience has convinced me it isn't a man's world after all."[4]

Young-Quinlan Company celebrated its fiftieth anniversary in 1944, and the following year, Quinlan sold her store to Chicago retailer Henry C. Lytton and Company. The *Minneapolis Daily Times* lauded Quinlan as one of the outstanding businesswomen of America: "Climaxing a business career that stretches back to the days when the wives of lumber and flour kings drove in their carriages to her shop. . . . [T]he sale of the famous Nicollet Avenue store still found

NEIMAN-MARCUS-YOUNG-QUINLAN

In his book *Minding the Store,* Neiman Marcus president Stanley Marcus wrote about a missed opportunity to acquire the Young-Quinlan Company at the time of Elizabeth Quinlan's retirement. It was 1945, the country was at war, and Stanley Marcus's brothers were in the service. There was a labor shortage, and the distance between Neiman Marcus's headquarters in Dallas, Texas, and Minneapolis was too great, Marcus wrote.

If the property was still available after the war, Neiman Marcus would consider the purchase. But Young-Quinlan was sold quickly to Chicago's Henry C. Lytton and Company.

Neiman Marcus did come to Minneapolis forty-six years later. The high-fashion luxury retailer set up shop in a 118,000-square-foot store at Gaviidae Common on Nicollet Mall in 1991. Twenty-two years later, it closed, following the footsteps of Saks Fifth Avenue, which was also located on Nicollet Avenue, and Bloomingdale's at the Mall of America.

Miss Quinlan hard at work, the active head of the enterprise until noon today."

In September 1947, Quinlan died at her Lowry Hill home after a short illness. Her funeral services were held at the Basilica of St. Mary in Minneapolis, and she was buried at St. Mary's Cemetery. The Young-Quinlan Company store was closed that day.

In a September 29 eulogy in the *Minneapolis Times,* Brenda Ueland countered Quinlan's own assessment that her success was the result of good timing and luck: Quinlan's success, she wrote, "might be due to an intuition, a sixth sense. She loved gambling—buying merchandise. Predicting fashions, etc., is gambling—and in such things she acted on this intuition which gave her 'an indescribable sense of certainty.' Besides that, she had courage."

The Lytton company's ownership of Young-Quinlan was short-lived. The store went back into the hands of a Minnesota company in 1949, when Maurice L. Rothschild and Company of Minneapolis bought it.

OPPOSITE: Young-Quinlan's fiftieth-anniversary booklet, 1944. THIS PAGE, RIGHT: Style show at Young-Quinlan, 1945. BELOW: Exterior view, 1948. *All Hennepin County Library.*

BOOKS ON WHEELS

In 1941, Young-Quinlan launched its Book Loge, a rental library that allowed a customer to borrow one hundred books a year for $7.50. A quick call to the store librarian would result in a home delivery within two hours.

The books were located on the second floor of the store and held two to thirty copies of each book. Each member could take out three books at a time. And the store kept lists of the more popular reads.

Golfer and Sportsman magazine reported in January 1941 that mysteries and fiction were leading the list at that time, and that there was a large waiting list for Ernest Hemingway's *For Whom the Bell Tolls.*

By March, the two stores had merged into the Young-Quinlan building, and advertisements in local newspapers were carrying the name Maurice L. Rothschild, Young-Quinlan Co. The store expanded to downtown St. Paul and eventually opened branches in Knollwood shopping center in St. Louis Park, Rosedale in Roseville, and Northtown in Blaine. In 1962, the stores were bought by the New York firm Cluett Peabody and Company, which changed the store's name to Young-Quinlan Rothschild Company. In 1969, it dropped the Rothschild part of the name entirely.

In an interesting turn of events, in 1978, Young-Quinlan became a division of another subsidiary of Cluett Peabody and Company: Lytton's, the Chicago firm that briefly owned Young-Quinlan in the late 1940s. As 1978 progressed, Young-Quinlan saw the closing of its branches in St. Paul, Knollwood, and Rosedale. The Northtown branch was converted to a "budget" operation.

In 1983, Young-Quinlan was sold to New York investor Daniel Shechtman. Long known as a top-end retailer, Young-Quinlan had become more of a discount operation under the new owners. When the lease came up in 1985, Cluett Peabody and Company—which still held the lease at the Nicollet Avenue building—chose not to renew it. The store closed in February to the dismay of many, including a group of longtime Fountain Room customers who created a petition to building owner Bob Greenberg to keep the tearoom open. But Greenberg claimed he could do nothing. It was Cluett Peabody and Company who made the decision to close the restaurant.

The building didn't sit empty for long. In 1986, Harold—an upscale women's store across the street that was co-owned by Bob Dayton (son of Donald Dayton) and Dolores DeFore—moved in for fifteen months. The original Harold building was being torn down to make room for a new shopping complex, the Conservatory, which would be the store's new home. "We moved the whole Harold store on Saturday night," DeFore said. "We closed on Saturday at five and opened Monday at Young-Quinlan's."

The Young-Quinlan building was renovated in 1988 by Bob and Sue Greenberg and their 614 Company. As for the women who launched the save-the-Fountain-Room petition, they were celebrated in October 1985 by the women's theater group At the Foot of the Mountain in *The Ladies Who Lunch,* a play based on the closing of the Fountain Room and a group of women who take up the cause to keep it open.

BELOW: Advertisement for fashions from the Gown Shop at Young-Quinlan, circa 1950s. OPPOSITE: Young-Quinlan catalog page and envelope. *All Hennepin County Library.*

The Gown Shop

at Young Quinlan draws upon an impressive roll call, with distinguished fashions from such talented fingers as

Pauline Trigere . . . Irene of Hollywood . . . Jo Copeland of Pattullo . . . Maurice Rentner . . . Nettie Rosenstein.

Second Floor

The Lacey Kerchief

Sponsored by Paris

Exquisite gift 'kerchiefs in perfect replica of rare old Rose Point, Reprouse, Lierre, Duchesse, Carrick Macross and Oriental Laces— 75c, $1.00 *to* $3.50

Real Lace 'Kerchiefs, Appenzell and unique applique effects—exclusive in motif— $1.50 *to* $65

Real Needlepoint embellishment on kerchief of natural crepe de chine—Binche trimmed. *Special* $2.50

White lacey 'kerchiefs—also pure linen with all-around spoke insert—an interesting miscellany of new patterns at—59c

Lace trimmed handkerchiefs—white Irish linen with one corner embroidery—French prints in smart colors—25c

Pure linen 'kerchiefs with sixteenth-inch hem and dainty corner initial. *Special* 25c

The utility 'kerchief, of very fine snowy white linen—petite hem— *Special* 19c

Handkerchiefs for Men and Youths!

Men's hand initialed kerchiefs in colors and white— 59c

Hand thread drawn, hand embroidered initial, outlined in white and colors— 75c *and* $1.00

French import monogram kerchiefs; six assorted tapes, hand rolled hem—all white— $1.50

Youth's handkerchiefs of fine, white linen; one-eighth inch hem, *Special* 25c

New colored prints for business wear $1 *to* $2.50

All linen plain goods and tape handkerchiefs— 75c *to* $2.50

Men's extra fine quality linen with sixteenth or one-eighth inch hem— *Special* 59c

White all linen Kerchiefs *Special* 35c

Children's kerchiefs—25c *upward*

'KERCHIEF SHOP—ENTRANCE FLOOR

Gifts which Give Comfort

Shoulderettes of soft zephyr yarn—delicate tints—orchid, madonna blue, conch shell pink and mist grey—also white—$3.95 $5.00

Convalescent or bed jackets in plain wool or zephyr and rayon silk combination—(the same dainty tints)— $5 *to* $8.75

Quaint Shawls in plain or rayon silk with zephyr blending—orchid, grey, pink, horizon blue, white, black; also grey-white and black-white combinations— $6.75 $7.75

"Swiss Miss" Sweater of brushed wool—a new turtle neck style—Hockey red, russet, fern, canary, and azure blue—$10. Jaunty tassel cap to match—$3.50.

SPORTS SHOP—ENTRANCE FLOOR

Gifts - Charmingly Personal for Persons of Charm

The "Coolie" Pajama (like Sketch)—fine quality crepe de chine—flesh or coral embroidered in contrasting tints *Special* $12.50

Pajamas and Pajama-negligees—$10.75 *to* $95

Soisette, broadcloth and crepe pajamas—$1.95 *to* $5.00

Exquisite Hand-made Lingerie—sheerest batiste, Ninon and lustrous silks embellished with real laces and hand embroidery— *Batiste* $3.95 *to* $15 *Silk* $6.95 *to* $65

Batiste Night Gowns—a host of attractive styles— $1 *to* $3.95

Munsing Rayon Vests— *Special* $1.35

Munsing Rayon Bloomers— *Special* $1.95

Heavier quality silk vests and bloomers are priced— $2.95 *to* $4.95

Effa Blanche Tailored Lingerie

Crepe de chine envelope chemise in flower-like tints— $2.95 *to* $5.00

Crepe de chine Night Gowns—tailored and trimmed styles— $6.95 *to* $15

Robes and Tea-Gowns

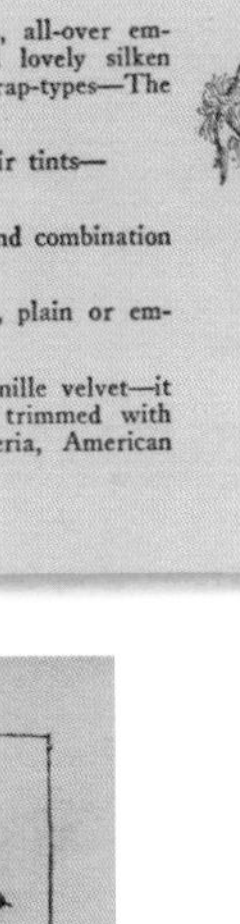

Glorious velvets, brocades, filmy chiffons, all-over embroidered coats, quilted satin robes and lovely silken negligees—Picturesque, floating and wrap-types—The gift of adoration! $12.50 *to* $95

Quilted satin Robes in the favored boudoir tints— *Special* $15

Tailored Flannel Robes—striped, plain, and combination effects— $12.50 *to* $29.50

Corduroy robes—lined and unlined types, plain or embossed— $3.95 *to* $18.50

Sketched is a flattering wrap-robe of chenille velvet—it is lined with Jap silk and luxuriously trimmed with matching ostrich. Colors—orchid, wisteria, American beauty and Flemish blue— *Special* $19.75

TRADITION AND TRAGEDY

In their early days, most of the downtown department stores in Minneapolis and St. Paul had elevator operators who greeted customers, worked the doors and the levers, and brought patrons to the different floors of their stores. But Young-Quinlan resisted automation, and the elegant wood-paneled elevators were operated by white-gloved humans up to the store's closing in 1985. The 614 Company, owner of the Young-Quinlan building, kept the tradition alive. Today, one elevator is still operated manually, although the operator no longer wears white gloves.

Many of the operators stayed at the job for decades, but one met a tragic death in 1981. Sixty-year-old Mary Evelyn Theis apparently stepped into what she thought was a waiting elevator and fell several floors through the shaft. A report in the December 20, 1981, *Minneapolis Tribune* said Theis had been checking an elevator that hadn't been working because of a broken key. Officials said they found the broken key in her pocket and a coat hanger at the bottom of the shaft. Theis had probably opened the elevator door with the hanger, as operators were instructed to do when keys break, and fell or accidentally stepped into the shaft, the newspaper said.

Maurice Rothschild, the founder of clothier Maurice L. Rothschild's, opened the Palace Clothing Company on Washington Avenue in Minneapolis in 1888. The Palace's claim to fame was that it was the first Minneapolis store to install electric lights. Rothschild moved his store to the 300 block of Nicollet Avenue in 1891 and later built a new store at Fourth and Nicollet. The company bought Young-Quinlan in 1949 and expanded to St. Paul, St. Louis Park, Roseville, and Blaine.

Boys' clothes

January special pricing.

We've re-grouped many lots. The "specials" are exactly what'll fit in with the boy's needs on resuming school.

They're some of the most driving values we've ever assembled. Don't overlook this.

Fancy Weave Suits—Fancy weaves in gray and brown effects; many have two pair knickers fully lined. Good, heavy weights and well made with taped seams. 15 to 18 sizes for big boys.

$5, $6.95, $7.95

Corduroy Suits—The boy wants to wear corduroy and there's nothing like it for winter service. Here's a lot of drab corduroys with full lined knickers, sizes 13 to 18. In a special at

$5 and $6.95

Corduroy Knickers Serviceable dark shade corduroy, made with double stitched seams, sizes 7 to 18. Regular $1.50 values that we've marked 85c

Mackinaws, $3.95

Warm, husky-looking mackinaws, shawl collars, belted all around, muff pockets. In browns, and red plaids. 8 to 18; at $3.95

Mackinaws, $6.50

Double-breasted sport style mackinaws of excellent heavy-weight materials, pockets big enough for skates or books, sizes 7 to 18; special; $6.50

Inband Caps in turban and golf styles, Skating toques and Angora tams, calues up to $2, several hundred bunched now at 85c

Knit Hockey Caps of combination college colors, four varieties, they're extra good and warm. A conspicuous snap, at 45c

SWEATERS; military style; strictly regulation O. D. shade; full button on pull-over shape; cadet sizes, 32 to 36 chest; $3.50, $4 values $2.65

Official headquarters Boy Scouts of America.

Maurice L Rothschild & Co
Palace Clothing House

Money cheerfully refunded

Minneapolis
St. Paul
Chicago

Minneapolis: Nicollet, cor. 4th. St. Paul: Robert, cor. 7th.

If you want a Buyer for your store, for your house, for real estate of any kind, for your business, for your launch, for your kodak, for your store and office fixtures, for anything that you've got for sale, get it by using a Journal Want Ad.

If you want a Roomer for that vacant room, get one by using a Journal Want Ad.

OPPOSITE, LEFT: Early trading cards from Maurice Rothschild's Palace Clothing. *Hennepin County Library.* OPPOSITE RIGHT AND THIS PAGE: Newspaper advertisements for Palace Clothing House. *Minnesota Historical Society Collections.*

Oval Room
Cotton
Carousel

4
The Last One Standing: Dayton's

Some of Catherine Dehdashti's most treasured memories of Dayton's department store begin with the bus rides she'd take from Wayzata to downtown Minneapolis when she was in her early teens. She would ride her bike from her home in Plymouth to meet friends in Wayzata and then bus from Wayzata to Ridgedale mall, "telling our parents we were going shopping at Ridgedale. Then we would transfer buses to go downtown.

"It was so exciting to be in downtown Minneapolis, pretending we were so much more grown up than we were. We would explore the whole store and eat in the Oak Grill, then go redo our makeup in the twelfth-floor bathroom with all the mirrors."

One of her teenage antics haunted Dehdashti when she applied for a job at the Minneapolis store at age nineteen: "I didn't think I'd be hired. I'd shoplifted at the Ridgedale Dayton's at age fourteen, and I'd been caught. I was trying to show off to my friend who had just proven that she could get away with slipping a Van Halen cassette tape into her Bermuda purse at the mall's Woolworth's store. I one-upped her with a bikini."

Five years later, Dehdashti told her story to the woman behind the desk in Dayton's human resources office. The woman smiled and said, "I'm sure you learned your lesson." And Dehdashti was hired to work in women's shoes.

Those early adventures at this storied department store piqued Dehdashti's interest in the history of the store enough that she's written a novel, *700 Nicollet,* that explores the store from 1990 to 2007.

Dayton's wasn't the first or the second major department store in Minneapolis, but it quickly became the Twin Cities' No. 1 store, and its name carried into the twenty-first century. The Dayton's logo has been gone from storefronts, shopping bags, and personal credit cards since 2001, but you can still catch a Twin Cities shopper referring to Macy's, the store that would come to occupy its many storefronts, as Dayton's.

In 1902, nearly two decades after Donaldson's and Powers got their start on Nicollet Avenue in Minneapolis, the store that would become Dayton's hung its shingle nearby. George Draper Dayton, a New York native who found success as a banker in Worthington, Minnesota, began looking for real estate investments in Minneapolis in 1890. He rented an office downtown, and over the next eleven years bought property along Nicollet Avenue, first at Sixth Street, then Seventh. After purchasing a tract in the 800 block of Nicollet and more frontage on Seventh Street, he built a six-story multiuse building at Seventh and Nicollet. Goodfellow Dry Goods, then the fourth-largest department store in the city, moved from its Third Street

OPPOSITE: The legendary Oval Room at Dayton's, April 1956. *Minnesota Historical Society Collections.*

location into the first three floors of the new building. Dayton financed the business and became a silent partner.

On June 24, 1902, Goodfellow Dry Goods Company opened at its new location to hundreds of shoppers who, according to one news report, "made purchases, listened to a splendid orchestra, and looked with delight at the beautiful goods and beautiful decorations." Known as the "Daylight Store," it was bright and open, and its long, broad aisles featured glass showcases with electric lights that illuminated the store's products. "The new Goodfellow Store," the news report continued, "is one of the handsomest and best appointed emporiums in the country."[1]

The store was just across the intersection from L. S. Donaldson and Company, the city's leading department store, and Goodfellow's management knew it faced stiff competition. The store invested heavily in advertising and strived to offer a variety of merchandise. But after a few months of declining profits, George Dayton bought out the other owners and changed the company's name to Dayton Dry Goods Company in 1903.

The new store launched a variety of promotions, including a three-day "Inventory Sale" in June, free concerts, and free lunches. The store motto—"What's Wrong We'll Right"—encouraged shoppers to alert management to any misleading advertisements, and customers received a dollar for each wrong they brought to the store's attention.

Several leased departments moved in that first year, including Merkham Trading Company's "hair-curler" parlor, Emma Read's drawing supplies, Mrs. Gertrude Stanton's optical service, and in the basement of the building, W. B. Sayre's hardware, china, and glassware. By 1906, the store expanded into all six floors of the building, nearly doubling the space from 63,000 square feet to 150,000. The store added a furniture department, a bookstore, a piano department, and the salon of local dressmaker "Miss Helen." George Dayton's oldest son, David Draper Dayton (who was known by his middle name, Draper), was named general manager.

TOP ROW: The store at 700 Nicollet Avenue opened as Goodfellow's in 1902 and within a year transitioned to Dayton's Goodfellow's and then to Dayton Dry Goods. *Hennepin County Library.* RIGHT: Dayton's models, circa 1915. *Minnesota Historical Society Collections.* OPPOSITE, TOP TO BOTTOM: Postcard view of the Dayton Dry Goods Company, 1912. *Minnesota Historical Society Collections.* Dayton's, corner of Eighth Street and Nicollet Avenue, 1915. *Hennepin County Library.* A fire in February 1917 shut down Dayton's for ten days. *Hennepin History Museum.*

That area of Nicollet Avenue was fast becoming a city center, and in 1909, the dry goods store added a new basement store that offered lower prices than the upper floors and stocked women's coats, suits, and dresses, along with linens, corsets, millinery, jewelry, underwear, notions, and laces. It also included a china department, a music department, a thirty-two-foot soda fountain, and a candy department.

Draper's brother, George Nelson Dayton (who, like his brother, went by his middle name), joined the business in 1911 as a blanket buyer. Nelson had graduated from the University of Minnesota's School of Agriculture in 1907 and had been trying to make a go of farming at Oak Leaf Farm in Anoka County before deciding to join his brother and father in the retail world.

Draper and Nelson Dayton led the store through continuing expansion. The building that stands at 700 Nicollet Avenue today is actually a mix of several structures. In 1910, a nine-story section was added in the rear of the original structure on Seventh Street to expand the store's offerings. The *Minneapolis Tribune* described the new floors as a "dream place for women": mahogany woodwork, green velvet carpet, private dressing and fitting rooms, millinery, suits, party dresses, skirts. The business's name was changed to the Dayton Company, meant to reflect that the store had moved from a "dry goods" enterprise to a department store. In 1913, an annex that included a sub-basement, a basement, and a one-story building was completed at the corner of Eighth and Nicollet, giving the store its first Eighth Street entrance. In 1914, eight floors were added to the annex, and in 1916, the store broadened its frontage on Eighth Street to 150 feet.

One year later, a fire destroyed some of the structure at the corner of Eighth and Nicollet, and rebuilding began almost immediately. The

DAYTON'S DELIVERY SERVICE GROWS WINGS

Dayton's made news in September 1919 for hiring airplanes to deliver goods to out-of-town visitors who had ordered the items at the Minnesota State Fair. Merchandise was flown to eighteen destinations northwest of Minneapolis that fall. The Dayton's aircraft even delivered a wedding present to an out-of-town destination just before the ceremony began.

ABOVE: Ray Miller and Charles Keys deliver goods via airplane to Dayton's, 1920. *Minnesota Historical Society Collections.*

The next spring, George Dayton took advantage of an express handlers' rail strike in New York to experiment with moving merchandise via air. Working with his neighbor William Kidder, owner of Curtiss Northwest Airplane Company, headquartered near the fairgrounds just north of St. Paul, Dayton hired two planes—painted with the words "Dayton's Delivery"—to fly from New York to Minneapolis carrying eight hundred pounds of merchandise.

Pilots Ray Miller and Charles Keys were already heading from New York to fly two de Havilland planes to Montana. They loaded the planes with the Dayton Company goods with plans to stop in Minneapolis en route.

When the planes landed at the Parade Grounds across from Dunwoody Institute in Minneapolis on May 10, 1920, their wings were removed and the pilots promptly drove the fuselages through downtown streets to make a street-side delivery to Dayton's. The merchandise—jewelry, lace, men's silk shirts, and other sundries—was immediately brought into the store, and every item—bearing tags that read, "By Airplane from New York to Minneapolis for the Dayton Co"—was purchased by shoppers looking for souvenirs from the historic flight.

The shipment wasn't a big moneymaker. It cost $2,500 to ship $6,000 worth of merchandise, but at the time, the two-thousand-plus-mile flight was the longest commercial flight on record, and the publicity was priceless.

The next year, Dayton's sent out planes to fly over the grounds of eighty-eight county fairs and the annual Paul Bunyan celebration in Brainerd, dropping foot-long red, blue, and yellow feathers that bore the Dayton name.

new construction extended Dayton's to the full length of Nicollet between Seventh and Eighth Streets. In 1920, the 1916 addition was raised to ten stories.

Catherine Dehdashti, who worked in the shoe department at Dayton's in the early 1990s, describes a deep sense of belonging that employees felt at the company. "We were trained to act like and to believe, 'It's my company,'" she said. Concern for the well-being of the employees was something that George Dayton stressed from the earliest days of the enterprise. In 1916, the store established a school for workers who had not finished high school. The company hosted employee parties and dinners. Workers joined baseball teams, bowling teams, glee clubs, orchestras, and other activities that fostered a community life there. When fifteen hundred employees were left without work for ten days following the 1917 fire, they were paid for those missed days. The men who enlisted or were drafted during World War I were offered their jobs back when they returned. Many of them did return, and some went on to become executives at the company. From the 1920s through the 1950s, the store provided a full-time nurse for sick employees and customers.

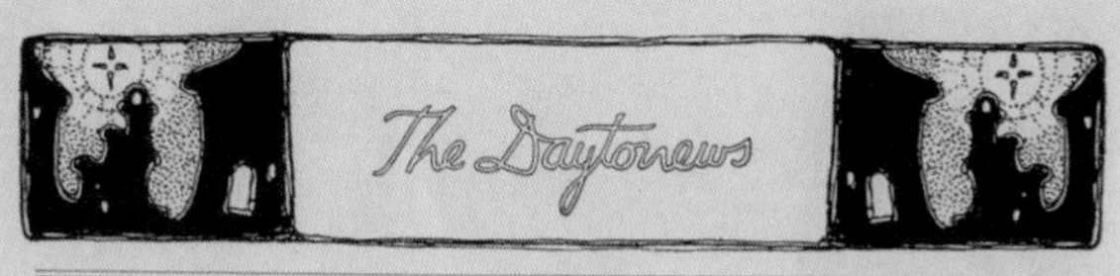

Vol. XI | January 1926 | No. 1

A little magazine published once a month by the employees of The Dayton Company, Minneapolis, Minnesota. It aspires to be a chronicle of store events and a cheer sheet for every one who reads it.

The price of The Daytonews is 3c per copy. On the day of publication it will be on sale at the 7th St. entrance, the 8th St. entrance, and the 10th floor cafeteria.

Happy New Year to You

How easy it is to say it! And we really mean it when we say it.

But did you ever stop to think that after all it is the other person who must put forth the effort necessary to vitalize the wish? Our "Happy New Year to you" is the expression of our kindly desire—it is the outcropping of our benevolence of thought—and we really, truly wish we could make the New Year very HAPPY indeed to all those we so freely "wish" it for. The "wish" often benefits us more than those to whom we say it— for our expression cheers, sweetens, broadens, ennobles us, and our lives are happier because we "wish" happiness for those about us.

But we all must bestir ourselves in order to achieve real happiness—it cannot come to any simply by our "wish," no matter how sincere that "wish" may have been. And haven't we all found by experience that the surest, and really the only way, to become happy is to forget ourselves in efforts to serve, cheer, encourage others?

Retroaction is a large word, but it covers a world of thought and philosophy—whenever we honestly seek to help any one we actually are more helped than is he, for it all reacts on us. I cannot explain it, but it is true that our simple wishing every one we meet a "Happy New Year" so reacts on us that before we know it we find ourselves "walking on air" and become conscious we are happy through and through because we have wished happiness to others. Let's fill the air the next few days with our wishes that all around us may have a really, truly very "Happy New Year."

With all my heart I wish it for every one connected with the Dayton organization. If I could, I would shield you all from anything that would make it less than a very "Happy New Year."

One longstanding familial tradition took place each Christmas Eve: store managers lined up to greet employees and wish them a happy holiday as they left the building at closing time. In the early days, George Dayton handed out boxes of candy to each worker, and in later years, it was his grandsons, each of whom were known by their first names—Mr. Donald, Mr. Bruce, Mr. Kenneth, Mr. Wallace, and Mr. Douglas—who made the gesture.

Dayton's celebrated its twentieth anniversary in 1922 with the launch of a one-day Golden Jubilee Bargain Day on October 11. Double quantities of goods were ordered, prices were slashed, and the sale was promoted heavily. It was such a success that for the first time the store pushed Donaldson's out of the No. 1 retail spot in the region, and the Jubilee Sale was established as an annual event.

Dayton's was at the top of its game in 1923, when Draper and Nelson bought their two sisters' shares of the store, but the course of the Dayton Company changed suddenly when Draper Dayton died of heart failure at the age of forty-three.

ABOVE LEFT: A letter from George Dayton to employees in the January 1926 issue of *Daytonews*, a "little magazine published once a month by the employees of The Dayton Company. . . . It aspires to be a chronicle of store events and a cheer sheet for every one who reads it." *Hennepin County Library.* ABOVE: Dayton's men's department, 1926. BELOW: Dayton's WBAH radio room orchestra, circa 1923. *Both Minnesota Historical Society Collections.*

LIVE FROM DAYTON'S

On May 11, 1922, the voice of Hugh Arthur, Dayton's advertising manager, went out across the airwaves of WBAH Radio live from the Dayton Company store. WBAH was the first radio station to be operated by a department store in the Twin Cities and the first in the area to use a battery rather than a generator to power it. It was one of only six radio stations in Minneapolis at the time. The station was well received by listeners, but after two years, WBAH was shut down.

Its last show featured music by soprano Tenie Murphy Sheehan and piano accompanist Lucille Frankman Murphy. Dayton's donated the station equipment to the Dunwoody Institute in Minneapolis.

Front-page headlines announced his death in the local papers, and many of the store's competitors ran mourning ads, including L. S. Donaldson Company and Powers Mercantile. The store closed on July 27 to allow employees to attend the funeral. A week later, George Dayton spoke to employees from the stairs leading to the balcony of the store: Nelson would assume many of Draper's duties. Nelson bought Draper's share of the common stock and began building a new executive team and refining the store's philosophy of service to the public.

The company celebrated its twenty-fifth anniversary in 1927 with a Silver Anniversary Sale that featured a store-window display of 43,022 coins—all minted in 1902. It also opened its first branch store that year: the three-story University Store near the University of Minnesota campus in Minneapolis. It sold only women's and men's wear, and an exotic tearoom on the third floor, called the Tent, was decorated to resemble a sheik's tent. Popular among the college crowd, it ran out of food quickly each day. Soon a second restaurant, the Dungeon, opened in the basement, decorated with balls and chains on the walls; its waiters wore prison stripes.

In 1928, the Dayton Company built a four-story parking garage on Eighth Street that could house three hundred automobiles. In summer 1929, the Dayton Company purchased J. B. Hudson and Son, a forty-five-year-old jewelry store. Just a few months later, the stock market crashed, launching the nation into the Great Depression.

The Dayton Company kept up an energetic fight during the Depression years by continuing to buy products in large quantities and then sell them at the lowest possible price. The basement store, now called the Downstairs Store, instituted "early bird" sales on Saturdays from 9 AM to noon. One of the lower-level store's main attractions was the daily bargain in the Red Arrow Booth, which customers could find by following huge symbols painted on the floor pointing the way.

Dayton's tried to pay for merchandise before it was received to save the money it would pay in interest. Those savings were passed on to the shopper. Management began focusing on specific departments to increase sales volume. In one example, a buyer filled a train car with 1,164

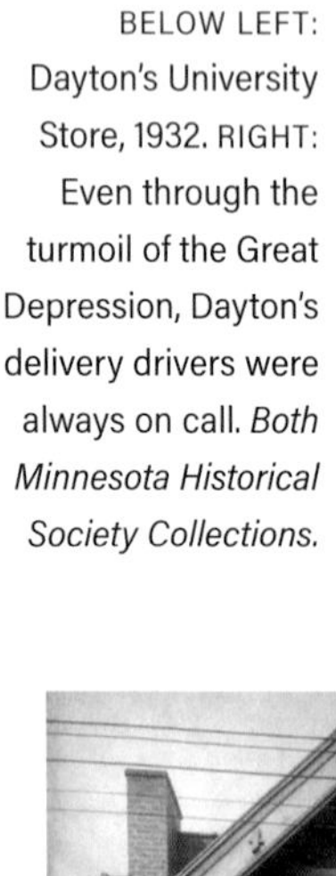

BELOW LEFT: Dayton's University Store, 1932. RIGHT: Even through the turmoil of the Great Depression, Dayton's delivery drivers were always on call. *Both Minnesota Historical Society Collections.*

overcoats from a mill in Gallison, Ohio, much to the delight of the small manufacturing town. When the coats arrived in Minneapolis, Dayton's advertised the coat sale and displayed nothing but those coats in its show windows and down the middle aisle of the store. The first day, enough items were sold to make the sale one of the store's most successful.

In December 1936, the company bought the land at the corner of Nicollet Avenue and Eighth Street, putting the entire block from Seventh to Eighth Streets under Dayton control. A few months later, Dayton's announced that it would raise the Eighth Street building to ten stories and the Nicollet corner to seven stories, improvements that would cost a total of $1 million.

Dayton's expansion project, 1937. *Minnesota Historical Society Collections.*

George Draper Dayton died on February 19, 1938, just before his eighty-first birthday. Headlines in the local papers lauded him as a "Leader in Northwest Business" and "Pioneer in Building of Agriculture in Minnesota." The store closed on February 21 for his funeral, which was held at Westminster Presbyterian Church.

By this time, a third generation of Daytons had begun to enter the business. Nelson Dayton's eldest son, Donald, joined the store in 1937, and his second son, Bruce Bliss Dayton, came on board in 1940. Before the decade ended, Wallace, Kenneth, and Douglas joined their brothers at the Dayton Company. Each began their careers in Dayton's receiving room. From there they went to the stockroom and then to the sales floor.

As the nation moved out of the Great Depression and into World War II, the Daytons continued to expand and add improvements to the store, including the installation of "moving stairways" from the street level to the fourth floor in October 1941.

Japan attacked Pearl Harbor in December 1941, launching the United States into World War II. The war had a curious effect on merchants like the Dayton Company. On one hand, buyers had a hard time obtaining goods to sell, but on the other hand, the scarcity of products available on the market drove more shoppers to Dayton's. When store buyers couldn't locate finished products, they hired manufacturers to make the products for them. The store bought raw materials like lumber and textiles—whatever was available—and contracted with vendors to produce articles to order.

When the government initiated a scrap-metal drive to increase resources for munitions in 1942, the Dayton Company complied. The large

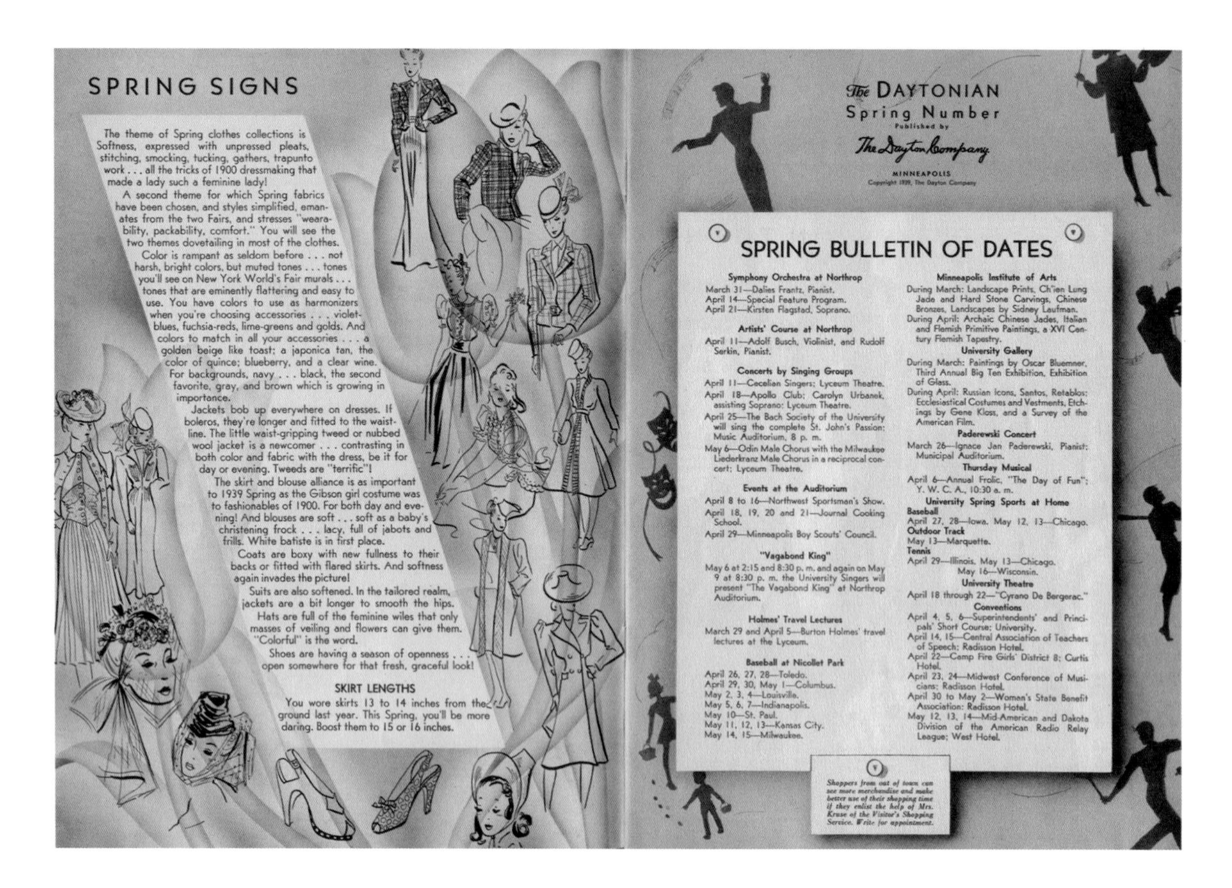

SPRING SIGNS

The theme of Spring clothes collections is Softness, expressed with unpressed pleats, stitching, smocking, tucking, gathers, trapunto work . . . all the tricks of 1900 dressmaking that made a lady such a feminine lady!

A second theme for which Spring fabrics have been chosen, and styles simplified, emanates from the two Fairs, and stresses "wearability, packability, comfort." You will see the two themes dovetailing in most of the clothes.

Color is rampant as seldom before . . . not harsh, bright colors, but muted tones . . . tones you'll see on New York World's Fair murals . . . tones that are eminently flattering and easy to use. You have colors to use as harmonizers when you're choosing accessories . . . violet-blues, fuchsia-reds, lime-greens and golds. And colors to match in all your accessories . . . a golden beige like toast; a japonica tan, the color of quince; blueberry, and a clear wine. For backgrounds, navy . . . black, the second favorite, gray, and brown which is growing in importance.

Jackets bob up everywhere on dresses. If boleros, they're longer and fitted to the waistline. The little waist-gripping tweed or nubbed wool jacket is a newcomer . . . contrasting in both color and fabric with the dress, be it for day or evening. Tweeds are "terrific"!

The skirt and blouse alliance is as important to 1939 Spring as the Gibson girl costume was to fashionables of 1900. For both day and evening! And blouses are soft . . . soft as a baby's christening frock . . . lacy, full of jabots and frills. White batiste is in first place.

Coats are boxy with new fullness to their backs or fitted with flared skirts. And softness again invades the picture!

Suits are also softened. In the tailored realm, jackets are a bit longer to smooth the hips.

Hats are full of the feminine wiles that only masses of veiling and flowers can give them. "Colorful" is the word.

Shoes are having a season of openness . . . open somewhere for that fresh, graceful look!

SKIRT LENGTHS

You wore skirts 13 to 14 inches from the ground last year. This Spring, you'll be more daring. Boost them to 15 or 16 inches.

The DAYTONIAN
Spring Number
Published by
The Dayton Company
MINNEAPOLIS
Copyright 1939, The Dayton Company

SPRING BULLETIN OF DATES

Symphony Orchestra at Northrop
March 31—Dalies Frantz, Pianist.
April 14—Special Feature Program.
April 21—Kirsten Flagstad, Soprano.

Artists' Course at Northrop
April 11—Adolf Busch, Violinist, and Rudolf Serkin, Pianist.

Concerts by Singing Groups
April 11—Cecelian Singers; Lyceum Theatre.
April 18—Apollo Club; Carolyn Urbanek, assisting Soprano; Lyceum Theatre.
April 25—The Bach Society of the University will sing the complete St. John's Passion; Music Auditorium, 8 p. m.
May 6—Odin Male Chorus with the Milwaukee Liederkranz Male Chorus in a reciprocal concert; Lyceum Theatre.

Events at the Auditorium
April 8 to 16—Northwest Sportsman's Show.
April 18, 19, 20 and 21—Journal Cooking School.
April 29—Minneapolis Boy Scouts' Council.

"Vagabond King"
May 6 at 2:15 and 8:30 p. m. and again on May 9 at 8:30 p. m. the University Singers will present "The Vagabond King" at Northrop Auditorium.

Holmes' Travel Lectures
March 29 and April 5—Burton Holmes' travel lectures at the Lyceum.

Baseball at Nicollet Park
April 26, 27, 28—Toledo.
April 29, 30, May 1—Columbus.
May 2, 3, 4—Louisville.
May 5, 6, 7—Indianapolis.
May 10—St. Paul.
May 11, 12, 13—Kansas City.
May 14, 15—Milwaukee.

Minneapolis Institute of Arts
During March: Landscape Prints, Ch'ien Lung Jade and Hard Stone Carvings, Chinese Bronzes, Landscapes by Sidney Laufman.
During April: Archaic Chinese Jades, Italian and Flemish Primitive Paintings, a XVI Century Flemish Tapestry.

University Gallery
During March: Paintings by Oscar Bluemner, Third Annual Big Ten Exhibition, Exhibition of Glass.
During April: Russian Icons, Santos, Retablos; Ecclesiastical Costumes and Vestments, Etchings by Gene Kloss, and a Survey of the American Film.

Paderewski Concert
March 26—Ignace Jan Paderewski, Pianist; Municipal Auditorium.

Thursday Musical
April 6—Annual Frolic, "The Day of Fun"; Y. W. C. A., 10:30 a. m.

University Spring Sports at Home
Baseball
April 27, 28—Iowa. May 12, 13—Chicago.
Outdoor Track
May 13—Marquette.
Tennis
April 29—Illinois. May 13—Chicago.
May 16—Wisconsin.

University Theatre
April 18 through 22—"Cyrano De Bergerac."

Conventions
April 4, 5, 6—Superintendents' and Principals' Short Course; University.
April 14, 15—Central Association of Teachers of Speech; Radisson Hotel.
April 22—Camp Fire Girls' District 8; Curtis Hotel.
April 23, 24—Midwest Conference of Musicians; Radisson Hotel.
April 30 to May 2—Women's State Benefit Association; Radisson Hotel.
May 12, 13, 14—Mid-American and Dakota Division of the American Radio Relay League; West Hotel.

Shoppers from out of town can see more merchandise and make better use of their shopping time if they enlist the help of Mrs. Kruse of the Visitor's Shopping Service. Write for appointment.

The spring 1939 issue of the *Daytonian* proclaimed the themes of the season to be "softness" and "wearability, packability, comfort." It also dared women to shorten their skirts: "You wore skirts 13 to 14 inches from the ground last year. This Spring, you'll be more daring. Boost them to 15 or 16 inches." *Hennepin County Library.*

electric rooftop sign that had long lit up the skyline with the company name, "Dayton's," was dismantled, and like the Donaldson's dome across the street, the materials were sent off to support the war effort.

In 1943, Dayton's shelved many of its annual sales, including the September Jubilee Sale, which was canceled "to comply with the government agency's request that we have no promotion sales of textiles and textile products which comprise a major part of our merchandise."[2]

The store canceled the anniversary sale again in 1944, but Dayton's still found a way to celebrate its forty-second anniversary and impress the crowds: it created a display of Twin Cities history in miniature in its store windows along Nicollet Avenue. Featured were a scale model of the round tower at Fort Snelling in 1820, a view of St. Anthony Falls and the nearby lumber and flour mills in 1857, street scenes from 1885, and a view of Nicollet Avenue looking toward the old Westminster church, the site of what would become the Dayton Company.

The Oval Room and the Studio of Interior Decorating and Designing were among the store's major innovations in the 1940s. The Oval Room was actually a remodel of what had been the Model Shop, a department that carried strictly American-designer clothing during World War II. After the war ended in August 1945, the Oval Room brought European designers back to Minnesota. The Studio, as it was called, was one of the first design studios to be placed in a department store. Its first attention-getting project was a penthouse apartment in the Radisson Hotel next door. The design of the new Town House quickly established the reputation of the studio, which sent buyers to Europe after the war to acquire furniture, Venetian glass, and art objects from across the continent.

In December 1945, Dayton's announced it would add five floors to the seven-floor corner at Nicollet and Eighth Street. It would also extend the escalator service to the seventh floor and install air conditioning on all floors. Plans for the twelfth floor included the Sky Room

LET THEM WEAR NYLONS

Nylon, a material introduced by DuPont in 1939, was in high demand during World War II. When Japan stopped exporting silk to the United States, manufacturers turned to nylon to create parachutes, airplane cords, and ropes. Nylon, it turned out, also made a pretty nice stocking, something that was in short supply throughout the war.

When DuPont shifted from manufacturing wartime material to nylon stockings in August 1945, the public was hungry for them. Dayton's began stocking nylons that fall, and in January 1946, it teased customers with a full-page newspaper ad letting the public know that Dayton's now "had enough" to host a nylon sale on February 6.

Thousands of people filled the streets surrounding Dayton's by six thirty on the morning of the sale, despite the cold and heavy snow—and a police alert that an accused murderer had just escaped from the Hennepin County jail. Fifteen police officers were posted at the store and twelve firefighters were on hand. The crowd was estimated at twenty thousand.

Employees prepared for the big sale for weeks, packaging the nylons in twos—the limit each customer would be allowed to buy—and locking them in the sub-basement fur vaults. When sale day arrived, Dayton's was ready with a plan to move shoppers through the store. Customers would be admitted through the Eighth Street door, then led by elevator to the third floor, where they would get into a queue that would make its way by escalator to the second floor. They then would be led through the toy department, the boys' and men's wear departments, and the yard goods section until they arrived at the cashiers' windows to pay for the nylons in advance. They would then take their receipt to the counters, where stockings were stacked by sizes and price. Eighty-eight salespeople were assigned to work exclusively on the nylon sale.

The store sold twenty thousand pairs that Wednesday and closed sales just after noon. The plan was to sell another twenty thousand pairs on Thursday and another twenty thousand on Friday. On Saturday, February 9, Dayton's ran an ad announcing, "There will be no sale of stockings today."

and Oak Grill restaurants, conference rooms, and an auditorium.

In April 1950, Nelson Dayton died of cancer, and the Dayton boys—Donald, Bruce, Kenneth, Wallace, and Douglas—all under the age of thirty-six, took the reins of America's second-largest privately owned department store. Their father had left each son 20 percent of the business. The brothers were joined by their cousin George Draper Dayton II, Draper Dayton's son, who served as executive general manager of the store.

ABOVE: Thousands lined up for the Dayton's nylon sale in January 1946. *Hennepin County Library.* LEFT: The five Dayton brothers and their cousin: (seated, from left) cousin George Draper Dayton II, Donald, and Douglas; (standing, from left) Wallace, Kenneth, and Bruce. *Minnesota Historical Society Collections.*

THIS PAGE: Advertisement for the Oval Room in the *Daytonian*, spring 1950. *Hennepin County Library.* OPPOSITE, CLOCKWISE FROM TOP LEFT: Women shoppers checking out the merchandise in the Oval Room, circa 1945. *Minnesota Historical Society Collections.* Famed photographer Erwin Blumenfeld shot photos for Oval Room advertisements, such as this one, which appeared in *Vogue,* circa 1950. *Goldstein Museum of Design.* Shoppers riding the escalators at Dayton's. Pop singer Mindy Carson worked the candy counter at Dayton's while promoting her appearance in Minneapolis, late 1940s. *Both Hennepin County Library.*

OVAL ROOM

TOP ROW, LEFT TO RIGHT: Dresses and coats department, circa 1949. Ladies' shoes, circa 1949. Men's ties and accessories, circa 1949. BOTTOM ROW, LEFT TO RIGHT: Frills and accessories, circa 1949. Sewing notions, 1956. *All Minnesota Historical Society Collections.*

Notions
Veilings
Plastic
skirt marker
dress form
SELF COVER BUTTON
Make Your Own
CONTOUR BELT
BOUND BUTTONHOLES
Baldwin
ADJUSTABLE

CLOCKWISE FROM TOP LEFT: Artist's rendering of the planned branch store in Rochester. *Minnesota Historical Society Collections.* Margot Siegel (left) and Jeanne Auerbacher; Jeanne Auerbacher in her office at Dayton's. *Both Goldstein Museum of Design.* A float in a Rochester parade promoted the city's new store, 1952. *Minnesota Historical Society Collections.*

The postwar economic boom in the United States brought a period of expansion to the Dayton Corporation in the 1950s and 1960s. The company opened a Rochester store in 1952, one in Southdale in 1956, and locations in St. Paul and South Dakota in the early 1960s. In May 1962—the same year Kmart opened in Garden City, Michigan, and Walmart debuted in Rogers, Arkansas—the Dayton Company opened its first Target store on Snelling Avenue in Roseville. By the end of the year, Target stores were opened in Duluth and the Twin Cities suburbs of St. Louis Park and Crystal.

In addition to the physical expansion, the company's penchant for marketing and style also ramped up beginning in the 1950s. The company went national with its marketing campaign, advertising in magazines such as *Harper's Bazaar* and *Vogue.* It was rare to see a retailer outside of New York City advertising in those publications. Dayton's brought in nationally recognized photographers, including Erwin Blumenfeld, for its Oval Room ads. And the department held annual spring fashion shows and trunk shows that included appearances by the clothing designers.

In the 1960s, Dayton's focused its merchandising approach on youth. It opened an auditorium on the eighth floor of the Minneapolis store in 1963 for annual Christmas exhibits and flower shows, but the venue soon became host to

LIKE MOTHER, LIKE DAUGHTER

One was known for her signature pillbox hat, alligator bag, and the black pearl earring she wore in her right ear, the white pearl in the left ear; the other for her remarkable collection of pop art on her walls and in her clothing. Madame Jeanne Auerbacher and her daughter, Margot Siegel, became fashion icons in the Twin Cities in the twentieth century, yet both fell into their respective careers quite by accident.

Auerbacher, who managed Dayton's downtown Minneapolis Oval Room from 1947 to 1956 and became known as the "Queen" of that venue, began her career after her husband's broom-and-mop factory hit hard times during the Great Depression.

Auerbacher was hired by her close friend Elizabeth Quinlan to work at the Young-Quinlan store's perfume counter, and she then went on to sell sportswear at Dayton's in 1934. She worked with merchandising manager Stuart Wells in the Model Shop, the forerunner to the Oval Room, through World War II. The Model Shop began as the French Room, a department that carried French designer clothes. After Germany declared war on France in 1939, French imports stopped, and Dayton's management renamed the venue the Model Shop and sold only American-made clothes. Siegel said her mother helped make American designers' work "important."

After the war ended, the Model Shop was remodeled and reopened as the elegant Oval Room—a beautiful oval-shaped room where designer clothes were kept in a back room and saleswomen brought them out to the customers.

Auerbacher was known as the Merchant Princess in the New York fashion market and as a buyer with impeccable taste. She was an extraordinary saleswoman who counted as friends some of the great names in the fashion world during the 1930s and 1940s, including Gilbert Adrian (MGM Studio costume designer who created Judy Garland's gingham pinafore in *The Wizard of Oz* and established his own fashion house during the war), Hattie Carnegie (first to introduce ready-to-wear and who launched many famous designers, including Norman Norell), and Philip Mangone (known as much for his elegant wool suits as his survival in the 1937 crash of the German passenger airship, LZ 129 *Hindenburg,* in New Jersey).

Siegel—who said she practically grew up in the fitting rooms of Dayton's—fell into her own fashion career when she was hired at *Women's Wear Daily* in New York after working as a news and feature writer for the Red Cross during World War II. She later worked as a Hollywood publicist and an overseas correspondent for Fairchild Publications before returning to the Twin Cities, where she became the public relations director at the Walker Art Center; founded her own public relations firm, SHE, with Gloria Hogan; and wrote features and a column for the *Minneapolis Star Tribune*. Many Twin Cities residents remember her for her pop culture column "Margot," published in *Skyway News* in the 1990s.

> **"The more elaborately you dress, the older you look. Never sacrifice dignity for youth. You should only look as young as your age allows."**
>
> *— fashion advice from Madame Jeanne Auerbacher in 1974.*[3]

Siegel wrote the book *Fashion* (*Looking Forward to a Career*), published in 1974, and founded the Friends of the Goldstein Museum of Design, which supports the University of Minnesota's design gallery. The Goldstein holds an incredible fashion collection, including the work of Coco Chanel, Christian Dior, Norman Norell, and Isaac Mizrahi. In 2012, the museum paid tribute to Siegel with the Margot Siegel Design Award, which honors emerging designers.

Siegel paid homage to her mother, who died in 1975, in a show of mid-twentieth-century fashion at the Goldstein in 2000. *Fashion Lives, Fashion Lives* displayed garments owned by Auerbacher and also featured a duplication of Auerbacher's office, with a life-size cardboard cutout of the Oval Room queen behind her desk in front of a wall of autographed eight-by-ten-inch photographs of the fashion luminaries with whom she worked.

In 2009, the Goldstein hosted *Intersections: Where Art Meets Fashion,* a show of art and apparel donated by Siegel to the museum. Pieces included a Louis Vuitton cherry blossom handbag designed by Takashi, a dress featuring Andy Warhol's Campbell's Soup can, and a woman's business suit featuring a print by Roy Lichtenstein. Siegel was eighty-six when the show opened.

Siegel said her mother never gave her advice on fashion. She figured that out on her own. "I always had terrific taste," she said in 2013. Siegel died in 2015 at age ninety-one.

BELOW, LEFT TO RIGHT: New York fashion models arrive in Minneapolis for the American Designers fashion show, held at Dayton's Sky Room in September 1957. A Nettie Rosenstein gown modeled in the Sky Room for the Friends of the Minneapolis Institute of Art's annual fashion show, September 1959. Stuart Wells is standing in the background. *Both Minnesota Historical Society Collections.* Woman modeling a Russian sable housecoat by Leo Ritter, December 1963. Star Tribune *photo, Minnesota Historical Society Collections.* RIGHT: Invitation to a showing of the Nettie Rosenstein Collection in Dayton's Sky Room, September 1958. *Hennepin County Library.*

The Friends of
the Minneapolis Institute of Art
invite you and your friends
to a showing by the Dayton Oval Room
of the
Nettie Rosenstein Collection
Thursday, the fourth of September
at three thirty o'clock.
Sky Room

TICKETS THREE DOLLARS
TEA WILL BE SERVED

PATRICIA MORRISON
OF "KISS ME KATE"
WILL BE A SPECIAL ATTRACTION

Saturday afternoon teen dances, concerts by local rock bands, and fashion shows featuring the latest teen trends. Youth was "an important, rapidly growing segment of the buying public," the store explained to employees in the December 1965 company newsletter. The store had hosted a monthlong "Youthquake" in August that featured appearances by young English designers, popular entertainers, and the introduction of London "mod" fashions. And the most important piece of all of this: Dayton's was the first department store in the United States to do it.

Dolores DeFore, the assistant fashion coordinator in the juniors department at the time, said it was all because she was in the right place at the right time. Her boss, Stuart Wells, had just returned from a trip to Europe in spring 1965. He came back and told her, "Dolores, you've got to go to London now." "I was on a plane within three or four days," she recalled. Once there, she bought clothes from designers Mary Quant, Angela Cash, and Gerald McCann and arranged for all of them to come to Dayton's for the back-to-school promotions later that year. Quant agreed to bring

Dayton's modern air door

MEET US AT THE WINDY DOOR

In 1959, the Dayton's Minneapolis store unveiled its new "Thermal Door," which kept heat in and cold out. The "doorless door" was a nineteen-foot-wide curtain of air flowing down from jets over the entrance to a grill on the floor, where the air was filtered, heated or cooled, and then recirculated by fans. The store claimed that the moving air insulated the interior of the store from outside dust, dirt, snow, rain, temperatures, animals, and insects. Sliding panes of glass were moved into place when the store was closed.

Vanessa Green, who would take the bus downtown for teen dances in the 1960s, said, "We would always meet by the 'windy door,' the air door. We called it the windy door because it was windy there."

The door was located at the Eighth Street and LaSalle Avenue entrance, next to the Dayton-Radisson parking ramp. When Dayton's opened its new store in downtown St. Paul, it included an "Air Door" at its main entrance.

Super Youthquake hit Dayton's during August and the vibrations are just beginning to subside after the month-long "soopah" series of shows for college students, teens, junior teens, and children.

Such headliners as Simon and Garfunkel, the Yardbirds, The Mitchell Trio and Gerry Mulligan entertained, and designers such as Luba, of pantsuit fame, Roger Nelson of London, and Denise of California showed their latest fashions.

During the first week of August, events were devoted to the teens with fashion shows, entertainers, and "live" radio broadcasts from Dayton's. Teen Board members arrived in all stores wearing new brick and heather brown military-looking outfits.

Junior Teen Board "Sound in '66" fashion shows highlighted the second week. Board members in all stores switched into their fall outfits of pow plaid hacking jackets and hipster skirts.

Fashion tips and beauty tricks for the back to college crowd were given at a "Beauty Beat" during the third week in August, and "Super '66" college shows were held at Minneapolis, St. Paul, and Southdale.

During the last week of the month Casey and Roundhouse Rodney, of "Lunch With Casey" fame, broadcast their WTCN-TV show live from the Minneapolis store auditorium daily.

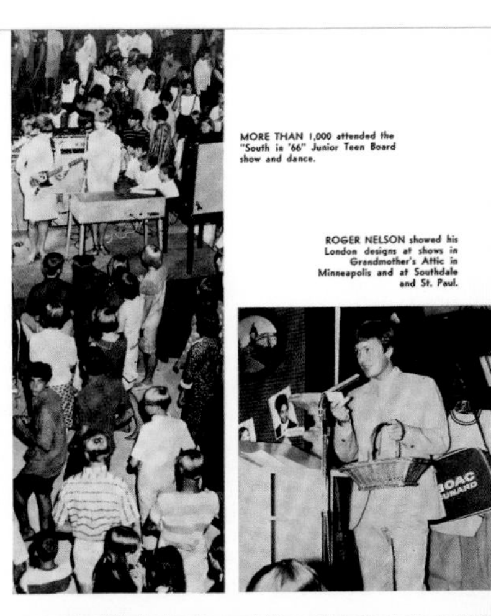

MORE THAN 1,000 attended the "South in '66" Junior Teen Board show and dance.

ROGER NELSON showed his London designs at shows in Grandmother's Attic in Minneapolis and at Southdale and St. Paul.

THE MITCHELL TRIO headlined the Minneapolis "Super '66" college show.

SUPER YOUTHQUAKE views members of of Dayton's youth boards in their new fall outfits. From left, Nancy Ross, Junior Teen Board; Chris Hunczak, Teen Board; Sophie Gruen, College Board; and David Brown, Varsity Board.

SUPER YOUTHQUAKE WAS HERE!

SEPTEMBER 1966 12

all of her models and fall fashion collection for a show in August. "It was the most fun thing in my whole career," DeFore said of the trip.

A few weeks later, DeFore was at a buyers' meeting in New York City when she was asked to speak about her trip to London: "I tell them about how these clothes were just phenomenal, and how I got all three of those designers to come over to Dayton's fall season," she said. "They couldn't get out of that room fast enough to see what they could do to get Mary Quant to come to them."

Quant, the British designer who is credited with creating the "mod" look, had her first show in the United States at Dayton's in August 1965. The Youthquake promotion included Gary Lewis and the Playboys performing at fashion shows in the store, a pop-up "Pizza Pub" for teens only, performances by Liverpool band the Remo Four, and, of course, shows with fashions by Quant, McCann, and Cash.

LEFT: Article in the *Daytonian* promoting "Youthquake," September 1966. *Target Corporation.* NEXT PAGES, CLOCKWISE FROM TOP LEFT: Easter window display of children's clothing, March 1940. *Minnesota Historical Society Collections.* Window display of the "RCA Whirlpool Miracle Kitchen," circa 1950s. *Hennepin History Museum.* Women's clothing window display, 1962. *Minnesota Historical Society Collections.* Window display promoting election voting, October 1956. *Hennepin History Museum.*

VOTE AS YOU PLEASE
BUT VOTE
LEARN HOW TO OPERATE
election
voting
machine
october 25-31
Vote November 6th

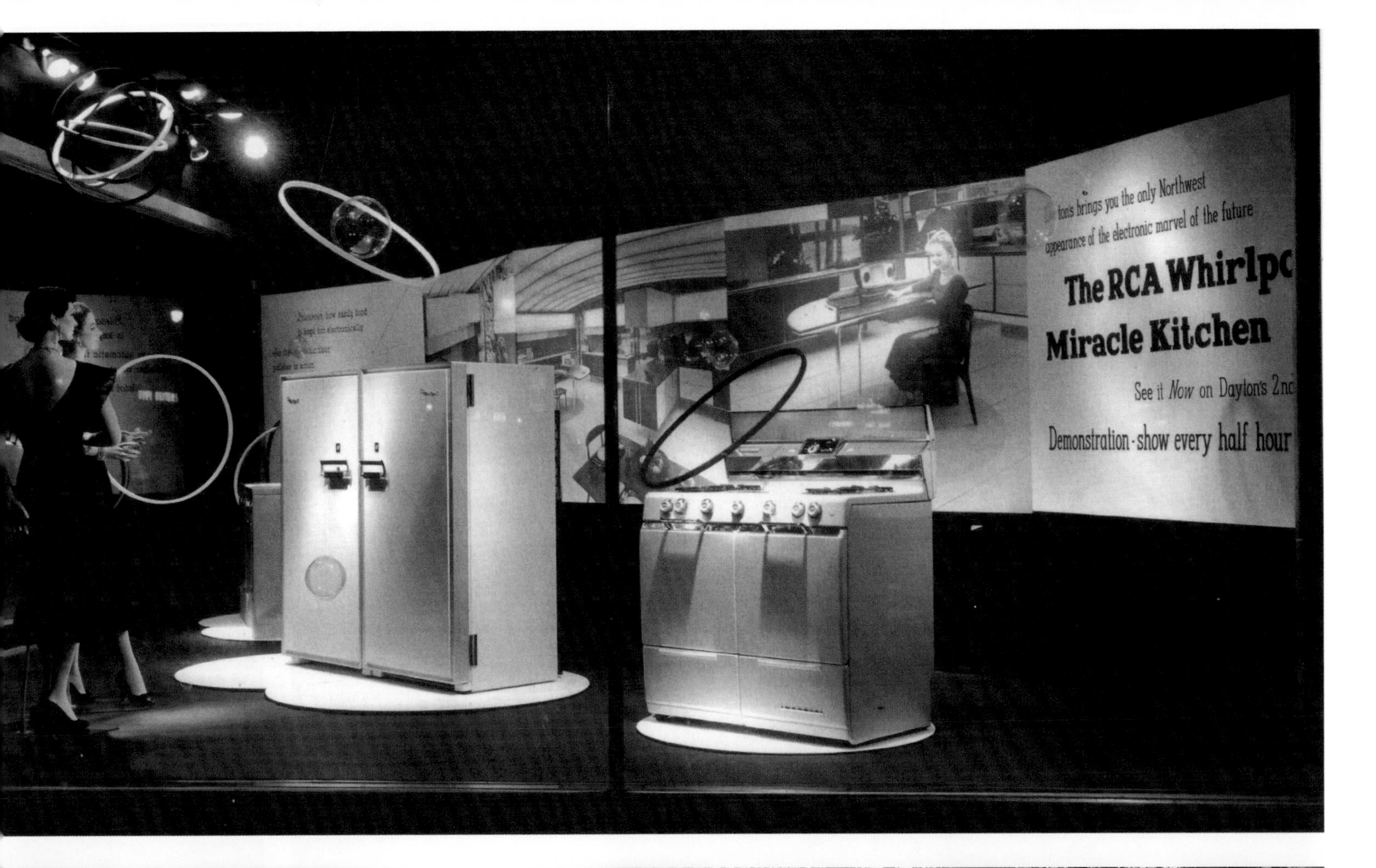
tons brings you the only Northwest
appearance of the electronic marvel of the future
The RCA Whirlpc
Miracle Kitchen
See it Now on Dayton's 2nc
Demonstration - show every half hour

suits on the
American Plan
blouses included!

ABOVE LEFT TO RIGHT: Window display of bowling gear, August 1949. Daisy Sale window display, May 1956. *Both Minnesota Historical Society Collections.*

"We beat the New York stores. Dayton's was the first one, and it was all because my timing was so great," DeFore said. "It was luck, and we made the right decisions. That was just a phenomenal fall season for us."

Dayton's didn't leave men out of the new fashions. The store opened the John Stephen shop on the second floor, which featured a new shaped look for men: pinched-waist jackets, trim button-down high-collared shirts, and skimpy low-slung trousers.

Dayton's ramped up back-to-school week in 1966 with Super Youthquake and "Soopah" fashion shows at a number of Dayton's stores. The downtown store hosted performances by the Yardbirds (featuring future Led Zeppelin guitarist Jimmy Page), Simon and Garfunkel, the Mitchell Trio (which included John Denver, who would become a hit 1970s folk singer), the Del Counts, and more. Super Youthquake was personified with a vinyl-clad motorcycle-riding character who visited Dayton's stores in Minneapolis, St. Paul, Southdale, and Brookdale aboard his vinyl-trimmed Honda.

A full-page advertisement in Twin Cities newspapers on July 31, 1966, proclaimed: "Faster than lighting, pow—here comes Super Youthquake! . . . Whenever you see the flash of vinyl, another Dayton's back-to-school bash begins." *Newsweek* called Dayton's "the swingingest spot in Minneapolis" in its August 22, 1966, issue: "To hear the folks at Dayton's tell it, it's right by the dishpans and ironing boards, and just left of the wicker rockers in Dayton's auditorium. This

week the 1,500-seat auditorium is in the middle of a month-long explosion in sound, billed 'Super Youthquake,' with tremors supplied by such groups as the Yardbirds, Simon and Garfunkel, the Mitchell Trio and thousands of their frenetic fans. . . . [T]o general manager Kenneth Dayton, they all produce the same sweet sound: clanging cash registers."

Speaking at a meeting of the Minnesota Retailers Federation in October 1966, Wells described the effect the country's youth was having on his store's merchandising methods: "The young are starting changes. The wealthy of Paris and London used to set the fashion, but today, it may be among the young and poor in Liverpool."[4]

IT WAS A MOD, MOD WORLD

Dayton's advertising department moved right along with the Optical Art movement in 1965 by creating ads with optical illusions. The store's Youthquake ads that year were shimmering, shaking, and moving—all because of the principles of Op Art being used in many of them. The store's employee magazine, the *Daytonews,* explained it: "It's a popular art movement called 'Op,' short for Optical Art. This kind of art has been so popular this year that it has titillated the fashion and home-furnishing market as provocatively as it has the eye of the gallery-goer.

"An Op design fools your eyes into seeing an *optical* illusion—something that is not really there. . . . Artists who started Op Art use science in their work. They measure lines and shapes to make designs that seem to move. They fold curves into curves. They slip triangles into squares. They zigzag straight lines. Their art shimmers and shakes."

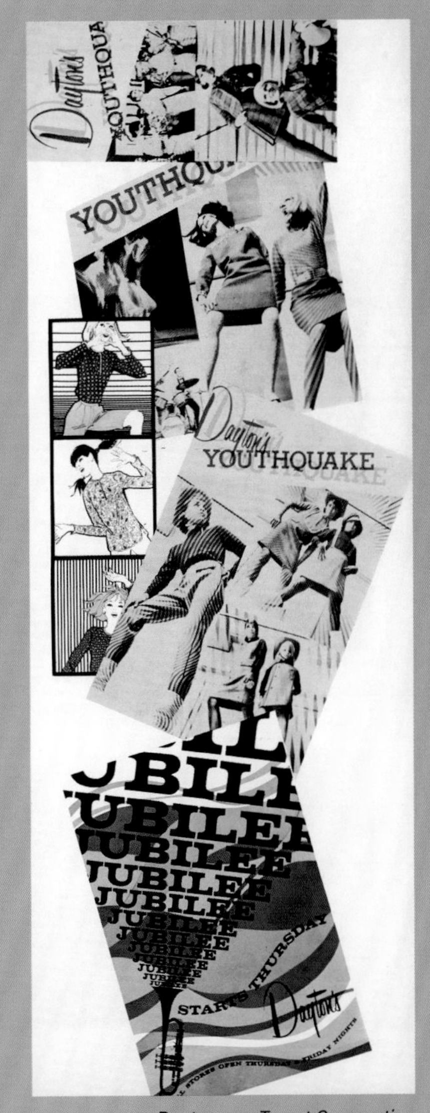

Daytonews. Target Corporation

Dayton's claimed to be one of the first department stores in the country to use this new style of ads.

Twiggy

TWIGGY!

She was cute. She was tall. She was very skinny. And she was a coup for Dayton's, the first department store outside of New York to get British supermodel Leslie Hornsby—known to the world as Twiggy—to visit on her trip to the United States in 1967.

When she arrived at the Minneapolis–St. Paul airport on April 22—dubbed Twiggy Day at Dayton's—the wispy seventeen-year-old was greeted by three hundred fans and eight very thin Twin Cities teens made up in Twiggy fashion and holding silver "Welcome Twiggy" signs. The girls were hired by Dayton's for Twiggy's two-day visit.

Just months after the popular and very British back-to-school Youthquake event, Dayton's arranged for the model to appear in a fashion show in the Minneapolis store's eighth-floor auditorium and make an appearance at its St. Paul store. Advertisements for "Twiggy types" were posted the month before. The qualifications: five feet, six inches tall, ninety-one pounds, a bust size of thirty-one inches, waist of twenty-two, and hips of thirty-two, and be willing to get a haircut a la Twiggy.

Todd Knaeble, just out of high school at that time, gave his friend Mike Barich a ride to the airport so Barich could photograph the event. "I remember this skinny little girl, big eyes, not much hair," Knaeble said. Barich spent the next couple of days photographing the model. His takeaway: she was young, she was sweet, and she liked to read comic books in her spare time.

"She was a cute, cute, cute little girl," said Dolores DeFore, the buyer for junior dresses. "She had this great face and this great-looking hair, and she seemed friendly and nice."

Dayton's introduced the "Twiggy Collection" of clothes, one of which Twiggy modeled at Dayton's. Vanessa Green remembers the dress. A fourteen-year-old at the time, Green was one of fifteen hundred who attended the April 23 fashion show, where the Twiggy look-alikes danced around portraying the model in various scenarios: Twiggy playing hopscotch, Twiggy coming home from school, Twiggy catching a butterfly.

"It was very crowded and hard to get close to the stage. I remember the models dancing down the catwalk and that dress with the horizontal stripe and pointed collar," which Green wanted badly. Her parents had an issue with the length, however. "It was a little too short," she said.

OPPOSITE: Mike Barich's photograph of Twiggy during her 1967 visit. THIS PAGE, TOP: Dayton's Twiggy lookalikes hold signs welcoming the British model to Minnesota. ABOVE: Justin de Villeneuve, the model's manager, led the way for Twiggy at the airport while protesters held signs raising awareness of body-image concerns around the slender model. *Both* Minneapolis Star *photos by William Seaman, Minnesota Historical Society Collections.*

ABOVE LEFT: In 1967, Dayton's re-introduced America's oldest soft drink, Moxie, as part of its back-to-school promotion. The concoction of gentian-root extract and twenty or so other flavors was said to taste somewhere between a cola and a root beer. Dayton's sold the drink by the bottle and carton. *Minnesota Historical Society Collections.* RIGHT: Bruce Dayton unveils the Alexander Calder sculpture on the new Nicollet Mall, November 2, 1967. Star Tribune *photo by Roy Swan, Minnesota Historical Society Collections.*

Shortly after Super Youthquake ended in 1966, the city broke ground on Nicollet Mall, which runs between Fifth and Twelfth Streets. Championed by Dayton's president Donald Dayton, the open-air pedestrian mall opened in October 1967 complete with trees, benches, and an eighteen-foot-high, fifteen-hundred-pound sculpture by Alexander Calder, commissioned by Dayton's at an estimated cost of $50,000. The store itself was remodeled so that passersby could look directly into boutiques rather than just at window-display mannequins. Inside, the cultural upheaval of the 1960s was making its way into the merchandise.

Dayton's kept up with fashion and cultural trends throughout the decade, holding yoga workshops, bringing in an astrologer who set up a computerized horoscope service in the store, launching B. Dalton Bookseller, and opening Gallery 12 on the twelfth floor. The in-house contemporary art gallery sold Tom Wesselmann nudes, Robert Rauschenberg lithographs, and sculptures by Marisol Escobar, among other artworks.

Also in October 1967, the Dayton Corporation went public with its first common stock offering: 450,000 shares at $34 per share. The new public company used the money raised to acquire new stores and expand B. Dalton. In 1968, the company acquired four Lipman Wolfe department stores in Oregon and two Diamond's stores in Phoenix, Arizona. And on May 20, 1969, the *Minneapolis Tribune* reported that Dayton shareholders had approved a merger with the J. L. Hudson Company of Detroit to form the Dayton Hudson Corporation. At the time, Hudson's operated the third-largest department store in the country, after Macy's Herald Square in Manhattan and Marshall Field's in Chicago. Hudson's was the largest privately held department store in the United States. The new corporation staged a huge flower show on Wall Street on September 9 to celebrate the Dayton Hudson listing on the New York Stock Exchange.

In the 1960s, Dayton's sold refrigerators, stoves, washers, and dryers; it had a hardware department stocked with power drills, belt sanders, and assorted sizes of ladders; and it sold sporting goods, including canoes, fishing equipment, and guns. The Dayton Hudson Corporation experimented and expanded with jewelry stores, a tire company (Lechmere Tires and Sales), consumer electronics (Team Central), and even a catalog showroom through the late 1960s and into the 1970s.

In 1978, B. Dalton Bookseller had 357 stores in forty-three states, including a flagship store on Fifth Avenue in Manhattan. That year, the Dayton Hudson Corporation bought Mervyn's, a midscale department store chain with stores in California, Nevada, and Arizona. In Minnesota, Dayton's opened its furniture Home Stores in Edina and Roseville.

By the end of the decade, Dayton Hudson owned stores in forty-four states—including Dayton's in Minnesota, North Dakota, and South Dakota; Diamond's in Arizona and Nevada; Lipman's in Oregon; J. L. Hudson's in Michigan and Ohio; and the John A. Brown chain in Oklahoma. Target was operating eighty stores in eleven states.

Dayton's was moving into a new era, and that became apparent for *Minneapolis Star* columnist Jim Klobuchar on the January morning in 1978 when he discovered Dayton's no longer sold buttons. "Never have I walked into Dayton's without my every need being satisfied and a few new ones being identified," wrote Klobuchar, who once described Dayton's as one of three institutions in which Minnesotans had an unbreakable faith (church and the potluck supper being the other two). The end of button sales at the Nicollet Avenue store that had been there before Social Security or Medicare, before shopping centers or credit cards, the store that had outlasted the League of Nations and the British empire—in Klobuchar's words—had just crushed an illusion for the writer: "If you couldn't find it at Dayton's, either it didn't exist or it was illegal."[5]

A Gallery 12 exhibit on Dayton's twelfth floor featured the work of Robert Rauschenberg in 1970. *Robert Rauschenberg Foundation.*

By 1976, the Dayton brothers and their cousin George had all stepped down from management, and in 1983, Bruce and Kenneth Dayton retired from the corporation's board of directors, ending eight decades of direct family involvement with the company. Three years later, the corporation sold B. Dalton to Barnes and Noble.

The Dayton's flagship store in Minneapolis began a remodel of the lower level in 1983 and transformed the bargain basement into an eighty-three-thousand-square-foot "open-air market" that included gourmet foods, a bakery, a candy shop, and an express-service café. The floor also included a pharmacy, a housewares department, a bed-and-bath department, and an electronics department. The budget merchandise that was once housed in the lower level was integrated throughout the store.

Through the final years of the century, the Dayton Hudson Corporation continued to expand by acquisition, but the Twin Cities institution was nearing its end. In April 1990, the company bought Chicago's leading retailer, Marshall Field's, for nearly $1.4 billion. This made the Dayton Hudson Corporation the second-largest department store retailer in the nation, just behind Macy's.

The Marshall Field's purchase came a month after Dayton Hudson announced it would refurbish the exterior of the Minneapolis Dayton's store, which came at the same time as a renovation of Nicollet Mall. Dayton's exterior would be restored by stripping six layers of brown paint and reopening twelve display windows that had been covered in 1984. The renovation employed the same color green around the façade of the store's new windows that George Draper Dayton used when the building was constructed in 1902. The work also included the renewal of the two-story granite colonnade that encompasses the building.

Under single corporate management, the three department stores—Hudson's, Dayton's, and Marshall Field's—began to see a merging of traditions. In 1991, Dayton's began sharing its eighth-floor holiday shows with Marshall Field's and Hudson's. Dayton's 1990 show, "Peter Pan," was staged at Hudson's in Southfield, Michigan, in 1991. That same year, the "Cinderella" set from the 1989 Dayton's Christmas show filled the windows at Marshall Field's flagship Chicago store.

In 1992, Dayton's announced it would drop its Spring Oval Room Show in Minneapolis and instead stage "A Cause for Applause," the Minneapolis version of Hudson's "Fash Bash" in Detroit.

LEFT TO RIGHT: Dayton's gift box, circa 1960s. *Minnesota Historical Society Collections.* Ad for the semi-annual Dayton's home sale, 1977. Artist's rendering of plans for the 1991 restoration of the exterior of the Dayton's building in Minneapolis. *Both Hennepin County Library.*

"A Cause for Applause" would benefit the Children's Cancer Research Fund and was held in July that year. In 1995, "A Cause for Applause" took the "Fash Bash" name. It branched out to Chicago in 1999 and was renamed "Glamorama" in 2003.

By 2000, Target had become the core business of the Dayton Hudson Corporation, and the company name was changed to Target Corporation to reflect that. The next year, the Dayton's name disappeared from the building at the corner of Seventh and Nicollet, as well as the locations at the Dales and in other parts of Minnesota and in North Dakota and South Dakota. All Dayton's and Hudson's stores were renamed Marshall Field's, a name better known nationally, Target executives claimed. But for many Minnesotans, a part of Minnesota culture had died.

"In twenty years, 20 percent of the population will still be calling the store Dayton's," Lee Lynch of advertising company Carmichael Lynch told *Star Tribune* writer Kristin Tillotson for her "Pop Stand" column. "I hope he's right," Tillotson wrote. "But in a generation or two, children will return from visiting Grandma to ask, 'Daddy, what's a Dayton's?'"

In 2004, Target Corporation sold its Mervyn's chain, and a year later, it shed its department store division, selling Marshall Field's to May Department Stores Company for $3.2 billion. Shortly thereafter, Federated Department Stores acquired the May company.

In 2006, all Marshall Field's stores became Macy's. In 2013, Macy's closed the former Dayton's store in downtown St. Paul, and four years later, the company closed Minneapolis's Nicollet Avenue store.

When Lee Lynch predicted that by 2020 Minnesotans would still be calling the building Dayton's, he was right. Nearly twenty years after the Dayton's name changed to Marshall Field's, the building that provided a century of shopping and tradition to Minnesotans was undergoing a transformation into an eclectic complex of stores, eateries, and offices, with promises that many of the historic building's iconic elements would be incorporated into the design. The new owner, 601w Companies of New York, had named what they hoped would become a retail destination the Dayton's Project.

ABOVE: In the late 1980s to mid-1990s, Dayton's provided free backpacks to kids entering kindergarten in Minneapolis and St. Paul. *Hennepin County Library.*

nn Milner. *Rae MacDonough.*

THE FIRST LADY OF RETAIL

It's a safe guess that Ann Milner saw more changes in retail in her career at 700 Nicollet Avenue than any Minnesotan, alive or not—because she worked there for eighty-five years.

Born in 1902—the same year George Dayton opened Goodfellow's Daylight Store at the corner of Nicollet Avenue and Seventh Street—she joined the staff at the store in 1919 at age seventeen. She began as a package wrapper and cashier but quickly moved her way up and spent the bulk of her career in the furniture department.

She took the bus to work throughout her eight and a half decades of employment, but on her last day, February 11, 2004, she was picked up at her home by a limousine that dropped her off at the Minneapolis Marshall Field's store, where she was greeted by Target Corporation managers and a host of coworkers and friends.

Milner continued to visit the store to have lunch at the Oak Grill up until her death on New Year's Day 2007.

CLOCKWISE FROM TOP RIGHT: Dayton's spring catalog, 1990s. Programs for Dayton's 1992 "A Cause for Applause," a benefit for the Children's Cancer Research Fund, and its successor, "Fash Bash," from 1995. Dayton's annual Jubilee Sale, 1978. *All Hennepin County Library.*

THAT MONKEY BUSINESS

Social media and news sites were abuzz in April 2018 when a demolition crew working on the remodel of the Dayton's building in downtown Minneapolis found the dried remains of a monkey in an air duct.

Adam Peterson, one of the people working at the site, posted a photo of the long-deceased monkey on the Old Minneapolis Facebook page. Speculation on the mystery of the monkey ensued.

Dayton's had a pet store on the fifth floor in the late 1950s. The pet department apparently moved to the eighth floor in the early 1960s, just before the floor was remodeled for a new auditorium. An advertisement in the *Minneapolis Star* in March 1963 promoted an exotic pet sale that included yellow-wing conure parrots, baby alligators, myna birds, and two types of monkeys: spider and squirrel.

The monkey mystery seemed to be solved after Steven Laboe posted on the Old Minneapolis page that while working for Target Corporation in the Dayton's building in the early 2000s, he heard a longtime employee tell a story of a monkey escaping the eighth-floor pet store.

"The guy told me that this took place sometime back in the '60s, over the weekend, because when they found the cage empty on Monday they knew something was up. They finally determined that the monkey had escaped in the air conditioning ductwork. Someone complained about a horrible odor a few hours later, and (as he explained it to me) the monkey tried to make a jump for it but managed to get caught up in one of the exhaust fan blades. Needless to say, it wasn't a pretty picture."

The monkey tale took a new turn when Robbinsdale mayor Regan Murphy shared a story that involved his late father. Murphy's dad and a junior high pal had skipped school one day, made their way to downtown Minneapolis, and at some point stole a monkey that was on display at Dayton's. They put the monkey in a backpack and took it to the friend's home, where the animal wreaked havoc. A couple of days later, the boys took the monkey back to Dayton's and let it loose in the store, Murphy said.

Minnesota governor Mark Dayton, the great-grandson of Dayton's founder George Draper Dayton, worked in the family store in the 1960s. He addressed the monkey in an unrelated news conference the week the remains were found: "I was not responsible," he deadpanned.

The monkey is just one of a number of treasures discovered during the remodel, including a stashed stolen wallet that was returned to its owner nearly fifty years later and ninety ten-inch-long papier-mâché Easter nesting eggs that project spokesperson Cailin Rogers said were probably from the 1950s or 1960s.

"The building has tons of surprises," Rogers said. "From windows that have been boarded up to the way all four buildings connect to make one giant floor plate, there are a lot of nuances in such a historic structure."

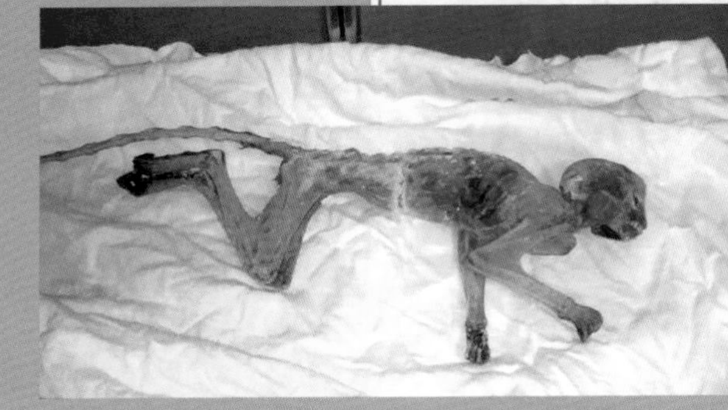

Old Minneapolis Facebook page.

TICKETS

5
All the Lines! Lines! Lines! Lines! Dayton's Eighth-Floor Auditorium

Walking into Dayton's downtown Minneapolis eighth-floor auditorium in December 1998 was like opening a giant version of Dr. Seuss's children's tale *How the Grinch Stole Christmas*. The entrance to the show resembled a walk-in book, and as visitors followed the path through the twenty-three vignettes of the show, the two-dimensional tale transformed into a three-dimensional extravaganza.

The brightly colored scenes included 109 animated figures in the fictional town of Whoville, complete with Who-houses, Who-shoppers, Who-feasts, and, of course, the Grinch and his dog, Max. Storyboards at each scene walked viewers through the narrative, which ends with the Grinch proclaiming that "Maybe Christmas doesn't come from a store. Maybe Christmas...perhaps...means a little bit more!"—a lesson that may have gone by the wayside as youngsters walked past scene twenty-three and into the Little Door Store, a child-size emporium where "kids only" could shop.

For more than half a century, Minnesotans made their way to Dayton's eighth-floor auditorium for a free annual holiday show created by a crew of talented theater veterans and artists who used cardboard and Styrofoam, plaster and paint, and some incredible creativity that often saw lines of people starting down at the fourth floor waiting to get in. (If people grumbled too much about the long waits, a couple of longtime ushers would gently suggest that the complainers could go over to Donaldson's across the street to see that store's Christmas displays, according to Todd Knaeble, who worked on the eighth-floor productions for more than three decades.)

As soon as the Christmas show ended, by New Year's Day, the crew began to assemble the spring flower show, a collaboration between

OPPOSITE: A mix of characters from previous eighth-floor Christmas shows at Dayton's came together for a disco scene in the 2004 show, "Snow White." *Dan Mackerman.* THIS PAGE: "How the Grinch Stole Christmas," 1998. *Macy's.*

Set detail and original sketch by Jack Barkla for "How the Grinch Stole Christmas," 1998. *Macy's.*

the store and nursery and garden retailer Bachman's, held in March or April each year.

One of Dayton's most distinctive features, and what set the store apart from all other Minnesota department stores, was the auditorium on the eighth floor of its flagship downtown Minneapolis location.

After Southdale opened in Edina with much fanfare—and free parking—in 1956, getting shoppers back downtown and into the stores was ever present in merchants' minds. In summer 1963, Dayton's moved the TV trays, Melmac dinnerware, coffee percolators, paint, vacuum cleaners, and a pet shop out of the eighth floor and created a thirteen-thousand-square-foot, walnut-paneled space that would become a memory maker for generations of Minnesotans.

"Dayton's built the auditorium to differentiate [itself] from the other department stores," said Knaeble, who retired from Macy's in 2017 after working in special events at Dayton's/Marshall Field's/Macy's for thirty-two years, first as a carpenter and then as a production manager.

Workers were still painting the ceiling of the auditorium when some two hundred floral designers, arrangers, growers, and members of the Minnesota Rose Society showed up in October 1963 to create the National Rose Show, an exhibit of more than one hundred thousand roses that coincided with the twenty-seventh annual convention of Roses Inc., a national association of commercial rose growers. Ralph Bachman of the Bachman family nurseries was co-chairman of the convention and the eighth-floor event.

Thousands of flowers were flown to Minneapolis from commercial growers in Europe, Canada, Australia, and Mexico, as well as every geographical corner of the United States. The show had nine elaborately decorated dioramas depicting a three-thousand-year history of the rose: the flower in ancient Babylon, in a Roman pagan festival, in Edwardian England. All of the human and horse figures were designed by Dayton's staff. *Minneapolis Tribune* columnist George Grim wrote that it was "the most spectacular fusing of flowers with spectacular display I've ever seen." And it was free for the lines of people who poured into the large hall to take it in.

Shortly after the October flower show, the inaugural Christmas exhibit featured a ride through Santa's Enchanted Forest, "a delirious fairyland of busy elves and animals," with two magic horses guiding visitors through a snowy tunnel, past glistening trees and hilltops, and then to Santa and Mrs. Claus, who waited at

Program for the 1987 Dayton's flower show, "Guthrie Gardens: A Salute to the Theater's 25th Year." *Hennepin County Library.*

Entrance to "Santa's Enchanted Forest" on the eighth floor, 1963. *Minnesota Historical Society Collections.*

their North Pole Castle ready to meet the children and give them a small gift.[1]

The auditorium soon became the spot where teens gathered on Saturday afternoons for free dances hosted by radio station WDGY (Wee-Gee) disc jockey Bill Diehl. It was the venue for elegant fashion shows, lectures, yoga workshops, and films by avant-garde directors. (Not everyone was impressed. *Minneapolis Tribune* columnist Will Jones wrote, on August 1, 1967, "Oh, those Dayton's. They've gone from the dry-goods business to the general-merchandise business to the small-loan business to the art business to the Carnaby-Street-clothes business to the rock 'n' roll and psychedelic concert business, and now look, . . . they're having a fling at the movie business.")

The eighth-floor auditorium once, in April 1965, hosted a live circus complete with three elephants, fifteen ponies, and five poodles, as well as seals, leopards, and other animals borrowed from St. Paul's Como Park Zoo. And in 1967, it was transformed into a simulated LSD trip when Fantasy Unlimited brought its "Sensations '67" to town, a concoction of lights, music, sounds, and images projected from slides and cameras aimed at creating a psychedelic experience.

DEFINE "PSYCHEDELIC"

Employees wanted to know: Why was Dayton's spending time, money, and talent promoting the psychedelic dance happening held Saturday, March 4, 1967? Thomas Jeglosky, publicity coordinator and special events director, answered that question in the March 1967 issue of the *Daytonian*.

Dayton's image is that of a trend-setting store that brings to the Twin Cities many "firsts." Among these firsts can be included Dickens Village, the Out of Sight shops, the Idea Center and Sensations '67.

The goal of presenting a series of Sensations '67 for teens and young adults is to bring to the Twin Cities the newest artistic concept, that of "multi-media." This is the concept of using lights, visuals, music and other artistic elements, e.g., light boxes, spinning discs together to create an environmental atmosphere. Other shows using such artistic elements are recently being held at a college in St. Cloud and the Walker Art Center.

The term "psychedelic" was used to describe the March 4 dance happening. The dictionary describes the term "psychedelic" as total involvement in an experience utilizing "all" the senses. "Psychedelic" may or may not be associated with drugs such as LSD. It has come to be used in quite loose interpretation, e.g. the terminology "psychedelic prints" to describe little girls 3x6 dresses! We used the term in this broad sense, and in no way intended the drug affiliation to prevail. Because of some of the responses we received, we now realize that many people misunderstood our program.

We will have two more such "dance happenings," as the first one was thoroughly enjoyed by 3,000 people who attended. They are strictly fun, *and we invite any employee to attend and see for himself.*

But the events that are etched most deeply in the collective memory and hearts of Minnesotans who visited the auditorium over its fifty-four years are the annual Christmas shows in November and December and the spring flower shows in March or April. Visitors were transported to Vienna, London, Hogwarts School of Witchcraft and Wizardry, Bourbon Street in New Orleans, Monet's garden, or the land of Beatrix Potter.

"It was totally immersive," Knaeble said. "You had to go through eight floors of merch to get there. They did a really smart thing. I'm sure they made a lot of money putting in this auditorium."

Indeed, by 1966, the "Dickens' London Towne" exhibit brought thirty thousand visitors into the store the day after Thanksgiving and 110,000 visitors through the show's run-up to Christmas Day.

After Dayton's became Marshall Field's and Marshall Field's became Macy's, the Macy's stores in New York and Chicago wanted what Minneapolis had, Knaeble said. Macy's had always had a spring flower show at its Herald Square store in New York, and Marshall Field's windows were legendary in Chicago, but neither had an auditorium like the one at 700 Nicollet Avenue. "New York wanted to have a wonderful auditorium like we had so they could do a wonderful thing like this," Knaeble said. "What was great about 'Pinocchio' and 'Wind in the Willows' and 'Alice in Wonderland' and the 'Nutcracker' is you were surrounded by it. It wasn't on top of a cosmetic counter."

LEFT: A re-creation of Diagon Alley for the "Harry Potter and the Sorcerer's Stone" Christmas show, 2000. *Macy's.* ABOVE: Program for "Dickens' London Towne," 1967. *Hennepin County Library.*

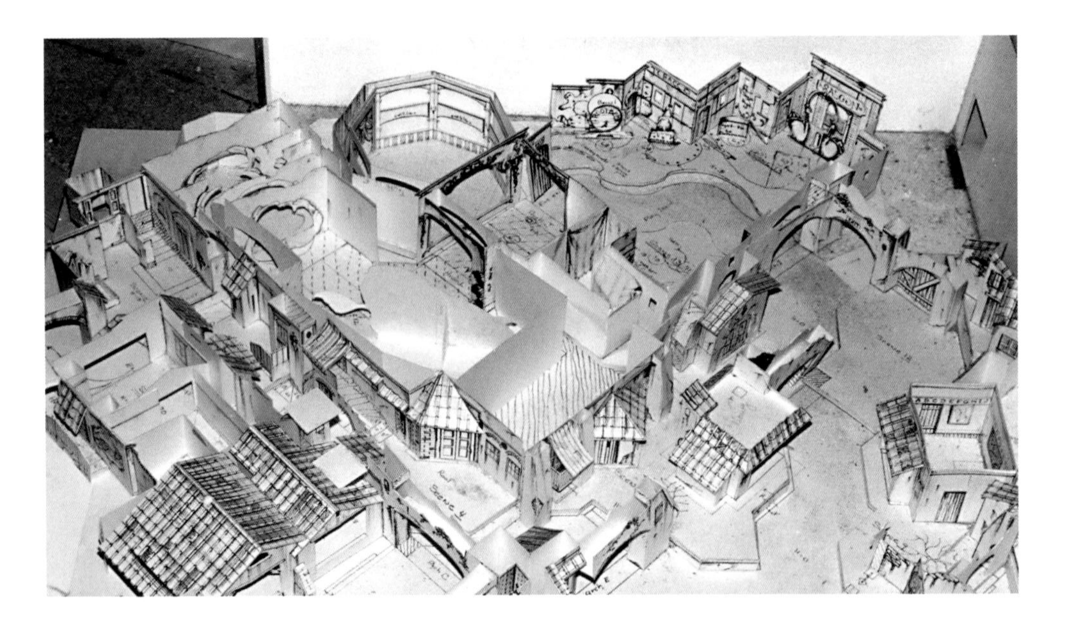

TOP: Paper model and poster of "Pinocchio." *Jack Barkla.* MIDDLE: Scene from "Cinderella," 1989. *Dan Mackerman.* BOTTOM: Scene from "Wind in the Willows." *Macy's.*

Knaeble's favorite show: "Pinocchio" in 1991, "because Jack [Edwards, the costume designer] and Jack [Barkla, the set designer] did such a great job designing. You really felt . . . [like] you were walking down the street of a small Italian town with beautiful architecture. You could be looking at scene one, and you'd see down the street and into the alley. Something would bring you there, and you wanted to just keep going on to see what was next."

The two Jacks came to Dayton's with extensive backgrounds in theater. Edwards was known for his costume work with the Guthrie Theater, pianist Lorie Line's holiday tours, and Prince. He began his career on Broadway in New York and then designed in Hollywood for television shows, including *The Carol Burnett Show* and the *Jim Nabors Hour*. Edwards died in January 2013 at the age of seventy-eight.

Barkla, a set designer who worked at the Guthrie Theater and the Children's Theatre Company, worked on Dayton's eighth-floor extravaganzas and fashion shows beginning in the late 1960s and remained up until Macy's closing of the store in spring 2017. He started out as a painter, creating large wall murals for the shows. "The auditorium is something like ninety by one hundred and sixty feet," Barkla said, "and it goes

up to eighteen-foot-high ceilings. Doing paintings that big is something you can only do when you're young."

When Dan Mackerman began working on the eighth-floor shows in Minneapolis as a painter in 1988, the figures and animation were created by an East Coast firm. It was Edwards's idea to start making the figures in-house, and Mackerman went from painter to sculptor. "The thing that was cool about that work is everything was experimental," Mackerman said. "We were constantly inventing things for the job. A need would arise, a job would come across our table, and we would find the easiest, quickest way to do it."

Experimentation was especially called for when Mackerman was asked to construct the carriage for the "Cinderella" Christmas show in 1989: "I had never sculpted before. I went through a ton of tools figuring out how to do this." In the end, the giant pumpkin carriage was made of Styrofoam, a product that became the medium of choice for many of the large stationary three-dimensional pieces of the shows—all of which were created on the eighth floor. And he used a chainsaw to sculpt it.

The weekend of the legendary 1991 Halloween blizzard that dumped twenty-eight inches of snow in the Twin Cities and shut down businesses and schools for days is when Mackerman honed his Styrofoam-sculpting chops. "I was working on the thirty-foot whale for 'Pinocchio,'" he said. "I pulled an all-nighter. I must have worked twenty hours straight."

The result "was just beautiful," Knaeble said. "It had Pinocchio on a raft inside Monstro's

(continued on page 97)

CLOCKWISE FROM TOP LEFT: Dan Mackerman's studio. *Dan Mackerman.* Scene from "Pinocchio." *Macy's.* Pinocchio and Geppetto inside the whale's mouth, 1991. *Dan Mackerman.* Animatronic Pinocchio figure from the 1991 holiday show. *Minnesota Historical Society Collections.*

THE MAGIC MAN

They call him Mr. Christmas. The Wizard. Someone who can create something astounding out of nothing, according to Minneapolis playwright Barbara Field.

A stage designer who has worked on just about every major stage in the Twin Cities beginning in the 1960s, Jack Barkla spent decades creating magic and illusion for Minnesota audiences. In December 1977, a writer for *Mpls.* magazine estimated that some five hundred thousand people would see Barkla's work that month alone.

At the time, he was knee-deep in designing sets for multiple shows. Barkla had created the set for the Guthrie Theater's *A Christmas Carol* and Minnesota Dance Theatre's *Nutcracker Fantasy.* His original designs were the foundation for that season's new production of *The Little Match Girl* at the Children's Theatre Company. He was also the guy who designed Dr. Seuss's "How the Grinch Stole Christmas," the eighth-floor holiday show at Dayton's downtown Minneapolis store that year.

It was his fifth year designing the eighth-floor shows, though he had begun working on the exhibits a few years before that.

Barkla, who grew up in Edina, remembers an animated circus that "went from window to window to window," in a Dayton's holiday display he saw as a child. Like many in the Twin Cities, Barkla and his family made it an annual event to go downtown to see the Dayton's Christmas windows, which were unveiled each Thanksgiving.

The sculpted papier-mâché figures in those store windows were created by Tommy Rowland in her Staten Island, New York, workshop. "I really understood what she was doing and why she chose the scale she chose," Barkla said. "It made quite an impression on me. There was something totally magic about it. I got that."

Years later, after studying art education at the University of Minnesota in the 1960s, Barkla picked up a part-time job at Dayton's, painting scenery and backdrops for $1.25 an hour—a wage he thought was "pretty decent" at the time.

Rowland and her husband were still creating the figures for the window displays and eighth-floor shows when Barkla joined the crew. "I worshiped what she did, what they both did," he said.

By 1973, Barkla was in charge of designing the sets for the eighth-floor show. His first complete show was "The Nutcracker." He chose to design that show in the style of architecture he had seen in Nuremberg, Germany. "I studied opera in Germany, and I

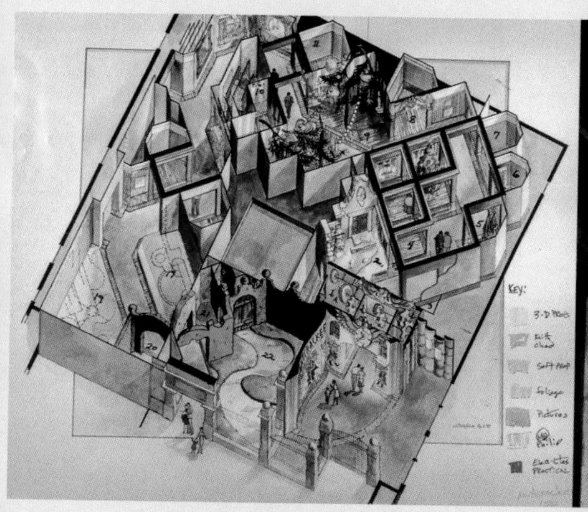

thought, 'This is wonderful.' I knew Nuremberg and I remembered standing outside [German Renaissance painter] Albrecht Dürer's home in the rain in Nuremberg."

That was summer 1967. Barkla was enrolled at the Bayreuth Festival Master Classes in Germany, an experience that ultimately pulled him out of a career teaching art and into his life's work as a set designer. In Bayreuth, he studied the work of Wieland Wagner—grandson of German composer Richard Wagner. "It was so brilliant. Wieland Wagner was the first to use modern lighting technology, and that was remarkable to see. It was so flawlessly done. There is no question it changed all of our lives for the better," Barkla said. "For me, it redefined the stage."

Barkla returned to Minnesota after that summer in Germany, left his graduate studies, and soon was hired at the Children's Theatre, then the Guthrie. Over the next three decades, he often had his hands in multiple productions at multiple venues at the same time—and always the Dayton's eighth-floor Christmas and flower shows, fashion shows, and other special exhibits.

When Minnesota governor Rudy Perpich declared December 7, 1989, Jack Barkla Day, the man had more than fourteen hundred theatrical sets to his credit, and that didn't include his commercial work at the Science Museum of Minnesota, the Renaissance Festival in Shakopee, St. Paul's Regions Hospital lobby, and the Festival of Nations, in addition to his work as production designer for several Super Bowl halftime shows, to name a few.

Born under the sign of Capricorn, he can't help but work hard, he said. Capricorns are loyal and resourceful, and they finish projects. They are builders. Add that to Barkla's ancestral lineage of mechanics, machinists, and craftspeople, and, it turns out, building things is stamped into his DNA.

Among his many prized possessions is a framed note from Theodore Geisel (Dr. Seuss), who said Barkla's work on the Children's Theatre production of *The 500 Hats of Bartholomew Cubbins* made him cry.

But the honors and tributes aren't why Barkla stayed with this work. He kept at it because he loves working with other artists. "[Theater is] a group art form, and it's an act of love, to care so much about doing work that is done for other people," he said. "I really believed in what we were doing."

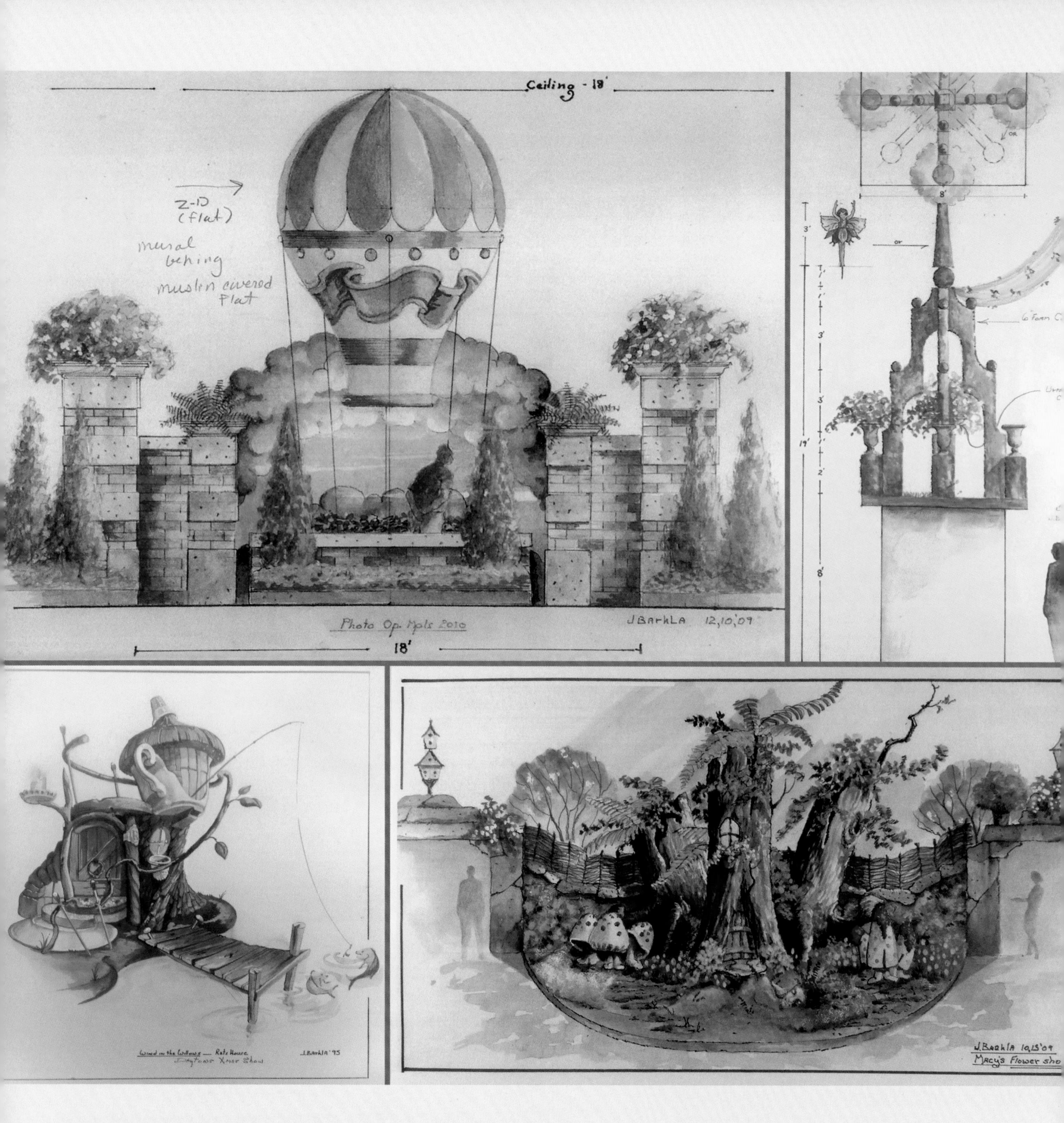

PREVIOUS PAGES, TOP ROW LEFT TO RIGHT: Jack Barkla in his Minneapolis home, 2017. *Mark Luinenburg.* Barkla's sketch for the 1998 Dayton's eighth-floor Christmas show, "How the Grinch Stole Christmas." Barkla's overview design sketch for Maurice Sendak's "Nutcracker," 1997. *Both Jack Barkla.* Maurice Sendak's "Nutcracker" Christmas show, 1997. *Macy's.* This door to a small telephone cupboard on the right side of the Dayton's eighth-floor auditorium was saved from the trash after Macy's sold the building at 700 Nicollet Avenue. The door was given to Barkla, who claimed it was "better than a gold watch" as a keepsake from his more than fifty years working on the eighth floor. The door, which is covered with layers of phone numbers, is now on display in Barkla's home, an homage to the people who worked with him. *Jack Barkla.* BOTTOM ROW: "The Nutcracker," 1973. *Hennepin County Library.* "Alice's Wonderland Christmas," 1980 Christmas show. *Jack Barkla.* THIS PAGE, CLOCKWISE FROM TOP LEFT: "Spring Is in the Air," 2010 flower show. "Flower Fairies," 2003 flower show. "Spring Is in the Air," 2010 flower show. "The Wind in the Willows," 1995 Christmas show. *All Jack Barkla.*

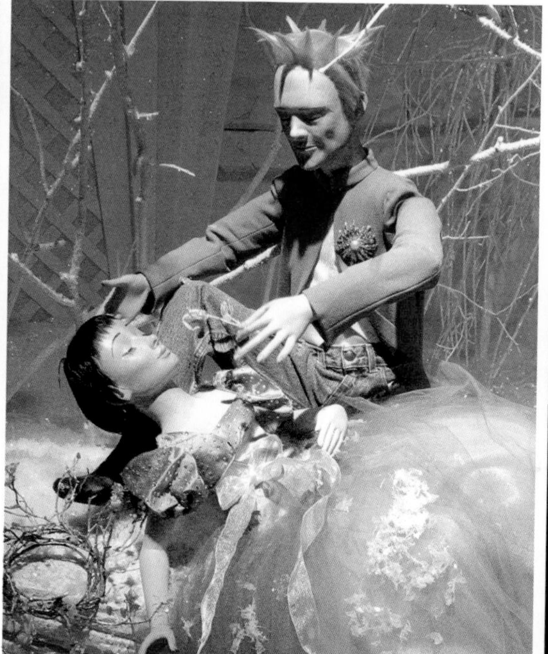

mouth and fish swimming in water below him. It was really wild."

"'Christmas Carol' [in 1996] was the first year I was allowed to just go nuts on the facial expressions," Mackerman said. "I had five different facial expressions for Scrooge." Scrooge's face was modeled after a "bachelor farmer" Mackerman knew as a kid growing up in rural Iowa. Sometimes Mackerman used his own face to help him sculpt.

"He'd work with a mirror and make all these faces," Knaeble recalled. And sometimes he used his coworkers. "The very last show we did ['A Day in the Life of an Elf'], I did a sculpture of Lyle [Jackson, the costumer who took over after Edwards retired] as an elf. Not sure he liked it," Mackerman said with a laugh.

Planning for each show began before the

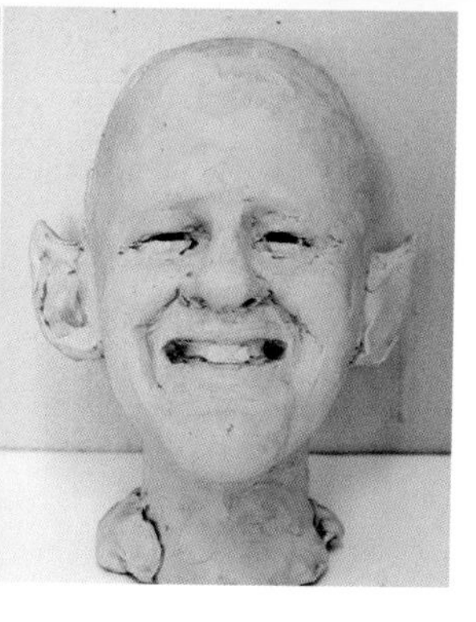

TOP ROW: Scenes from 1989's "Cinderella" show. *Dan Mackerman* (LEFT) and *Macy's* (RIGHT). CENTER: For the 2004 Christmas show, "Snow White," costume designer Jack Edwards asked Dan Mackerman to make Snow White look like Audrey Hepburn and the prince look like Justin Timberlake. Mackerman said he did his best. *Dan Mackerman.* Two of the many faces of Ebenezer Scrooge, from 1996's "A Christmas Carol" show. *Macy's.* BOTTOM ROW: Lyle Jackson (left), model for "A Day in the Life of an Elf," 2008. *Dan Mackerman.*

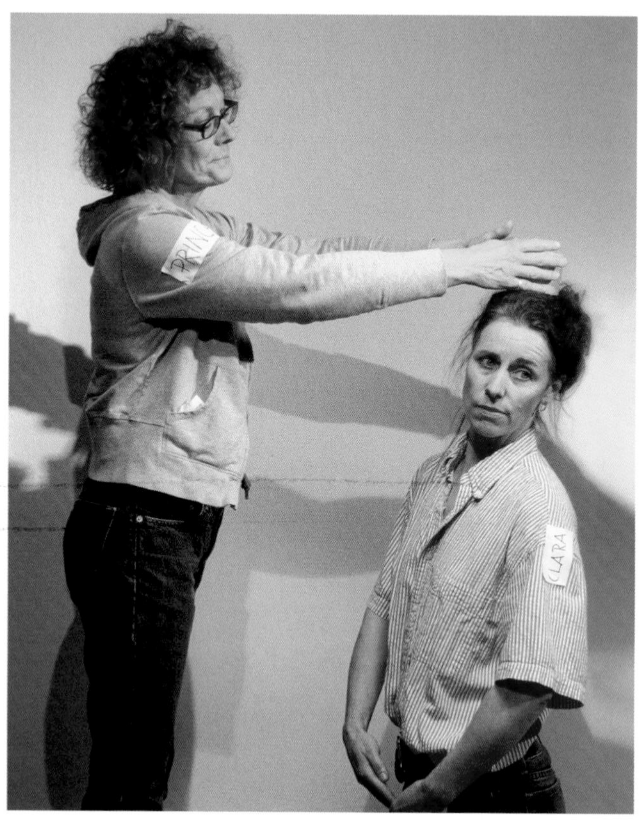

ABOVE: Rick Walsh working on the 1990 flower show, "Babar's Kingdom of Flowers." Star Tribune *photo by Bruce Bisping, Minnesota Historical Society Collections.* RIGHT: Eighth-floor artists Kate Sullivan and Constance Crawford act out a scene from "The Nutcracker." *Dan Mackerman.* BELOW: "Mary Poppins," the first Christmas show under Macy's ownership, 2006. *Macy's.*

previous show closed. Knaeble would meet with the two Jacks (and later Jackson), Mackerman, prop manager Connie Crawford, builder Rick Walsh, and other crew members. "We'd sit around a table and figure out the scenes and the action in the story in each of those scenes, and it would get wild as we figured out what each character did, how they related to one another. We tried to be comical." And sometimes, their silliness was edited by management, like when "we had a guy in drag with a mustache" lined up with all the women in "Cinderella," waiting to see if the shoe fit. "We had to pull the mustache off," Knaeble said.

And sometimes, it wasn't. "We had a Barbie doll in every show," Mackerman said. "We

THE EIGHTH-FLOOR CHRISTMAS SHOWS

- 1963: Santa's Enchanted Forest
- 1964: Land of Trolls
- 1965: No name (featured animated animals preparing for Christmas)
- 1966: Dickens' London Towne
- 1967: Dickens' London Towne
- 1968: Under the Giant Christmas Tree
- 1969: Peter Pan
- 1970: Santa's Toy Workshop
- 1971: Santa's TV Studio
- 1972: Joy to the World by Joan Walsh Anglund
- 1973: Nutcracker
- 1974: Grandma Moses' "Christmas in the Country"
- 1975: 'Twas the Night Before Christmas
- 1976: Charlie and the Chocolate Factory
- 1977: How the Grinch Stole Christmas (Dr. Seuss)
- 1978: Once Upon a Christmastime
- 1979: Babes in Toyland
- 1980: Alice's Wonderland Christmas
- 1981: Hansel and Gretel
- 1982: Pippi Longstocking
- 1983: Babar and Father Christmas
- 1984: Animalen, "The Peaceable Kingdom"
- 1985: The Velveteen Rabbit
- 1986: Santabear's First Christmas
- 1987: Santabear's High-Flying Adventures

would dress it up to match a scene and bury it in [that] scene."

Designing and planning for the flower show would begin while the team was still building the Christmas show. "The strike of the Christmas show would take like ten days, and as soon as you were done striking, you'd start building the flower show," Knaeble said.

The eighth-floor Christmas show in 2006, the year Macy's took over the downtown store, was "Mary Poppins." In 2007, "Nutcracker" was on display, and in 2008, "A Day in the Life of an Elf" debuted, and that same show continued each year (with changing titles) until 2016, the last Christmas show on the eighth floor at 700 Nicollet Avenue.

ABOVE LEFT: Jack Barkla's sketch for "A Day in the Life of an Elf," 2008. *Jack Barkla.* RIGHT: Display window on Nicollet Mall, 2001 flower show, "Linnea in Monet's Garden." *Sue Hartley.* BELOW: "Paddington Bear and the Christmas Surprise," 2002 Christmas show. *Macy's.*

1988: The Polar Express
1989: Cinderella
1990: Peter Pan
1991: Pinocchio
1992: Puss in Boots
1993: Beauty and the Beast
1994: The Wizard of Oz
1995: The Wind in the Willows
1996: A Christmas Carol
1997: Nutcracker (Maurice Sendak)
1998: How the Grinch Stole Christmas
1999: The 12 Days of Christmas
2000: Harry Potter and the Sorcerer's Stone

MARSHALL FIELD'S ERA

2001: 'Twas the Night Before Christmas
2002: Paddington Bear and the Christmas Surprise
2003: Charlie and the Chocolate Factory
2004: Snow White
2005: Cinderella

MACY'S ERA

2006: Mary Poppins
2007: Nutcracker
2008–2016: A Day in the Life of an Elf

"Bourbon Street in Bloom," 1982. *Jack Barkla.*

In April 1967, Dayton's eighth-floor auditorium was transformed into a scene reminiscent of the Alabama Azalea Trail, complete with blooming magnolias, live oak trees dripping with Spanish moss, a forty-foot lagoon filled with real frogs and turtles, and thousands of blooming tulips, hyacinths, and narcissus—as well as southern belles in hoop skirts and the smell of fried chicken wafting through. For visitors to the Dayton's-Bachman's flower show "Southern Gardens," it was like "stepping off a steamboat and into this southern town," according to longtime flower show designer Jack Barkla.

Dayton's hosted its first spring flower show on the main floor of its downtown store in 1960. A *Minneapolis Morning Tribune* article from that year described the eight gardens, which included a Japanese garden and flowers from around the world. Rosebushes, eight-foot-tall Hawaiian palms, fuchsia trees, and exhibits extended the length of the Nicollet Avenue side of the store and along the Eighth Street side: "More than 100,000 blooms were moved into Dayton's Monday," according to the *Tribune* article. "Since the store opening that morning, visitors have been 'wall-to-wall' with peak crowds at noon."[2]

The spring shows and Christmas shows were Dayton's thank-you to the community, Barkla said. "The Daytons were just so socially responsible. [The family] grew up with a keen awareness

of their responsibility in their community and tried to use it in the best way possible."

Shortly after that first floral show, Minneapolis nursery and retailer Bachman's partnered with the store and continued through the store's transitions to Marshall Field's in 2001 and then to Macy's in 2006. The eighth floor saw its last flower show in spring 2016.

Through the years, the show spotlighted different geographic regions in North America and around the globe and had themes that included children's tales, such as *Alice in Wonderland* by Lewis Carroll in 1999 and *Linnea in Monet's Garden* by Christian Bjork in 2001.

In 1996, the flower show was dubbed a

ABOVE: "Linnea in Monet's Garden," 2001. *Sue Hartley.*
LEFT: "Alice in Wonderland," 1999. *Macy's.*

"stay-at-home" show featuring seven small gardens that Minnesotans could replicate in their own yards. "Garden Varieties" was based on a similar show held annually at London's Kew Gardens, Barkla said. "Every fountain, plant, and flowerpot had a price on it. People loved it. Often people would go to the show and see things and think they can't afford it. It was nice to say, 'No, you can do these things. It's not that expensive. With a little imagination, the average person can do it.'"

One of the more spectacular shows was the 1991 "Fiori d'Italia" (Flowers of Italy). Barkla had always wanted to travel to Italy. Instead, he took the Twin Cities on a tour of the country.

In a March 15, 1991, *Star Tribune* article by Mary Abbe, Barkla described the show as "a *Reader's Digest* condensed tour of Italian gardens." It featured a cascade of water tumbling through a series of basins into a pool along with seventeen fountains and water jets, a Temple of Apollo with statues representing the four seasons, benches, frescoes, vine-draped pergolas, and two loud macaws in an aviary in the middle of the piazza. It also featured "stonework" carved from wood and Styrofoam and painted to look like marble, granite, and even lichen-covered rock.

Barkla's all-time favorite was the 1995 show, "Tivoli Gardens," which was designed after the famous amusement park and pleasure garden in Copenhagen, Denmark. Barkla designed it in honor of his college mentor, George Olson, and his wife, Gladys, who had recently died of cancer, he said. Gladys was from Denmark.

The show replicated pieces of the historic park, including amusement rides for children and a pantomime theater in honor of Tivoli's Peacock Theatre. The flower show's version

ABOVE: "Tivoli Gardens," 1995. *Dan Mackerman.* RIGHT: Program for the "Tivoli Gardens" flower show, 1995. *Hennepin County Library.*

featured a large peacock head that rose up out of the floor of the theater and turned to survey the crowd before each show.

"Tivoli" and "Fiori d'Italia" were two of the more popular shows, according to Dale Bachman, the current CEO of Bachman's and producer of the flower show beginning in 1981. "Italian gardens was a huge effort. The thing you can count on with Jack [Barkla], and it's true with the Christmas show, too, he would create the sets, but it was all in the detail, the propping, the finishing touches, his artful eye."

Each year in January, Bachman and someone from Dayton's would head to California, Oregon, or Florida to buy plants that could be forced out of season, Barkla said. A longtime Bachman's employee, expert gardener Timo Juujarvi, saw to that. He was a "seer of plants," Barkla said. "I could walk through the greenhouse with him and he would point to a little twig coming out of the ground and say, on the week of July 2—to the day—this will bloom. He was just amazing."

That knack for knowing when something will flower was important in the construction of the flower show, which was always in March or early April, a time when there's often snow still on the ground in Minnesota.

Juujarvi was interviewed in 1999 by *Star Tribune* writer Ingrid Sundstrom just as the "Alice in Wonderland" show opened. He had been in charge of monitoring the progress of the plants for the show for twenty years by then. "One winter, we had a huge 25-foot magnolia, with big flower buds that looked like they were going to come out too soon," Juujarvi told Sundstrom. "I went and got my front-end loader, drove it out to the parking lot and got a load of snow, which I dumped right on the magnolia. That stopped the blooming for a while."

LEFT: "Fiori d'Italia," 1991. *Dan Mackerman.*
ABOVE: Flower detail from 2013's "The Painted Garden." *Sue Hartley.*

Japanese Crimson Queen

Once the drawings and floor plans for the flower shows were made, the soil and any large trees were moved into the auditorium. More than 150 cubic yards of soil were used for the planting beds. About five days after the soil was brought in, potted shrubs were installed, and several days before the show opened, flowering bulbs, perennials, and other flowers were planted. While the landscapers were tending to the gardens, the eighth-floor special events crew built the sets and the scenery.

A number of past shows featured live animals. The 1993 flower show, "Flowers and Fjords," included two Norwegian fjord horses showcased in a Scandinavian-style barn. And there was a time when live birds, frogs, and butterflies filled the auditorium.

"Years before we were more culturally sensitive to animals, [staff] would go out in the park and trap live birds and put the birds in the auditorium in the flower show," Barkla said. "It was wonderful to have these birds flying in the shows, but what people don't like to think about is, ultimately, they would fly into the air-conditioning system."

Minneapolis Star columnist George Grim wrote about a good intention gone awry in the 1965 show. Apparently, three hundred Hawaiian butterflies were netted near Honolulu and jetted to Dayton's, along with two British Columbian jays. On the Saturday of the show, the jays and the butterflies, along with canaries and cardinals, were flying free over the flower show's English garden. By midafternoon, staff noticed the disappearance of the butterflies. Turns out, the jays were eating the butterflies. After the show closed that day, the jays were netted and put in a cage.

Barkla has a similar story from the mid-1970s, but this one involves a species of red bird from South America. "I don't remember which show, but someone had the idea to have red birds, and they found a source in South America. They thought, 'That's wonderful.' But you have to quarantine the birds when they arrive."

So the birds arrived in Minneapolis and were quarantined, but the folks in charge of the show were nervous that the red birds wouldn't be out of quarantine in time for the show's opening. They added some local sparrows and robins to the show.

A special showing for senior citizens had been scheduled the day the red birds got out of

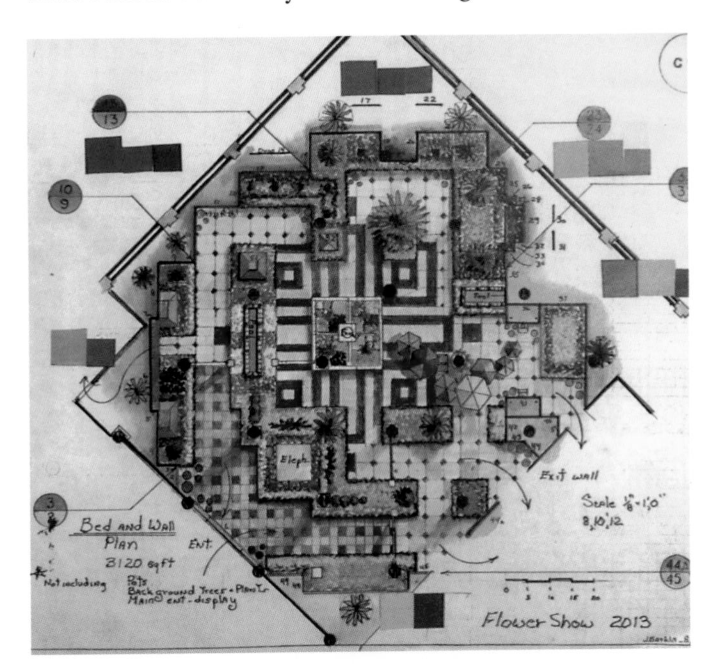

quarantine and arrived at Dayton's. Barkla was standing in the hallway with the store's special events director as the birds were released and the senior guests were making their way down the hall.

Suddenly, there was a great commotion, "and we look down there and there were senior citizens waving their canes and umbrellas, and there were muffled sounds and a couple of screams, and people came running out."

Turns out, the South American red birds were carnivorous and had begun attacking the

OPPOSITE: "The Painted Garden," 2013. *Sue Hartley.* THIS PAGE: Site plan for "The Painted Garden," 2013. *Jack Barkla.*

TOP: "Gardina Africana" was displayed on Macy's first floor in 2007. ABOVE: The flower show returned to the eighth floor with "Dream in Color" in 2009. OPPOSITE: "Dream in Color," 2009 flower show. *All Sue Hartley.*

domestic birds and then the senior guests. The seniors made their way out of the auditorium, the auditorium was shut down, and the birds were caught and caged. "It was just bizarre," Barkla laughed.

Here is one more animal story: "We got some wonderful ducks—beautiful creatures—and we brought them into the auditorium a couple of days before the show opened," Barkla said. "By the time the show opened, the ducks were in heat because all this foliage was growing very fast, and the birds thought it was spring. The male ducks were hopping on the female ducks, and we decided, rather than have parents be forced into talking to their children about sex, we took all the male ducks out and kept the female ducks."

Macy's brought the flower show back to the

1963: National Rose Show
1964: Flower Festival, National Rose Show (fall)
1965: English Garden
1966: Italian Garden
1967: Southern Garden
1968: Dutch Garden
1969: Sculpture Gardens (spring); Not So Far East (summer)
1970: Springtime Park
1971: New England Spring
1972: Camelot
1973: An Old-Fashioned Garden
1974: It's Cherry Blossom Time
1975: California Flower Market
1976: Springtime on the Mississippi
1977: Scheherazade: Exotic Gardens of Morocco
1978: A Flowering Woodland
1979: Hollywood in Bloom
1980: Gardens of Picasso's France
1981: Gardens of the Midnight Sun
1982: Bourbon Street in Bloom
1983: Island Gardens of the Aegean
1984: Minnesota Wild
1985: An English Country Garden: The Gentle World of Beatrix Potter
1986: Form and Flower: The Garden of Hiroshi Teshigahara
1987: Guthrie Gardens: A Salute to the Theater's 25th Year with Desmond Heeley
1988: Salute to the Sculpture Garden
1989: Scenes From Tomie dePaola
1990: Babar's Kingdom of Flowers
1991: Fiori d'Italia
1992: Flowers and Fjords
1993: An English Country Garden
1994: Flores Mexicanas
1995: Tivoli Gardens
1996: Garden Varieties for Your Backyard
1997: Gardens of Vienna
1998: Beatrix Potter's A Storybook Fling
1999: Alice in Wonderland
2000: Curious George Goes to the Flower Show
2001: Linnea in Monet's Garden

MARSHALL FIELD'S ERA

2002: Provence in Bloom, Christian Tortu
2003: Flower Fairies
2004: The Garden of Make Believe
2005: Music in the Garden
2006: Avantgarden

MACY'S ERA

2007: Gardina Africana (moved to first floor)
2008: Floranova (first floor)
2009: Dream in Color (moved back to eighth-floor auditorium)
2010: Spring Is in the Air
2011: Towers of Flowers
2012: Brasil: Gardens in Paradise
2013: The Painted Garden
2014: The Secret Garden
2015: Art in Bloom
2016: America the Beautiful

building's main floor in 2007 and 2008, but returned it to the eighth floor in 2009. Plans were in the works for a carnival-themed show in 2017 when the company announced in January of that year that the Nicollet Avenue store had been sold to a developer. Dale Bachman and Jack Barkla didn't wait long to resurrect a spring flower show. "Spring Is in the Air," a two-week "floral experience," opened at the Galleria shopping center in Edina in March 2018. Flower lovers were once again treated to the sweet smells of spring blooms, and this time, the parking was free.

The spring shows changed when the store became Macy's, Knaeble said. "Dayton's was more willing to spend money. Macy's was a little more economical about their money, and maybe that's the reason why they are still in business.

"There was a lot of excellent, great work that came out of [the eighth-floor shows]," Knaeble continued. "I don't think you could get that kind of product without all the wonderful people who put out. People's souls were in this stuff."

LEFT: The last garden show in the eighth-floor auditorium: "America the Beautiful," 2016. RIGHT: "Art in Bloom," 2015. *Both Sue Hartley.*

Emporium
JUNCTION
212

6
Capital City Shopping: St. Paul's Department Stores

Sure, Minneapolis was the home for the flagship Dayton's, Powers, Donaldson's, and Young-Quinlan stores, but St. Paul had its own homegrown department stores long before those giants of Minnesota retailing set up shop in the capital city.

A shopping trip to downtown St. Paul in the first six decades of the twentieth century could mean buying fabric and notions or sweets from the in-store candy kitchen at the Emporium; having your feet x-rayed in a shoe-fitting fluoroscope in the children's shoe department at Field-Schlick; catching a spring African violet show at the Golden Rule; or attending a preview tea for the Minnesota Artists exhibition at Schuneman's.

The stores were elegant with their high ceilings, elevator operators calling out the floor numbers at each stop, and salespeople at the ready in every department—like Mr. Pierre at the Golden Rule, where Norene Stovall worked in the early 1960s. He was the floorwalker on the main floor, the man who greeted customers and resolved problems. "He was a real character: small, thin mustache curled up at the ends, black pinstripe suit, always a red carnation in his lapel," Stovall said. He spoke with a French accent, "but my sixteen-year-old ears couldn't tell if it was fake or not."

Toni Johnson, who grew up in the 1950s north of St. Paul in what is now Shoreview, remembers the marble and glass, the chandeliers, the fancy metal grills of the elevators, the extensive fabric selections ("because Mom sewed most of our clothing"), and the book departments. "When we went downtown it was an all-day adventure since my mom didn't drive. We would go in the morning with my dad, who worked at a photo studio downtown, and meet him to go home at the end of the day," she said. Those all-day trips also meant "a treat at the River Room at Schuneman's! *Big* treat!"

Mary Liebelt Jensen never shopped much at Schuneman's as a girl growing up in St. Paul or after she married and had children. The store was out of her price range. But in spring 1958, she found herself in Schuneman's picking out a full wardrobe after winning a contest on the *Bee Baxter Show* on KSTP Channel 5.

Baxter had asked viewers to write in about what they would like to do to improve themselves. Jensen wrote a letter describing how she'd wanted to lose weight so that she would feel better about herself. She was brought on the show once a week for six weeks and given diet tips ("not very healthy diet tricks," she says in retrospect). She ended up losing twenty pounds and was awarded a $250 wardrobe that included five dresses; a navy blue suit; white gloves, purse, hat, and shoes; and undergarments. The clothes came at a great time, as not long after that, Jensen went to work as an accountant for the state of Minnesota. Jensen remembers Schuneman's as a beautiful store, featuring a piano player on the first floor.

OPPOSITE: Downtown St. Paul street scene in front of Emporium department store, November 28, 1952. *Minnesota Historical Society Collections.*

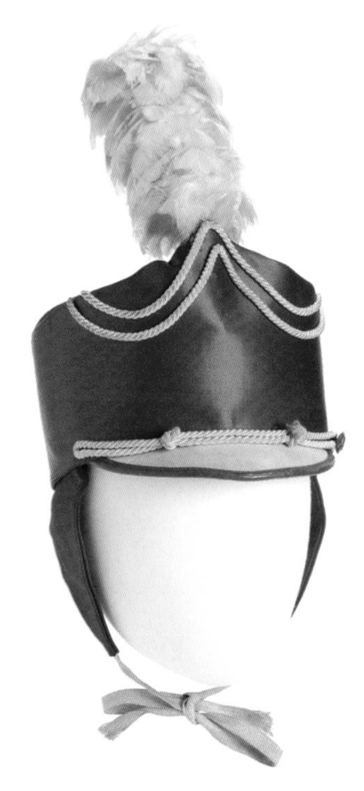

Schuneman's opened in 1888 as a small dry goods store called Schuneman and Evans on the north side of Third Street near Robert. Third Street was in the heart of St. Paul's shopping area at the time, and the store was in good company: Field, Mahler and Company (which later became Field-Schlick) was at Third and Wabasha; Mannheimer's was at Third and Minnesota; and Dryer Brothers was on Third between Minnesota and Robert.

By 1891, owners Charles Schuneman and B. H. Evans took over two floors at a large new building at Sixth and Wabasha Streets. Charles Schuneman's brother, Albert, joined shortly after, and the store expanded to another two floors, adding furniture and floor covers to the merchandise. Evans sold his interest to the Schuneman brothers in 1912. In 1926, Schuneman's Inc. consolidated with Mannheimer Brothers, a dry goods store that opened in 1871. The merged store was called Schuneman-Mannheimer for a time. Carl T. Schuneman, Albert's son, led the firm through the next three decades of changes and improvements.

"General nuisance" is how he described himself in the October 31, 1956, *Inside Schuneman's* newsletter. Carl Schuneman spent a summer vacation working his first job at the store in the wholesale carpet department. He was twelve years old. Two years later, he worked the Schuneman's booth at the Minnesota State Fair, gathering addresses from out-of-town visitors. He described it as "the longest week I ever spent." It was busy. The booth was right next to the Midway.

TOP LEFT: Schuneman and Evans, circa 1890. TOP RIGHT: Schuneman employees, 1901. ABOVE AND RIGHT: Hat and jacket for Schuneman's employee marching band, circa 1946. *All Minnesota Historical Society Collections.*

TOP LEFT: Saleswoman and model showing stockings to Schuneman shoppers, 1948. TOP RIGHT: Entrance to Schuneman's beauty salon, 1938. *Both* St. Paul Dispatch *photos, Minnesota Historical Society Collections.*

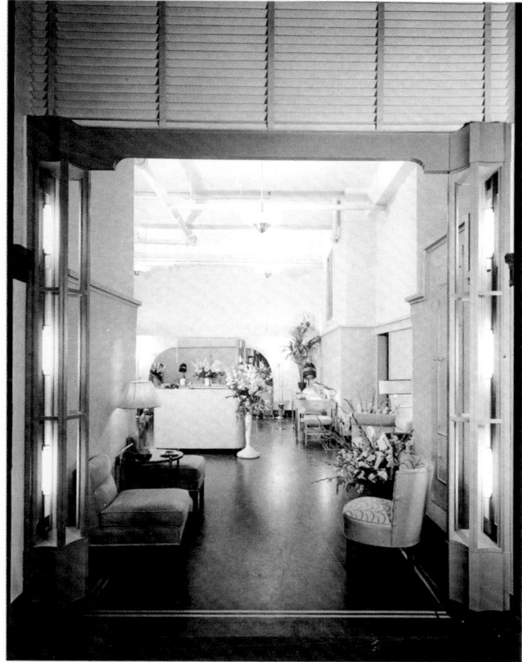

After serving in the military in World War I, Carl returned to the store in 1919 and oversaw the construction of a building that connected Schuneman's to the neighboring Hamm Building on St. Peter Street. He left the store again in 1926 to serve for three years as the US assistant secretary of treasury, where he oversaw the building of public post offices, including the ones in St. Paul and Minneapolis.

Schuneman's was sold to the Consolidated Retail Corporation in the early 1930s, but the family acquired it back in 1935, after the chain, hit by the Depression, was unable to complete the purchase. Carl T. Schuneman was named president that year.

Schuneman's grew fast beginning in the late 1930s. By 1952, it had 300,000 square feet of floor space and, by 1958, employed nearly 900 regular employees. That number grew to more than 1,600 during the Christmas shopping season.[1]

Schuneman's time as a Schuneman-owned business came to an end on November 28, 1958, when Dayton's president, Donald Dayton, called a press conference at the nearby St. Paul Hotel to announce his company's purchase of the St. Paul department store. The Minneapolis company also acquired most of the block across Wabasha Street from Schuneman's as a site for a future Dayton's location, as Schuneman's owned its building but leased the land it was on from the Catholic Archdiocese of St. Paul and Minneapolis.

In January 1959, the store bore the name Dayton's-Schuneman's. Two years later, Dayton's purchased what was considered one of St. Paul's

ABOVE LEFT: Schuneman's models, 1955. ABOVE RIGHT: Schuneman's model kitchen at Home-a-Rama, St. Paul Auditorium, September 1958. *Both* St. Paul Dispatch *photos, Minnesota Historical Society Collections.*

ABOVE: Dayton's-Schuneman's store manager Robert Bertholf, Donald Dayton, and Bruce Dayton look over a model for the planned five-story Dayton's store in St. Paul, February 9, 1962. Star Tribune *photo, Minnesota Historical Society Collections.* RIGHT: *Christine Johnson.*

most valuable corners: two buildings at Seventh and Wabasha Streets. United Properties, the real estate company that controlled the Emporium, a major competitor to Dayton's-Schuneman's, had owned the property.

Dayton's hired Victor Gruen, the architect for both the Southdale and Brookdale shopping centers, to design the new building. By August 1963, the name *Schuneman* was gone, and a brand-new Dayton's opened at 411 Cedar Street.

The Golden Rule, whose tagline was "St. Paul's Dominant Store," did dominate the shopping district at Seventh and Robert for decades. Founded in 1886 by three Ohio men, Jacob Dittenhoffer and brothers William and Joseph Elsinger, the store moved into a three-story building on Seventh Street in 1891 and saw several additions under the direction of architect Clarence H. Johnston in 1901, 1910, and 1914.

In its early days, the store was known as "The Santa Claus Store": a figure of St. Nicholas stood at the Seventh Street entrance, and the stock consisted largely of toys. An ad in the African American newspaper the *Appeal*, on Saturday, December 23, 1899, announced Santa's visit to the Golden Rule, Santa's "headquarters," that very day: "Let all the good little boys and girls know that they can come and talk to me. I will bring my big book and take their orders for what they wish for Christmas. You can also say that I will bring The Golden Rule the finest exhibit of Holiday Goods and at the lowest prices ever heard of in Minnesota. Yours truly, in haste, Santa Claus." The ad also encouraged children

(continued on page 118)

Donaldson's–Golden Rule, 1966. *Minnesota Historical Society Collections.*

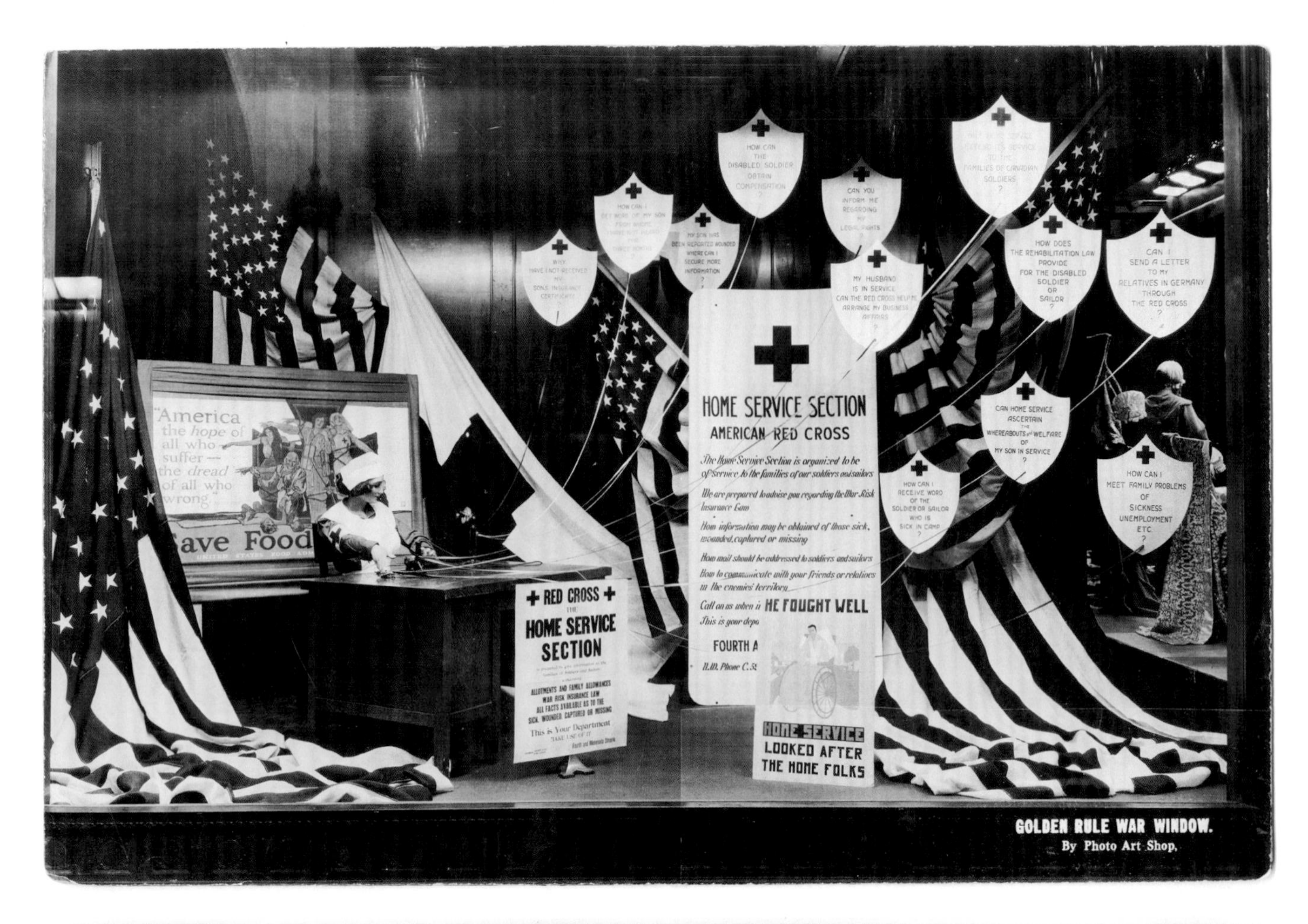

Golden Rule display windows supporting the war effort during World War I. *Minnesota Historical Society Collections.*

GIFT RECOMMENDATIONS FOR GOLDEN RULE EMPLOYEES

The December 1923 issue of the Golden Rule's employee newsletter, *Store News,* included tips on becoming a good salesperson ("The first thing required to give service is to know your line thoroughly"), a list of new year's resolutions that included advice on opening a savings account, and a little fun, such as these gift suggestions for Golden Rule employees. We wonder: Did Mr. McDonald ever get that sweet disposition?

If I Were Santa Claus I'd Bring

Miss Ludwig—A megaphone.
Miss Line—A pair of riding boots.
Mr. Bartlett—Six more warehouses to build.
Mrs. Randolph—Respectable discount checks.
Mr. Blodgett—A magnifying glass.
Mr. Buchman—A baby doll with pink knees.
Miss Driscoll—A rest.
Miss Burger—A husband.
Miss Kenny—Some "Three Star Hennessy."
Mr. Fink—A wife.
Mr. Cannon—A beard.
Mr. Smith—A double chocolate sundae.
Miss Strelow— A Mah Jongg set.
Mr. Zoller—A Victor record.
Mr. Newbauer—A loud speaking radio horn.
Mr. Broeker—Cold weather.
Miss Hawker—One cool summer.
Mr. Rosenberg—An easy inventory.
Mr. Gray—A prize-fighter to manage.
Mr. Lundberg—A bowling ball.
Mr. McDonald—A sweet disposition.
Mr. Stolberg—A three cushion billiard cue.
Mr. Strauss—A fishing rod with a fish.
Mr. Muldoon—A new Reo.
Mr. Schwartz—Another doll sale.
Mr. Penrose—A wedding ring.

THE GOLDEN RULE'S TEN COMMANDMENTS OF SERVICE

From the Golden Rule employee newsletter, *Store News,* December 1923.

1. *Understanding and Sympathy.*
2. *Courtesy and Civility.*
3. *Anxiety to please and not patronizing.*
4. *Good salesmanship.*
5. *Absence of impatiency.*
6. *Intelligence and Helpfulness.*
7. *Reliability.*
8. *Frankness that avoids muddles.*
9. *Conveniences.*
10. *Reliable and business-like principles.*

Gift box from the Golden Rule department store, St. Paul. *Christine Johnson.*

to send letters to Santa to the Golden Rule, and they would be answered in person.

By the store's fortieth anniversary in 1926, the Golden Rule was known for its innovative "remote delivery" system. The store stocked samples of products, and when a purchase was made, the merchandise was delivered from the store's warehouse by a shuttle of trucks that ran every fifteen minutes. The store claimed its system had been copied by stores in New York and one unnamed large Minneapolis department store.[2]

In 1928, the Golden Rule joined the nationwide Hahn Department Store Company chain, which consisted of twenty-two department stores from around the United States, including L. S. Donaldson Company across the river in Minneapolis.

In 1938, the Golden Rule added escalators and a "Street of Little Shops" on the Robert Street side of the store's main floor. The small shops stocked women's lingerie, shoes, hats, hosiery, bags, blouses, and sportswear and men's shirts. The store's 339-seat luncheonette in the basement was decorated in red, black, and blue, with venetian blinds and chromium metal trim. A marble staircase "wide enough for two automobiles to drive abreast down its slope" in the center of the store created a grand entrance.[3]

For Mary Liebelt Jensen, the Golden Rule was the place to buy piano sheet music for her children's lessons in the 1950s and 1960s and, once in a while, to treat herself to the lunch counter's delicious Friday fish fry.

The Golden Rule wallpaper department, 1951. *Minnesota Historical Society Collections.*

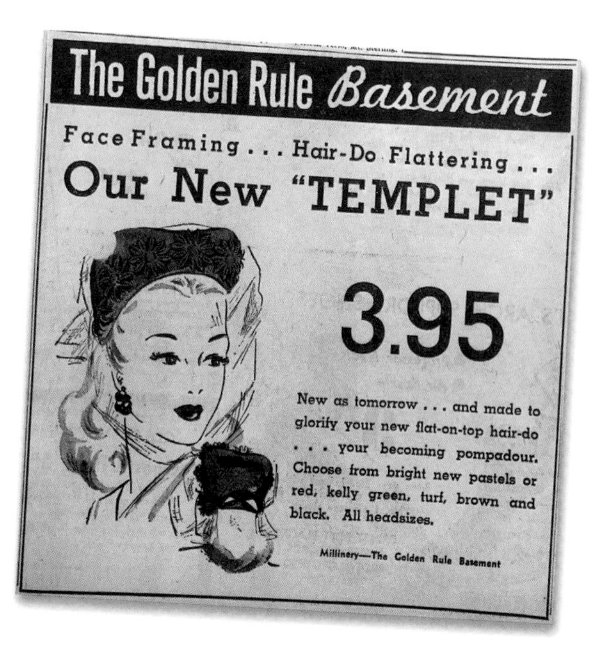

ABOVE LEFT: Woman trying on wigs at Myndall Cains salon in Donaldson's–Golden Rule, 1962. *Minnesota Historical Society Collections.* RIGHT: Late 1940s Golden Rule advertisement. *Author's collection.*

The name changed on the marquee in 1961, when Donaldson's merged with the Golden Rule. The store was called Donaldson's–Golden Rule until 1970, when the name *Golden Rule* was dropped. In 1980, Donaldson's moved out of the Golden Rule building and into a new space in the Town Square complex at Cedar and Sixth Streets. The new development looked so much like a suburban shopping center that it was given an unofficial nickname of "St. Pauldale." Town Square included shops, restaurants, a hotel, and two office towers. City leaders had hoped the development would lead to an invigorated downtown St. Paul. Nearly thirty years later, the city's leaders were still working on that. By 2018, no major retailers were located in downtown St. Paul, and Town Square's tenants included a bank, a convenience store, two state offices, and a handful of fast-food restaurants. The former Dayton's/Macy's on Wabasha Street, however, had been renovated into a mixed-use project with offices, a brewery, and practice ice for the Minnesota Wild hockey team, and that, along with the renovation of the hundred-year-old Palace Theater nearby and the revitalization of the Lowertown Historic District, has many St. Paul leaders and residents hopeful that the downtown can be reenergized.

Although the Golden Rule name has been gone from department stores for decades, the original turn-of-the-nineteenth-century building at Seventh and Robert still stands and is called the Golden Rule Building. It was converted to an office building in the early 1980s and continues to serve that function.

The Emporium, St. Paul's "Fresh Air" store, made headlines in 1902 with the announcement of the March 1 opening of an "immense new department store" on East Seventh Street. Proprietors J. T. and W. S. Kennedy, Angus McLeod, and P. McCarthy opened a thirty-five-thousand-square-foot store that featured twenty-two departments and employed 150 salespeople.[4]

Seven months later, this popular new store had a second opening of its expanded "beautiful daylight store," which was now double the size of when it first opened. An advertisement in the *Minneapolis Journal* listed a "sensational silk skirt sale," with one hundred black silk dress skirts, made of extra-good taffeta silk, very neatly trimmed, priced at $7.95, and five hundred dozen boys' heavy fleece-lined shirts and

LEFT: Emporium flower department, 1925. *Minnesota Historical Society Collections.* BELOW: Advertisement for Emporium's furniture upholstery service. *Author's collection.*

Emporium
ST. PAUL'S ONLY LARGE HOME-OWNED STORE

GIVE YOUR HOME A BRIGHT SPRING LOOK!

Reupholster Your Furniture

NOW TO CONSERVE WHAT YOU HAVE!

Beautify and conserve your furniture by having it reupholstered. Save that precious spring filled sofa and chair. We'll call for it anywhere in St. Paul, sterilize it, reweb bottom, retie springs and replace filling where needed. Then we'll top it off with striped or figured rayon and cotton damask, or textured fabrics. There'll be an additional charge for nailheads, tufting or oversize pieces. All the work will be done in our workroom by our expert staff.

FINE SELECTION OF FABRICS.

Rayon and cotton damask, in floral or striped effects. Beautiful textured fabrics in pleasing colors. Yard 1.95

Sofa . . . . 54^{50}
Average 3 cushion

Chair . . . 26^{95}
Average 1 cushion

DRAPERIES EMPORIUM, THIRD FLOOR

drawers, all sizes, priced at twenty-one cents apiece. A woman could buy a Royal Worcester corset made of imported sateen with extra garter attachments for eighty-five cents.[5]

In 1925, William Hamm, president of the Theodore Hamm Brewing Company, purchased a substantial interest in the Emporium. His son, William Hamm Jr., joined him on the store's board of directors. Just eight years after acquiring the Emporium, the senior Hamm was kidnapped in June 1933 after leaving work at the brewery. The kidnappers were members of the Alvin Karpis–Ma Barker gang. He was released four days later unharmed near Wyoming, Minnesota, after paying a ransom of $100,000.

Hamm's had a real-estate division that owned bars and managed properties, including the Emporium property. After the state banned breweries from owning bars, the division was spun off from the brewery in 1937 and renamed United Properties.

The business continued to grow in the ensuing decades. In 1949, the company spent $2 million remodeling the interior and installing escalators at the store at Seventh and Robert Streets. A decade later, the store's exterior was refaced with beige aluminum plating on the top four floors, the first-floor façade was trimmed in brown marble, and ten display windows were added. In the 1960s, the Emporium opened branch locations at Signal Hills, a West St. Paul shopping center, and

OPPOSITE, TOP TO BOTTOM: Postcard view of St. Paul's Emporium department store. Street view of Emporium, circa 1917. *Both Minnesota Historical Society Collections.*

NEWS FROM “THE FRESH AIR STORE”

In 1917, customers at the Emporium could get their photographs developed the same day; buy a Grafonola, an early-twentieth-century phonograph; and have their purchases delivered to their lake home. This excerpt from the July 1917 Emporium newsletter, *News from “The Fresh Air Store,”* describes those amenities.

DAY AND NIGHT KODAK SERVICE — *We now maintain a service that is par excellent. At the main entrance of Seventh Street there is a drop box for films. Leave your films there at any hour of the night. When received by us before 9 a.m., they will be ready at 4:30 p.m. same day. If left between 9 a.m. and 2 p.m., they will be ready at noon next day. A complete showing of Kodaks and cameras will be found here at all times. Any advice or information will be gladly given upon request.*

COLUMBIA GRAFONOLAS — *A talking machine will be enjoyed at either town house or lake cottage. It will provide good, wholesome, entertainment for old and young anywhere and everywhere and it is inexpensive amusement. World famous artists may be heard over and over again at less than the cost of hearing them in person once. You can hear great bands and orchestras, opera singers, comedians, in fact the best of the world’s artists. Come to the Talking Machine Department in the balcony annex and ask to hear any piece you wish. Our assortment of records is unusually large just now and new ones are arriving frequently.*

DAILY LAKE DELIVERIES — *We make daily deliveries to all White Bear and Bald Eagle lake points. Take advantage of this service.*

a budget store in Highland Village in St. Paul.

The flagship Emporium was a major department store that had a bakery in the basement and sold groceries and meats. St. Paul schoolchildren knew it as the place to buy their grade-school textbooks. In March 1958, the Emporium received a gold award for excellence in sales promotion from the National Retail Merchants Association for best in exhibits, fairs, and shows.

In 1963, United Properties sold the three Emporium stores to Kerr's Inc., an Oklahoma-based chain with stores in Oklahoma, Kansas, and Chicago. United Properties maintained ownership of the building and the land. At that time, the Emporium was one of the three largest department stores in St. Paul, along with Dayton's and Donaldson's–Golden Rule.

Three years later, Emporium officials filed a Chapter 11 petition in US Bankruptcy Court. The store had $1.6 million in debts. The downtown store and its two branch stores closed February 27, 1967, with no plans to reopen unless "a substantial amount of capital can be raised to rehabilitate the company," attorney Frederick C. Douglass said in a statement to the press. "There is no money available to pay any of the employees or any other creditors, and unless money can be raised there will have to be an orderly liquidation of the assets." The downtown store did open in May that year to move stock that had been on hand since the bankruptcy hearings began, and in February 1968, a Chicago businessman formed a new corporation to take over the bankrupt Emporium. The store opened February 12, 1968, under the name Emporium; however, it never regained its footing and closed permanently just a few months later, in June 1968.

IT'S ALL ABOUT ST. PAUL

The Emporium celebrated "St. Paul week" in June 1957 with St. Paul products promoted throughout the store. Store displays and show windows featured products made by 241 St. Paul companies, including UNIVAC (producer of the first commercial computer in the United States), Toni (maker of home hair permanents), Hamm's beer, and Armour hams. There were interactive displays, including one from Northern States Power Company in which onlookers were asked to try their hands at pedaling a bicycle hard enough to generate enough energy to light a hundred-watt bulb.

It was a popular show, even for women, one unidentified organizer told the *Minneapolis Star.* Boosters had worried that women would not attend, he told reporter Scott Donaldson, but "we were wrong. Maybe it's because Poppa works at the plant."

OPPOSITE, TOP TO BOTTOM: Emporium's popular bakery, 1940. Advertisement for Emporium's sixty-first anniversary sale, 1963. *Both Minnesota Historical Society Collections.* Bobby Goldman and Carol Schneider look at the closed sign at Emporium's downtown St. Paul store, February 27, 1967. Star Tribune *photo by Charles Bjorgen, Minnesota Historical Society Collections.* THIS PAGE: The Emporium's Signal Hills branch, September 1961. Star Tribune *photo, Minnesota Historical Society Collections.*

Field-Schlick was a boutique department store with an emphasis on fine fashion for women. It began as D.W. Ingersoll and Company at Third and Wabasha in 1856, the enterprise of New York merchants D.W. Ingersoll, T.C. Field, and C.F. Mahler. Frank Schlick Jr. joined the company in 1877, and in 1882, the store's name was changed to Field, Mahler and Company. Ingersoll left the interest in 1889, and Field acquired his share of the business. John Field, a nephew of T. C. Field, joined the firm in 1886, and by 1896, Mahler had left, and John Field took control of Mahler's interests. Grain sacks, blankets, and hoop skirts were a big part of the store's stocks in those early days.

By 1890, the firm opened a new store bounded by Fourth, Fifth, Wabasha, and St. Peter Streets, where it continued to operate over the next forty years. The store was remodeled in 1930, and on November 30 of that year, Field-Schlick ran an advertisement in the *Minneapolis Tribune* inviting "the people of Minneapolis and the Northwest to inspect one of 'America's Most

LEFT: Field-Schlick's Wabasha Street entrance, 1925. BELOW: Field-Schlick's Man's Shop, circa 1940. *Both Minnesota Historical Society Collections.*

Beautiful Stores'" at a formal opening of the new store on December 1.

"No expense has been spared to give the people of Saint Paul a beautiful store," read a souvenir booklet prepared for the opening. The store used a combination of rare woods in its design. The cabinets in the Fifth Street shops, where one would find hosiery, handbags, scarves, toiletries, and luggage, were made of black beanwood from the lowlands of Australia. The chocolate-colored wood was trimmed in teakwood from "Siam, Burma, and India."

The lingerie and underwear shops used East Indian satinwood from Ceylon. "Satinwood was popular in France during the period of Louis XIV," the booklet said. "It was originally used in Italy and often found in the ruins of Pompeii."

The men's furnishings and boys' wear shops off Wabasha Street were appointed with silky oak from Australia. The St. Peter Street shops—linens, silks and yard goods, women's shoes, bedding, small wares—saw the use of a number of woods from around the globe: French walnut in small wares, laurel in the shoe shop, English harewood in the negligee and corset shops.

From its beginnings, Field-Schlick offered high-end fashions, jewelry, cosmetics, and more. An advertisement in the April 29, 1900, *Minneapolis Tribune* promoted Black India Silks at $1 to $1.25 a yard and tailor-made suits at $30. Nearly eight decades later, a *St. Paul Dispatch* article on August 3, 1979, described it as a "mecca for women seeking high-fashion clothes, furs, hats, and handbags. It also had a busy counter for entertainment and sports events."

The store celebrated its centennial on January 29, 1955, with a dinner buffet at the Hotel Lowry adjacent to the Field-Schlick store. Employees were honored for their years of service, including twenty-four women and seven men

OPPOSITE, TOP: Interior of Field, Mahler and Company, 1890. BOTTOM: The Field-Schlick drum corps, 1954. *Both Minnesota Historical Society Collections.*

Charge-a-plate for several St. Paul department stores. *Mary Joan Ricci.*

who had worked there for more than twenty-five years. Three days later, St. Paul mayor Joseph Dillon unveiled a centennial crest at the store. The crest featured a golden needle and thread, symbolizing fashion; the North Star, symbolizing the future; the state capitol, honoring both the city and the state; and an hourglass, symbolic of the first one hundred years.

Field-Schlick opened its first branch store in 1961, in St. Paul's Highland neighborhood. By the late 1970s, it had stores at HarMar Mall in Roseville, Southview Shopping Center in South St. Paul, and Maplewood Mall in Maplewood, but the end was near for the longtime St. Paul retailer. In April 1979, the company ran public notices in city newspapers announcing an "Emergency Cash Raising Sale to raise immediate operating capital." By August, downtown St. Paul had lost its oldest retail store.

In addition to the beloved local department stores that established themselves as St. Paul institutions beginning in the late nineteenth century, two major national chains also left their imprints on Minnesota's capital city.

In 1921, Montgomery Ward and Company completed construction on a 1.2-million-square-foot catalog house on University Avenue, about three miles west of downtown St. Paul. The building, with its lofty 257-foot-high tower, was a landmark in the city's Midway area. It underwent various renovations as Montgomery Ward shifted its business focus from mail-order to retail. The structure was demolished in 1996 to make way for the Midway Marketplace, where a new Wards store was built with a seventy-foot replica of the old tower.

Montgomery Ward went out of business in 2001, but a few years later, the company that

FIELD-SCHLICK WAS HER STRAWBERRIES AND CREAM

Spring without at least one tour of Field-Schlick's was like strawberries without cream, or waffles without syrup, reported the *Minneapolis Tribune* in its March 22, 1936, column "Peg About Town."

For two weeks now, we've heard about the Field-Schlick March of Fashion twenty times a day. Upshot of looking it over: Our proud Minneapolis eyes are a violet green over the following Field-Schlick coups: (1) Carlin Comforts, formerly obtainable only in New York. A special room full. Exclusively. (2) Literally slews of miracles called Accessory Affinities. . . . Scarfs, bags and gloves that match perfectly. In shades of British Tan, Scottish Brick and Parma Violet that will set you to writing poetry. All the result of special work of Field-Schlick stylists with leading leather companies since way last fall. (3) Even shoes with matching bags. Yes, a March of Fashion through Field-Schlick is pretty irresistible. (Right by St. Paul's Lowry, stranger!)

TEEN POWER

Teenagers were where it was at for major retailers in the mid-twentieth century, and several department stores in the Twin Cities recruited high school girls from across the metro area to serve on their teen boards. The teens staged fashion shows, worked shifts in the stores' juniors departments, and served as great public relations tools that encouraged other teens to come into the stores.

Field-Schlick's Youth Snap Council was made up of fourteen girls who met once a month on Saturday mornings to plan events. The council—whose members did not work in the store—was one of the last of the teen boards in the Twin Cities, and Field-Schlick continued to take applications into the 1970s.

In the mid-1960s, Dayton's held contests for its teen board members at Minneapolis, Southdale, and St. Paul to serve on the Bobbie Brooks National Fashion Board. Winners received scholarships, new wardrobes, and all-expenses-paid trips to New York. Dolores DeFore accompanied the winners on the New York trips for several years. The first time she went was also her first time in New York: "It was a pleasure trip: go to the theater, take a boat ride around Manhattan." DeFore toured stores and the fashion market with the teens. "We had a packed week, and we really had fun doing it," she said.

In 1965, the official uniform for Donaldson's teen board included an A-line skirt, matching cutaway jacket, knee socks, and a burgundy paisley-print blouse, with blue heather the official color. Shoes were the Miss America brand. Donaldson's teens published a monthly newsletter, *Teens on Parade,* which featured a "question of the month." Board members quizzed students at their schools and printed answers in each issue. In September 1965, the question was, "What do you look for in a prospective date?"

Joan Frederick asked students at Orono High School, and the results were varied. Boys' answers ranged from good-looking legs to personality to sex appeal. Girls' answers ranged from "a little bit of everything" to "if he's got money." Toné Frank, of Vocational High School in Minneapolis, wrote: "I was surprised at some of the answers I received when I asked this question. The thing that surprised me was the fact that the answers weren't all in the 'good looks' category. Anybody knows that first impressions are many time lasting ones and that a person's appearance is the first thing to meet the eye, but according to the answers I've listed here, if a person is clean and neatly dressed and has a friendly way, he'll not have to worry about sitting home on Saturday nights."

Powers used a panel of twelve high school boys to judge a spring teen fashion show in 1946. The show, held at the Nicollet Hotel in Minneapolis, included "crooning" by Frank Gelsone, announcing by *Calling All Girls* fashion editor Nancy Pepper, and music by Bud Strawn's Band.

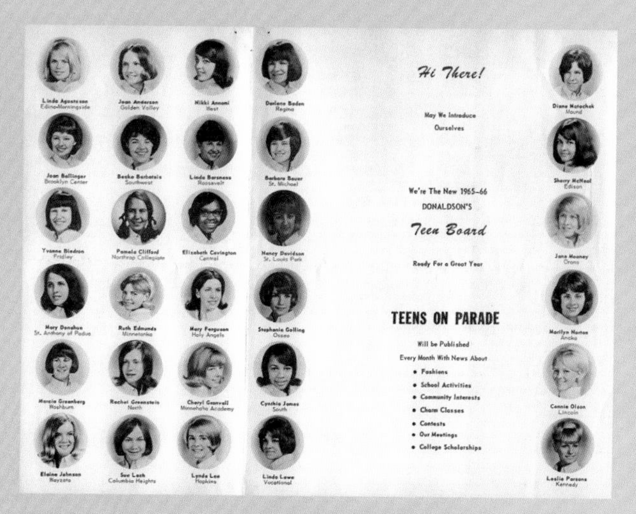

Linda Agustsson, Edina-Morningside
Joan Anderson, Golden Valley
Nikki Annoni, West
Darlene Baden, Regina
Joan Ballinger, Brooklyn Center
Becke Barbatsis, Southwest
Linda Barsness, Roosevelt
Barbara Bauer, St. Michael
Yvonne Biedron, Fridley
Pamela Clifford, Northrop Collegiate
Elizabeth Covington, Central
Nancy Davidson, St. Louis Park
Mary Donahue, St. Anthony of Padua
Ruth Edmunds, Minnetonka
Mary Ferguson, Holy Angels
Stephanie Golling, Osseo
Marcia Greenberg, Washburn
Rachel Greenstein, North
Cheryl Granvall, Minnehaha Academy
Cynthia Jones, South
Elaine Johnson, Wayzata
Sue Lach, Columbia Heights
Lynda Lee, Hopkins
Linda Lowe, Vocational

Hi There!

May We Introduce Ourselves

We're The New 1965–66 DONALDSON'S *Teen Board*

Ready For a Great Year

TEENS ON PARADE

Will be Published Every Month With News About

- Fashions
- School Activities
- Community Interests
- Charm Classes
- Contests
- Our Meetings
- College Scholarships

Diane Matochek, Mound
Sherry McNeal, Edison
Jane Mooney, Orono
Marilyn Norton, Anoka
Connie Olson, Lincoln
Leslie Parsons, Kennedy

CLOCKWISE FROM TOP RIGHT: Florine Muska, Karen Anderson, and Mary Lou Lavicott at the first meeting of Dayton's-Schuneman's Teen Board, 1960. Lavicott is modeling the board's three-piece uniform. St. Paul Pioneer Press and Dispatch *photo, Minnesota Historical Society Collections.* Donaldson's Teen Board for 1965–66. Dayton's Teen Board on the cover of the *Teentonian,* 1965. *Both Hennepin County Library.*

owners went to court in 1958 to try to stop Sears, Roebuck and Company—the company that got its start when Richard Sears began selling watches from a train depot near Redwood Falls, Minnesota, in 1886—from building a new store near the state capitol. The group of independent business owners sued the St. Paul Housing and Redevelopment Authority over its sale of a thirteen-acre tract of redeveloped land to Sears, Roebuck.

The businesses maintained that they would suffer if the Sears store was built, and the suit claimed that the original purpose of the Housing and Redevelopment Authority was to provide public housing, not sell renewed land for commercial

bought the Ward name brought it back on the internet as Wards.com. Now, Montgomery Ward, a company that began as a mail-order business in 1872 is, once again, a mail-order business of sorts. As for the Midway Wards location, it was occupied by Herberger's until 2018, when Bon-Ton Stores Inc., the Minnesota-founded chain's parent company, announced it was bought out of bankruptcy by liquidators.

Another national retailer's plan to expand its presence in St. Paul was a source of controversy for local businesses in the middle of the twentieth century. Seventy-four downtown business

purposes. The suit also alleged that the price obtained from Sears for the land had been too cheap. Sears paid ninety-five cents a square foot for the land—a total of $586,736.

The case made its way to the Minnesota Supreme Court, which ruled on June 26, 1959, that the sale of redeveloped land to Sears, Roebuck was legal and valid. That cleared the way for construction of a $4.5 million Sears department store, which opened the day after Dayton's opened its five-story downtown St. Paul store.

Sears's sprawling two-story store included 98,280 square feet of sales space, a service station,

ABOVE: Montgomery Ward on University Avenue, St. Paul, circa 1925. RIGHT: Sears Building on Lake Street, Minneapolis, circa 1929. FAR RIGHT: Interior of the Sears department store, St. Paul, 1970. *All Minnesota Historical Society Collections.*

a garden shop, and parking space for more than 1,400 cars. Dayton's had 380,000 square feet of sales space and a 615-car enclosed parking ramp. The Sears store was still operating at 425 Rice Street as of 2018.

Back across the river in Minneapolis, the towering Sears Building on Lake Street has seen renewed life as a mixed-use site that is home to the Midtown Global Market, the Chicago Lofts and Midtown Exchange Apartments, the headquarters of Allina Health, and other uses. Built in 1928, the longtime Sears catalog center and retail facility sat vacant for more than a decade after the company closed its operations there in 1994. The Midtown Global Market, which opened in 2006, features diverse offerings of food vendors and specialty merchandise.

BELOW, CLOCKWISE: The front wall of Bannon's Department Store collapsed on March 10, 1950. Firefighters rescue birds from Bannon's after the collapse. *Both* St. Paul Pioneer Press and Dispatch *photos, Minnesota Historical Society Collections.* The day after the collapse. Star Tribune *photo, Minnesota Historical Society Collections.*

STORE'S WALL PLUNGES TO STREET

As workers prepared to tear down an old building on Seventh Street in St. Paul that formed part of Bannon's Department Store, a fifty-foot section of the front wall crashed to the street midmorning on March 10, 1950.

Workers said they heard sounds within the wall that indicated it was cracking and had less than a minute to clear pedestrians before the crash. No one was injured.

Bannon's had operated in St. Paul since 1883. In 1906, George and William Bannon purchased a four-story brick building at Seventh and Minnesota Streets. In 1946, Gamble Stores purchased Bannon's. The company operated 521 stores throughout the United States and Canada.

The store was forced to move after the wall collapse. It found a temporary spot on Robert Street, but a year later, in April 1951, the store began liquidating its entire stock of merchandise.

NELSON BROS
& CO

7

On the Road: Retail Stories from around the State

During the first seventy-five years of the twentieth century, Minnesotans couldn't take a road trip across the state without driving through the downtown business districts of the towns on the paths of many state highways and county roads. Dotting these main streets were the merchants that had been established as the towns were built in the late 1800s. These shops grew and brought commerce and culture to the communities—and, by the turn of the twenty-first century, most of them were gone.

Travelers heading into Winona in the 1860s no doubt saw the signs on all the main roads marking each mile toward town: "8 Miles to Choate's Cheap Cash Store," "7 Miles to Choate's." Traveling by horse and wagon and using a crude odometer, merchant and master marketer Hannibal Choate began promoting his new store in his new town probably as soon as the ground thawed.

H. Choate and Company opened in December 1861 in what was then a small steamboat landing, where mud streets were filled with wagon-wheel ruts, and the business district consisted of a handful of weathered wooden buildings. Born in New York, where he was trained in the mercantile business, Hannibal Choate came to Winona to take over a store he had purchased for $900.

That enterprise would become a landmark and cultural institution in this river town for the next 120 years. Choate's was the store that sponsored Miss Winona each year during the summer Steamboat Days, the store that broadcast the *Choate's Musical Clock* radio hour from station KWNO from its third floor, and the community booster that created a lot of sweet memories with its red-and-white Santa House located on "Santa Lane" downtown, a December delight that opened in 1963.

When the business began at 117 Main Street in 1861, Choate stocked the shelves with groceries, yard goods, boots and shoes, crockery, and "Yankee Notions." It saw fast success, and it soon moved to larger accommodations

OPPOSITE: Nelson Brothers and Company Department Store, Luverne, Minnesota, circa 1890. *Rock County Historical Society.*

ABOVE: H. Choate and Company department store, Winona. RIGHT: Teens take part in *Choate's Musical Clock* radio hour, 1950s. OPPOSITE, TOP: Choate's models, 1950s. BOTTOM: Choate's display window, 1940s. *All Lynne Hartert.*

at Second and Center Streets. By 1888, Hannibal Choate had built the stone Romanesque Revival building that still stands at the corner of Third and Center.

The store was five stories tall with four granite columns, large plate-glass windows twelve feet wide, oak detailing inside, and a passenger elevator, which was run by an attendant well into the mid-twentieth century. The 1888 grand opening made the front page of the *Winona Daily Republican*, and advertisements inside the paper promised "a veritable bargain in dress goods, . . . 50 cents is the magic word that will bring a new serge dress to your household. Woolen underwear . . . woolen hosiery, seamless for 25 cents a pair . . . Fosterina lacing hooks, kid gloves, carpetings, oil cloths, cloaks at $15." The store featured a dressmaking department and a variety of yard goods in 1888: sateens, camel hairs, silks, whipcords, alpacas, and mohairs. As the century turned, however, Choate's brought ready-to-wear to southeastern Minnesota, a trend that had already made its way to Minneapolis at the Young-Quinlan Company on Nicollet Avenue.[1]

The new Choate's building included offices on the fifth floor, and in 1896, Choate expanded with a new addition, increasing the store's floor space and office rental space.

Hannibal Choate died in 1923. His sons, Charles (known as Chokie) and Hannibal Jr., took over and added home furnishings and gifts to the inventory. Chokie had a reputation for being a fun-loving manager whose silly promotions were good marketing for the store, said Lynne Hartert, who now owns the building. Shoppers in the 1960s and 1970s remember purchasing records in the basement, where they could listen to a 45 before buying, or heading to the upper floors for orthodontist and dentist appointments.

"The Old Store on the Corner," its nickname since the early 1900s, was sold in 1958 to the La-Crosse Group. H. Choate and Company continued under that name until 1980, when Allen Stores bought it. Allen's Department Store moved out just a few years later, and the building sat empty until Hartert and her husband, Steve, bought it in 1994 to house their growing retail business, Heart's Desire. The Harterts spent nearly a decade restoring the forty-thousand-square-foot building, which was listed on the National Register of Historic Places in 1976. The main floor is now anchored by the Hartert's gift store, while the upper floors include apartments rented by students from nearby Winona State University and St. Mary's University, as well as a variety of business offices, including the local branch of the Social Security Administration.

LEFT: Choate's employee gathering, 1940s. BELOW: Charles "Chokie" Choate. *Both Lynne Hartert.* BOTTOM: Heart's Desire, in the former Choate's building, 2017. *Wikipedia Commons.*

Some twenty years after Hannibal Choate landed in Winona, Frank Fandel got off a wagon train in St. Cloud, about 180 miles to the northwest, and began one of the first chapters in that area's retail history.

The Luxembourg native came to the United States with his parents at age twelve in 1871. The family settled in St. Paul, where Fandel spent a few years waiting tables at the St. Paul Hotel, saving money, and looking for an opportunity to leave Minnesota and open a mercantile in Montana. That opportunity came in 1879. Fandel

EVERYBODY WAS DOING IT

After Nicollet Mall opened in 1967 in Minneapolis, communities outside of the Twin Cities followed the trend of creating a pedestrian-friendly shopping area in their downtowns.

Winona banned all motorized traffic when it opened the four-block Levee Plaza in 1969 between Walnut and Main Streets. H. Choate Company president Al Krieger told a *Minneapolis Tribune* reporter it was "one of the best things Winona ever did. After three years, people still comment on it continually."[2]

"The effect on business? My sales are up 20 to 25 percent over the last (pre-mall) year, and that's a direct result of Levee Plaza," Krieger said.

St. Cloud banned all traffic, including buses and taxis, from its three-block Mall Germain, which opened in November 1972. The new mall even barred cross traffic on the busy Sixth Avenue intersection next to Fandel's.

Twenty-three years after it was built, Winona's Levee Plaza proved not to be working, and the city ripped it out and rebuilt Third Street in an effort to make parking easier and to woo shoppers back downtown. By 1998, St. Cloud, too, had opened up St. Germain Street to make room for parking.

boarded a westbound wagon train, and according to family lore, he found the journey so uncomfortable that he got off just sixty-five miles past Minneapolis. Three years later, he opened the Empire Store with Michael Nugent. By 1885, Fandel became sole owner and changed the name to Fandel's.

St. Cloud was the frontier at that time, and Fandel prospered by supplying goods to settlers in Stearns County. In 1914, more than two thousand people attended the grand opening of Fandel's new three-story commercial block on the corner of Sixth Avenue and St. Germain Street. The multicolored brick-and-red-granite building cost $50,000 to construct. A local newspaper called it "a monument to the enterprise and success of its owner."

Fandel's featured a self-service elevator and pneumatic tubes that routed customers' money to another floor, where a worker made change and sent it back to the sales clerk.

Frank Fandel had five children, Victor, Julius, Sylvester, Pauline, and Hortense. The three sons ran the company for a time. By the 1950s, Victor's son Frederick "Fritz" Fandel was president of the store, a position he held until the early 1980s, when his son, Peter, took the reins.

Jett Heckler was hired at Fandel's in 1959. She worked in the intimate apparel department, called lingerie at the time, and that's where she stayed until Fandel's closed in 1985. One of her more humorous memories is how busy the lingerie department got on Christmas Eve. Every year,

Fritz Fandel being interviewed by a local radio station. *Peter Fandel.*

ABOVE: Fandel's, circa 1890. RIGHT: Fandel's carpet department, circa 1900. *Both Peter Fandel.*

men rushed into the store toward closing to buy their wives presents in Heckler's department, she said, and the day after Christmas, most of the women who received those last-minute gifts were in line to return them.

Peter Fandel was the last president and general merchandise manager at Fandel's. He grew up in the store and has fond memories of exploring all the nooks and crannies of the building. He also remembers the calls customers made to his family home every year on Christmas Eve. "We closed at four o'clock, and every Christmas Eve without fail, there would be a number of people

TOP TO BOTTOM: Fandel's basement store, circa 1920. Christmastime at Fandel's, 1960s. Christmastime at Fandel's, 1960s. *All Peter Fandel.*

who forgot their wrapped Christmas presents in the store," Fandel recalled. "They would call the house at four-thirty, five o'clock, six o'clock. 'Oh, we're so sorry, didn't realize you were closing early,' or whatever the excuse was, but basically the question was, 'Can you help us out?' Obviously, the answer was yes."

Members of the Fandel family would meet the customers at the store, unlock the doors, and walk them through the dark building to the lower-level gift-wrap section. "We'd find their presents and carry them up, and some years if we didn't get that call, we'd worry," he said. Working long hours and weekends, making emergency deliveries, it was all part of the job. "It was just the way it was. It was all we knew."

Fandel's had expanded to four operations by the 1980s: the flagship store in downtown St. Cloud, which included home goods, furniture, and carpeting, as well as clothing; a women's specialty store at St. Cloud's Crossroads Center; and two women's specialty stores, called Intrigue, in Fergus Falls and Alexandria.

Retailing changed a lot from the 1950s to the 1980s, Peter Fandel said. In the mid-twentieth century, Fandel's sent its buyers to the garment district in New York City, where "you could walk into the showroom and see all those things available for the season, in the next room would be the person who designed those things, and then in the back door comes the person who is running the business on Long Island. It was all local—maybe all within the state of New York—that these goods were designed, sewn, produced, sold, and shipped. And that went for the furniture too." Buyers were

OPPOSITE, TOP: Interior, Fandel's, 1950s.
BOTTOM: Fandel's clerks, 1950s.
Both Peter Fandel.

FANDEL'S

Exclusive Styles--Famous Makes--Luxurious Qualities
Golden Jubilee Brings All of These in Your

SPRING COAT

At the Lowest Price in Years!

$21

Most all of them one-of-a-kind styles! Regular $29.75 to $35.00 qualities. All those famous makers you know so well made extreme price concessions—we chose only the best selling styles. Luxurious fur collars, spongy diagonal weaves, scarfs, full sleeves, fitted waists—in a range of colors and sizes to satisfy every woman.

—Fandel's Second Floor

Cast a Knowing Eye at this

Your Pick of C

TEN DOLLAR Froc

During Golden Jubilee Celebrati

You know as every woman knows TEN DOLLAR frocks are a buy any time—at **$8.00** they are a steal—a downright steal! They bring everything that's new at the very time you want to wear it. 3-piece silk and wool suits are included. Sizes 12 to 56.

—Fandel's Seco

FANDEL'S

Golden Jubilee Corset Values

Lovely Silks and Laces—Brand New Styles
Famous Makes—Perfect Fitting

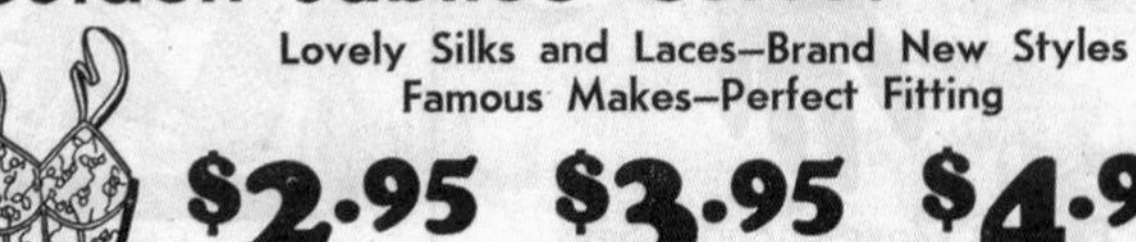

$2.95 *Values* to $5.00
Combinations, lace-trimmed step-ins, corsets. Fine materials in new, fitted styles of satin and crepe silks with silk elastic. All sizes.

$3.95 *Values* to $7.95
Lace-top combinations, side-fastening girdles, corsets. Lovely materials trimmed with fine ecru lace. Complete selections in all sizes.

$4.95 *Values* to $10.00
Combinations with inner-belts, lace-trimmed combinations, brocaded combinations for larger figures. Fine garments at low Anniversary prices.

—Fandel's Second Floor

Two Special Prices On Undies

Fandel's Standard Quality - - Most Wanted Styles

95c

$1.59 *Values!*

All silk washable French crepe pantie and brassiere sets trimmed with ecru lace. Also Munsingwear fine rayon embroidered bloomers and panties.

—Main Floor

$1.59

$1.95 *Values!*

$1.95 quality washable French silk crepe undies—pantie sets, teddies, step-ins, panties in brief 1932 styles. Lace trimmed. All sizes.

—Main Floor

Girls' Cotton Dresses

Anniversary Selections Larger Than Ever

79c 98c $1.49

Broadcloths, batistes, voiles, organdies, meshes, rayon silk—all washable—guaranteed fast. Sizes 1 to 16 years. A great assortment of styles.

—Fandel's New Addition

Special!
Girls' Bloomers
39c

Little girls like them because they fit perfectly. Fine rayons — regular 50¢ quality. Sizes 2 to 12.

—Main Floor

ABOVE AND RIGHT: Advertisements for Fandel's fiftieth anniversary, 1932.
Peter Fandel.

sent to furniture-manufacturing towns like High Point, North Carolina, where some businesses had been making furniture for hundreds of years.

"We would come to know the manufacturers. They became like family," Fandel said. "Now, the model is completely different."

Fandel's was often compared to Dayton's, which Fandel says was the store's chief competitor. His father was sometimes referred to as the Donald Dayton of St. Cloud. "We were like them in not only product lines but provided the same level of service: personal shopping, gift wrap, free alterations, delivery," he said.

Bill Morgan, a retired history professor from St. Cloud State University, said Fandel's "had an elegance that was very special," adding, "it was like downtown [Minneapolis] Dayton's."

ABOVE: Fandel's exterior, 1940s. OPPOSITE, TOP: Fandel's store window, 1946. BOTTOM: Fandel's display windows supporting the war effort during World War II. *All Peter Fandel.*

And like Dayton's, Fandel's management enjoyed employing marketing gimmicks to draw in the crowds. One example was the Noritake bone china promotion in the 1970s: to prove the strength and durability of the new china, Fandel's created a display on the main sales floor where they rested a Volkswagen Golf on four teacups. "We got a couple of jacks and put down sheets of Plexiglas under each tire, then placed an upside-down bone china teacup on each of these pieces of Plexiglas," he said. As they began to rest the car on the teacups and Plexiglas, the cups exploded one by one.

"I think we went through eleven of them but eventually got the car settled on four delicate bone china teacups, got the car raised, and put up red velvet ropes and stanchions." It made a memorable display.

"We sold bone china like crazy," Peter Fandel said.

In the department store world, all good things come to an end. Jeanne Malley, who worked in the china and crystal department (also known as the never-call-them-dishes department), recounted the day Peter Fandel called the staff into her department to deliver bad news. Herberger's was buying Fandel's.

"It was a sad day," Malley said. "We were all there. We cried and cried."

"It was like a death in the family," Fandel said. "It was the demise of an institution, and that was a sad affair, not only for those of us who

1st National
April — 1946
GIRL SCOUTING BUILDS WORLD FRIENDSHIP
NORTH AMERICA
EUROPE
ASIA
AFRICA
Pacific Ocean
Pacific Ocean
AUSTRALIA
Pennies collected by Scouts for World Friendship Fund in St Cloud. This year these pennies will be used for the rehabilitation of Scouting in the War torn areas.
ST CLOUD

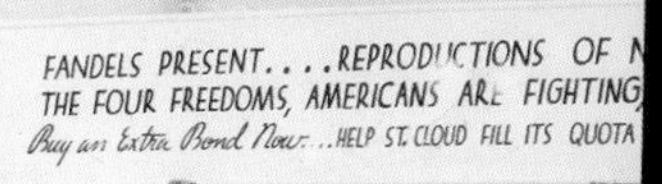
FANDELS PRESENT.... REPRODUCTIONS OF N MAN ROCKWELL'S FAMOUS PAINTINGS OF
THE FOUR FREEDOMS, AMERICANS ARE FIGHTING ORKING AND BUYING BONDS TO PRESERVE
Buy an Extra Bond Now... HELP ST. CLOUD FILL ITS QUOTA MERICA'S 13-BILLION DOLLAR SECOND WAR LOAN DRIVE!

OURS... to fight for
FREEDOM FROM
BUY MORE BONDS
SAVE FREEDOM OF WORSHIP
BUY WAR BO
BUY MORE BONDS

OURS... to fight for
REEDOM FROM WANT
BUY MORE BONDS
SAVE FREEDOM OF SPEECH
UY WAR BONDS
BUY MORE BONDS

worked in the company but for the customers."

The store was not faltering financially, Fandel said. In fact, it was on a bit of an uptick. But Herberger's, the multistate chain department store that got its start in Osakis, Minnesota, when brothers George and Frank Herberger purchased the Fry Store in 1889, wanted to build a flagship store in downtown St. Cloud, where it was headquartered. So it entered into negotiations to buy both the Fandel's property and its retail operations.

"I tried to stop it," Fandel said. But in the end, he owned only a small percentage of the family's business. There were twenty-two shareholders, all of whom were descendants of Frank Fandel. The building that both Fandel and Morgan called a "jewel" was razed shortly after the sale.

"History unfolds, and it's not unique to us," Fandel said. Indeed, Bon-Ton Stores Inc., owner of Herberger's, Younkers, and two hundred other regional department stores in the United States, announced it was going out of business in April 2018. Herberger's fourteen Minnesota stores would close, including the downtown St. Cloud store on St. Germain Street, where Fandel's had stood.

Fandel's once belonged to a retail group that consisted of nine stores similar in size and character to Fandel's, and they are all gone: "They've gone bankrupt, been bought out by a large competitor, or simply decided to close their doors," Peter Fandel said. One of those stores was Brett's in Mankato.

Fandel's sidewalk sale, 1970s. *Peter Fandel.*

When Mankato native Maud Hart Lovelace wrote about the Lion Department Store in her 1943 book *Betsy and Tacy Go Downtown*, many Betsy-Tacy fans believed she was writing about Brett's Department Store, a Mankato institution for nearly 125 years. Lovelace's first eight books, published from 1940 to 1948, feature the adventures of Betsy Warrington Ray, Tacy Kelly, and Tib Muller, three girls growing up in Deep Valley, Minnesota, a fictional town based on Lovelace's childhood home of Mankato.

When Betsy and Tacy wander through the departments at the Lion store, they look at rhinestone side combs, jeweled hat pins, fluffy collars and belts and pocketbooks, black lace stockings, taffeta petticoats, and embroidered corset covers—all items George E. Brett likely stocked when he established George E. Brett Dry Goods on Front Street in Mankato in 1868. Lovelace was born in 1892, the year before Brett built his store at 329 Front Street twenty-five years after opening his business.

Brett's stayed a family business for five generations after George Brett traveled from Maine to Minnesota to open the mercantile. In 1915, George's son Edward became president. By 1926, Brett's occupied three floors and a basement on Front Street and had

TOP: Postcard view of George E. Brett Dry Goods in Mankato. ABOVE: George E. Brett Dry Goods, circa 1870. *Both Blue Earth County Historical Society.*

THIS PAGE, RIGHT: George E. Brett Dry Goods interior, circa 1885. BELOW: Brett's ladies and misses apparel section, circa 1915. *Both Blue Earth County Historical Society.* BOTTOM: Dress department at Oreck's, Duluth, 1930s. OPPOSITE, TOP: Interior of Freimuth's, circa 1950s. BOTTOM: Freimuth's, Duluth, circa 1910. *All St. Louis County Historical Society.*

opened a store in Albert Lea. The Brett baton was passed to Edward's nephew Brett Taylor, who became president of the store in 1930.

Brett's was one of the first retailers in southern Minnesota to install escalators in the 1950s. By 1973, it was the largest independent retailer in Mankato. Brett Taylor's son, Brett Taylor Jr., became president in 1971 and oversaw the expansion of Brett's to the southern Minnesota towns of New Ulm, Hutchinson, Fairmont, Faribault, and Owatonna. By 1990, when Brett Taylor Jr.'s son, Scott Taylor, took over the company, retail winds had changed, as the country faced a recession, and River Hills Mall was about to open in Mankato. Many Front Street stores relocated to the new retail center on the northeast edge of town.

The store's name changed to Brett's Specialty Store in 1991, reflecting the company's decision to drop several departments that were lagging in sales, including housewares and home products. That year's holiday season was lackluster, and soon after the new mall opened in Mankato in 1992, Brett's announced the closing of all its stores after nearly 125 years in business.

Downtown Duluth was once home to several department stores: the upscale Wahl's and Oreck's Gold Room, the more affordable Freimuth's, and the Glass Block, which featured a bakery known for its sweet rolls and its lunch counter in the basement.

Freimuth's was the oldest of Duluth's family-owned retail firms. Founded as a general store in 1883, it moved to 1900 Superior Street, where it operated until October 18, 1961, when the business closed. The building sat vacant for several years before it was razed in 1968.

The Glass Block was a Superior Street landmark for eighty-nine years. It was opened by John Panton and Joseph Watson as a one-room dry

goods store in 1887 at Superior and First Avenue; the merchants moved to a larger store at 118 West Superior Street within months. In 1892, Panton and Watson built a two-story red Tiffany brick building with sandstone trim at 128 West Superior Street and moved the business there. In 1896, William White took over Watson's share of the business, and the store was named Panton and White, but it was nicknamed the "Glass Block." Panton had apparently worked at Donaldson's

Glass Block in Minneapolis before moving to Duluth. By 1902, three stories had been added to the building, and it was named the Panton and White Glass Block Store. The business was purchased in 1911 by the F. A. Patrick Company, and the name changed officially to the Glass Block Store. A second store was opened at Miller Hill Mall in 1973, but in 1981, the Glass Block closed. The downtown building was demolished shortly after.

Corneilus (Con) O'Brien arrived in Brainerd in 1883 and soon established a saloon on Eighth Street. The business prospered quickly, and O'Brien turned the saloon into a general store, which grew into O'Brien Mercantile Company. O'Brien's remained a family-run business until it closed in the 1970s.

In January 1898, the O'Brien store burned, along with the Sleeper Opera House next door. O'Brien claimed he'd rebuild, and he did. By April of that year, a new one-story brick building with a steel roof, a plate-glass front, steam heat, and modern appliances opened for business. By 1905, the mercantile was stocking ladies' ready-to-wear garments, women's and men's shoes, men's clothing, groceries, meats, and provisions of all kinds: "In this mercantile emporium one may purchase every article of apparel or food necessary to man, woman or child, rightly priced and of a standard of quality that cannot be surpassed."[3]

Con O'Brien—who served as Brainerd mayor twice—died in 1932, and his oldest son, James, became president of the O'Brien's store. After James died in 1944, his son, Tom O'Brien, became president.

The store moved to the corner of Laurel and Broadway, the former site of a Montgomery Ward store, in the 1960s. And in February 1973, the O'Brien Department Store closed its doors.

Sarah Gorham, who grew up in Brainerd, recalls the store's pneumatic tubes used to bring change to customers. She described Tom O'Brien, her across-the-street neighbor, as "an elegant, dapper man," who wore tweed suits and bowties.

She also recalls the dilemma of an adolescent girl in the mid-1970s: "In a small town, where everyone shopped at the same few stores, someone else was probably going to wear the same clothing as you. So the cool kids got to go to St. Cloud." Where did they shop? Fandel's.

BELOW LEFT: The Glass Block, Duluth, circa 1910. RIGHT: Glass block, 1963. *Both St. Louis County Historical Society.* OPPOSITE, LEFT TO RIGHT: Shoe department, O'Brien's, 1950s. Customer and clerk at O'Brien's, Brainerd, 1950s. *Both Crow Wing County Historical Society.* O'Brien's ad from *Kitchen Kapers,* a cookbook published by the St. Francis Guild, the Brainerd Council of Catholic Women. *Kim Avenson.*

A MAN OF MANY TITLES

He was a merchant, a psychologist, an educator, a builder, a radio executive, a landlord, a silviculturist, a traveler, and a musician.

Tom O'Brien was a man of many titles, including president of O'Brien Mercantile Company in Brainerd from 1945 to 1973. The *Minneapolis Star* featured O'Brien in its July 5, 1956, edition, with an article titled, "Brainerd's Tom O'Brien Can't Kill Time: Meet a 1-man 'Business District.'"

One of Minnesota's busiest men, O'Brien is forty-nine, a bachelor and a holder of many titles

"One of Minnesota's busiest men, O'Brien is forty-nine, a bachelor and a holder of many titles," the paper said. Besides the Mercantile Company, he was president of O'Brien Minerals, which dealt in mineral rights; president and founder of Brainerd Broadcasting Company, which operated station KLIZ (named for his mother, Elizabeth O'Brien); copartner in O'Brien Properties, holding company for many of Brainerd's downtown business properties; state vice chairman of the American Red Cross fund campaign; member of the advisory committee of the College of St. Scholastica; director of Build Brainerd Inc.; and past president of the Brainerd Rotary Club. Did we mention his time on the Brainerd school board, the Minnesota State School Board, and his work lobbying for public schools at the Minnesota Legislature? O'Brien also helped establish a program in the 1950s that brought foreign students as guests to Brainerd each year to discuss international issues and give "one half an idea of how the other half lives." In May 1956, students from sixty-one countries visited the town.

O'Brien told the *Star* he didn't know what it was like to have to kill an evening, or even a single hour.

Like his father, Con O'Brien, Tom O'Brien served as mayor in Brainerd as well as city council president. O'Brien died in 1982 at age seventy-six.

Donaldson's
YOUR FRIENDLY CHRISTMAS STORE

8
The Most Wonderful Time of the Year: Department Store Holidays

Before the turn of the twentieth century, Minnesota dry goods stores knew the marketing power of Christmas and Santa Claus. Many claimed to be *the* Santa and holiday headquarters, and it worked.

In 1882, Donaldson's ran a small ad in the December 7 *Minneapolis Journal* announcing it would open its Christmas window display a day early "to prevent overcrowding." The window would be open through Christmas and "give you ample opportunity to see everything at your leisure after the opening," the notice said.

By the 1890s, many Minnesota department stores were hosting Santa himself for special visits. In 1892, he visited Santa Claus's Fairyland in the basement of Donaldson's Glass Block, which was filled, of course, with "dolls, games, musical goods and toys of every description." He came to St. Paul's Golden Rule, which dubbed itself "the Santa Claus Store," in 1899 for a day to answer all the letters children had written to him and brought to the store before his scheduled appearance.[1]

Donaldson's began bringing the merrymaker

OPPOSITE: Donaldson's Christmas display, 1957. *Minnesota Historical Society Collections.* THIS PAGE: *Painting by Nita Anderson.*

to Nicollet Avenue by train in the 1920s. Skeptics who insisted there "ain't no Santa Claus" were encouraged to head to the Milwaukee Depot at two o'clock Saturday, December 1, 1922, to see Santa come in on a special train and then parade down the avenue in a gaily decorated float to the store, where he'd made his headquarters in Donaldson's Christmas Treasure House.

Mr. James Foster, the travel agency headquartered at Donaldson's, had to make special arrangements for Santa because there wasn't enough snow to travel by sleigh on his trek down from the North Pole (this must have been before reindeer could fly). A specially routed train would bring him into Minneapolis, according to news reports and advertisements printed in area

OPPOSITE: Donaldson's "Christmas Gift Book," 1925. THIS PAGE, ABOVE: Dayton's "World of Toys" Christmas catalog, 1952. LEFT: Powers's "Toytime" Christmas catalog, 1955. *All Hennepin County Library.*

LEFT: Five-year-old Lynn Sonnichsen shopping in Dayton's For Children Only Shop, 1964. Star Tribune *photo.* BELOW: Entrance to Donaldson's "Toyland," 1957. OPPOSITE, TOP: Donaldson's Santa parade, 1915. BOTTOM: Jane Marie Heaton with Santa Claus at Schuneman's, 1950. *All Minnesota Historical Society Collections.*

DONALDSON COMPANY GIVES TO YOUNGSTERS

Eight Thousand Little Hearts Made Happy By Store

December 18, 1915 — The L. S. Donaldson Company filled 8,000 little hearts with joy yesterday. And a welcome burden was placed in each of the 16,000 little hands. It was only one of the Donaldson ways of making Christmas real to children.

The schools held their final session before the holidays yesterday and in the lower grades there were Santa Claus impersonations and Yuletide programs. Donaldson delivery wagons visited every school and kindergarten and each child in first grade and kindergarten received a Santa Claus doll, with a bag of candy tied to his or her shoulders, and a wooden toy automobile. Eight thousand children were thus remembered.

In addition, the company is continuing its last year's practice of receiving orders for Christmas stockings. Patrons purchase candies and gifts for families in need, and the company furnishes the stockings to be filled and delivers them to the addresses designated.

A continuous moving picture show, exhibiting Santa Claus and Yuletide films, is conducted in the subway of the Glass Block store with free admission to youngsters.
—*Minneapolis Morning Tribune*

newspapers the day before. The next year, Santa faced similar circumstances, and once again, Mr. Foster stepped in to secure a train to get him to the store. Donaldson's broadcasted radio messages leading up to the day of St. Nick's visit to keep children apprised of his schedule.

Department stores pulled out all the stops inside and out at Christmas. Window displays became a cultural event in downtown Minneapolis, as the major retailers worked hard to one-up each other. On November 28, 1914, Donaldson's ran an ad in the *Minneapolis Morning Tribune* encouraging "Boys, Girls and Older Folks" to come see the "great goings at your favorite store. . . . First you should see the windows then the wonderful main floor decorations. Then Toyland in the basement. Then investigate the subway 'surprise,' but do not forget the second floor bazar [*sic*], where you will find *everything* you just wanted so much."

PUT UP YOUR JOLLY DUKES

Things weren't always so happy and festive during the holiday season downtown. In December 1910, a brawl broke out between two Santas, according to the December 22 *Minneapolis Morning Tribune*. The day before, children walking down Nicollet Avenue came across two men dressed in Santa Claus outfits engaged in a fistfight. The Santas had been working for Volunteers of America soliciting funds for the poor of Minneapolis when one of them threw a taunt at the other, saying he didn't look like Santa Claus. Some verbal back-and-forth ensued, and then the red-costumed, white-whiskered fellows began to duke it out.

A group of boys passing by joined in by doubling up their fists and taking sides. A police officer at Hennepin Avenue and Third Street heard the commotion, came over, and put an end to the fracas. The two Santa Clauses went back to their respective posts, and when adjutant John O'Neal of the Volunteers of America was asked how he would handle the situation, he said the participants "had made up" with each other, and he would take no action.

In 1926, Dayton's set up an entire zoo, including lions, leopards, bears, and camels, in its street windows at Christmas. Some decades later, the store featured a family of chimpanzees in a cage, but after two days they had to be removed because "we were not in the business of teaching children the facts of life," Dayton's president Donald Dayton said in an interview in the December 3, 1965, issue of the *Minneapolis Tribune.*

By the 1940s, crowds filled Nicollet Avenue the night before Thanksgiving when the stores' windows were unveiled, revealing the animated Christmas displays. In 1945, Powers's windows were filled with characters from Charles Dickens's *A Christmas Carol,* the Dayton Company displayed animated scenes from *Alice in Wonderland,* and Donaldson's displayed a holiday toy land.

(continued on page 160)

OPPOSITE, TOP: Crowds fill the sidewalks outside Dayton's Christmas windows, 1923. *Hennepin County Library.* BOTTOM: "Santa's Workshop" window display at Donaldson's, 1957. THIS PAGE, TOP: Dayton's Christmas window featuring "Santa's Circus," 1957. *Both Minnesota Historical Society Collections.* BELOW, LEFT: Powers Christmas window display, 1947. Star Tribune *photo, Minnesota Historical Society Collections.* RIGHT: Dayton's Christmas window featuring "Santa's Workshop," 1962. *Minnesota Historical Society Collections.*

I WAS A DEPARTMENT STORE SANTA

A week in the belly of the beast with Santa Jim

By Jim Walsh

Twin Cities writer Jim Walsh spent three weeks in 1989 working as one of several Santas at Dayton's downtown Minneapolis store — what Walsh described as "one of the most prestigious gigs an inexperienced but thoroughly willing Santa could hope for." He wrote how he was always fascinated by department store Santas: "I've always wanted to know what life is like in their big black boots, and now, for the next three weeks, I'm the man." He chronicled his first week in the Santa suit for City Pages *in an article that appeared on December 27, 1989. Following are some excerpts from the piece.*

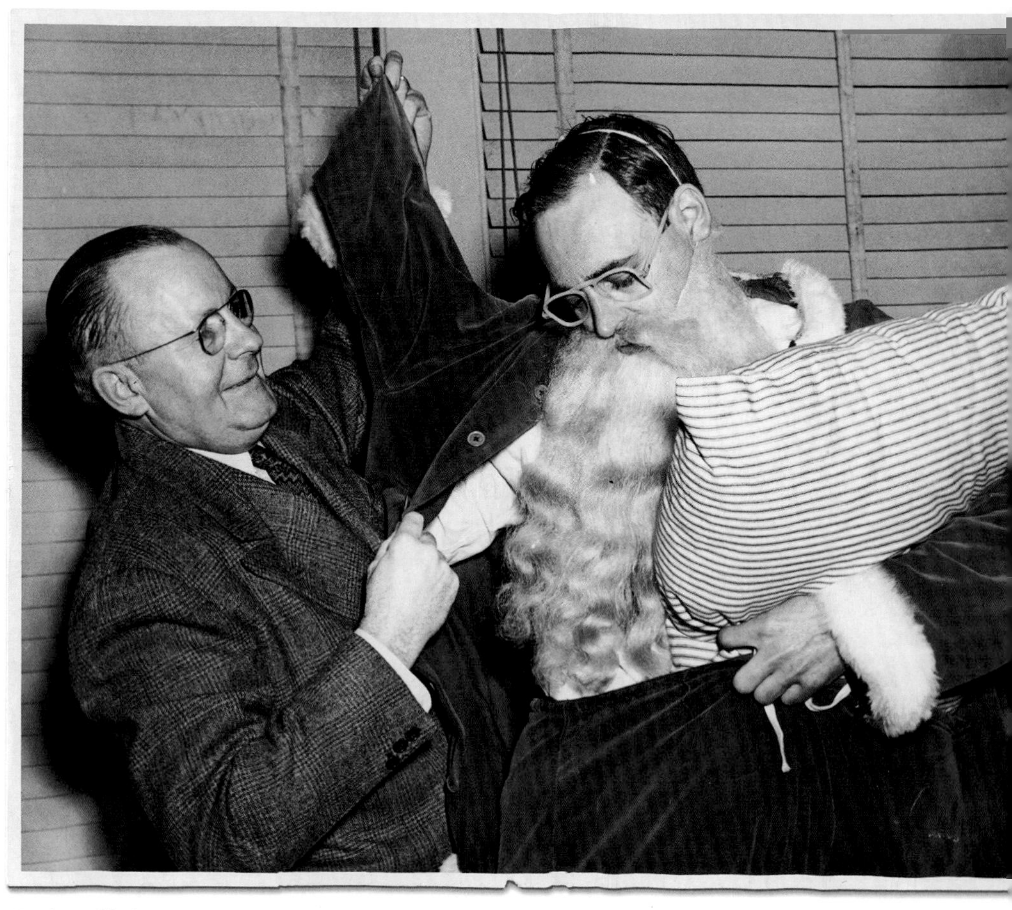

Gordon Mikkelson, Powers's Santa, getting into costume, 1947. *Hennepin County Library.*

MONDAY

I got on the bus this morning and studied my set of suggested clauses, given to me by Trixie, the young woman who runs the show at Dayton's. The rules are pretty meticulous: "Never allow the child to think or feel you aren't real; remember, once the costume is on — you are Santa Claus. Keep in character at all times: you never know who may be near. Drinking alcoholic beverages before or during your shift is cause for immediate termination.... Use good judgment if you're out the night before, also. Never promise a child anything. Be aware of your hand positions as you lift or hold a child. Try to remind children, 'Santa loves you.'"

I was a little nervous.... As I changed into my gear — padding, beard, wig, hat, suit, spats, and belt — and rubbed rouge on my cheeks and white greasepaint on my eyebrows, I got tips from Bob, a veteran Santa. Bob addressed me as "Santa Jim" at one point; he said it in the way you might call someone "father" or "padre" or "sister." Apparently this is a pretty sacred fraternity I've hitched up with. Bob and Trixie told me not to worry, that I was going to be great. Then they threw me to the wolves.

For the first hour, a whole series of kids cried, screamed, kicked and clawed to get away from Santa Jim. Trixie, who acts as photographer and cashier as well as Queen of Santa's Helpers, said I was doing fine. But she admitted it was weird—she'd never seen such a long string of frightened kids.

These kids weren't just scared, they were freaked. I started taking it personally. I thought they were on to me — they sensed I was a fake, a paper Santa. One kid said I was only dressed like Santa. I choked. I asked him how old he was.

The breakthrough came when a five-year-old girl climbed up on my lap, huge eyes lit up so bright they looked almost artificial. I asked her what she wanted for Christmas and she said sweetly, "Nothing — I have everything I want." When I asked her if she was sure, she reconsidered and said modestly, "Weeeelll . . . some new mittens." That was it? Nothing else? She scrunched up her face, thought for a second. "A notebook," she finally added. I gave her a Cin-

A Donaldson's Santa conducts interviews, which are transcribed on a special record for the children's parents, December 1947. Minneapolis Tribune *photo by Duff Johnson, Minnesota Historical Society Collection.*

derella coloring book, she hugged me and waved goodbye, and [as] the next bunch of kids jumped on my lap asking for Teenage Mutant Nintendo Super Mario Barbies, there was still a lump in Santa Jim's throat.

TUESDAY

Hung around after my shift tonight to watch Bud, who—along with Bob and Howard—is one of the kings of Dayton's Santas. Bud was interviewed by WCCO-AM on Thanksgiving night, and *Life* magazine is planning a spread on him for December 1990, entitled "A Day in the Life of Santa Claus." Bud's a pro, a Santa's Santa. He's been doing it for eight years, and as I sat talking with him in the dressing area tonight, he actually became Santa Claus upon donning the wig and beard. (Me, I became a guy in a Santa suit.) I'm getting pretty good at making the kids feel comfortable, but I haven't really found my groove yet. At least I'm calm. Late today, I mustered my first respectable "Ho-Ho-Ho," but it was lame compared to Bud's naturally jolly laugh.

Santa with Jill Kyvig at St. Paul's Golden Rule, circa 1960. *Jill Kyvig.*

It's a little hard to believe, but every Santa I work with seems genuinely to want to impart a certain amount of magic. Sitting for four hours a day in the Clan of the Santa Bear (mercifully the little rodent has been shelved this year), I thought I'd be sickened by the commercialization of Christmas. I expected a "herd 'em in and herd 'em out" ethic, but I've been pleasantly surprised.

For example, there are two working Santas per shift at Dayton's, but you'll never see them in the same room together because of the two sets of curtains, two aisles and two separate rooms where the kids come to visit. (It's an experience not unlike Catholic confession.) And when Santa goes on lunch break in the middle of his five-hour shift (I'm told the mall Santas work four hours straight, which no doubt makes for some pretty cranky Santas), everyone makes a big deal about how "Santa's going to feed the reindeer now."

I blew the reindeer thing today. A seriously dubious kid asked me how many reindeer I had, and I blanked. "Twelve, of course," said Santa Fake, whose dog had obviously eaten his notes on reindeer lore. The kid looked at me suspiciously, so I quickly added, "But I use eighteen on Christmas Eve, because I have so many toys." That seemed to genuinely intrigue him. I know it's eight; I had a weak moment followed by panic, that's all. Anyway, I think he bought it.

Which brings up the credibility thing. Most babies are just there—they have a great time tugging at your beard, and they'll gladly sit still for the picture, because they have no clue about what's going on. One- and two-year-olds are absolutely terrified—even if they make it up on to your lap, there's no guarantee that they'll stay there long enough for a picture or chitchat. Three-year-olds straddle the line between terror and wonder, and four- and five-year-olds are the most fun. They believe in you with all their hearts, they're fairly bold, and they know exactly what they want for Christmas. With kids six, seven, and beyond, you run into growing skepticism.

WEDNESDAY

Sheer chaos greeted me as I got off the elevator on this, the morning of the Feast of St. Nicholas. One of Dayton's heinous 13-hour sales was in its first hour, and the line to see Santa and the Cinderella display was backed up past the elevators and wrapped around the escalator. "Poor sod," I thought of the Santa, who would see 150 to 200 kids during his four-hour shift. Then I realized that poor sod was me. . . .

Every morning as I put on my costume, I'm struck how this place sounds like a doctor's office. If you close your eyes, you'd swear you were in the waiting room of an infirmary during a mass flu vaccination. Moms' soothing voices go, "It'll only take a second, honey; he won't hurt you," which inevitably is followed by shrieks, wails, and babes' sonic "Noooo!'s." All for what? A photo.

The picture is everything. At the expense of all else—the kids' emotional well-being, Santa's thighs, knees, shins, and sanity—everything revolves around getting the picture and preserving the memory of how it really wasn't: *"Here-Joey-look-over-here-Joey!"* they cry; *"Smile, Joey! C'mon, Joey—if you don't sit on Santa's lap, Santa won't bring you anything."* (I always stay Silent Santa Jim on that one.)

This morning, one especially idiotic dad tried to get his son to smile by doing a dance that made me want to laugh and puke at the same time. Then, this afternoon, I spent fifteen minutes with four creepy thirty-something moms and their screaming, petrified kids. To the moms, I was a prop to be folded, spindled, and mutilated any which way they wished. To the kids, I was Freddie Krueger in a red suit. When they're that scared, the advice from the Santa experts is to become neutral and remain passive. Don't reach out for the kids: let the parents run the show.

But obnoxious parents are the exception, not the rule. Most of them appreciate it when you're patient and gentle and you try to talk the kid into a picture ("I want to bring a copy of it up to the North Pole to show Rudolph," I sometimes say). The fear probably wouldn't be so intense if the operation wasn't so intimate. The kids stand in line, jumping up and down, rehearsing what they're going to say to Santa, and the anticipation drives them over the edge. Though I haven't yet received the professional Santa's official baptism (no one's wet their pants on me yet), a two-year-old did some serious drooling on my hand yesterday.

Breakfast with Santa at Dayton's, 1961. *Minnesota Historical Society Collections.*

Trixie says the event is easier for the kids at malls, where Santa is in full view and they can get a good long look at the big guy as they wait in line. They see other kids sitting and talking with Santa, whereas in the downtown store they're sequestered until the moment of truth. When they turn that corner and come face to face with the almighty and powerful Claus, it's a mind-blower.

Another element of the fear factor is the contradictory messages the Santa trip sends out. After Trixie and I weathered a seemingly endless sequence of scared kids today, she pointed out that we confuse our children by telling them to be very afraid of strangers and then insisting they sit on this weird guy's lap and have a picture taken with him. The reality of that paradox is never too far away—I sit in the chair every day with a poster of a smiling Jacob Wetterling positioned just to the left of the camera.

THURSDAY

One of the most bizarre aspects of this gig is going out on lunch break and moving, ghost-like, amid my "victims." Unseen. Unheard. Uncostumed. Invisible.

Call it Santa paranoia, but today when I was eating lunch in the first floor deli, I think one of the kids I'd just had on my knee (he asked me for a candy cane and I told him I had a house full of 'em at the North Pole) recognized me. He was sitting in a booth facing me, and he gave me the twice-over and looked hard at my semi-white eyebrows and still-rouged cheeks. He started tugging at his mom—I think he was about to blow my cover—but mom was dealing with his crying baby brother and told the would-be snitch to shut up.

One of the younger Santas told me he enjoys milking this alter ego for all it's worth. When young women come up to sit on this guy's lap and ask him for Porsches and men, he'll flirt with them later as they shop. Out of costume, he approaches them with something like "I'm sorry to hear you've been a good girl this year, but Santa promises to bring you the Porsche you asked for anyway." The surprised women, this propositional Claus contends, love it.

FRIDAY

Finally, today, Santa Jim got a little grumpy. Throughout this first week, I've chosen not to think about the real reason why the kids love me—because, truth be told, I'm the Great Buddha of Gimme. Anyway, today I started thinking about it and it got to me; it brought Cranky Santa Jim down.

Then, about a half hour into my shift, that feeling evaporated. A group of ten deaf kids came in with their teachers. They pawed at me and hugged me and kissed me and all at once bombarded me with lyrical grunts and indecipherable wishes. They told me what they wanted by way of their teachers' sign language, and I told them what Rudolph and the elves had been up to. As they left, one of the teachers showed me how to sign "I love you" (at first, I did it with just the forefinger and pinky—like the metal "Rock With Satan"—until the teacher told me to extend my thumb), and they squealed with delight. It was pretty cool.

Breakfast with Santa at Donaldson's, 1975. Star Tribune *photo by Roger Nystrom, Minnesota Historical Society Collections.*

So I guess it hasn't been all that disillusioning. For every greedy kid that's rattled off a list of expensive wants like a human FAX machine, there have been just as many moments when I've looked into some kids' eyes and seen unconditional love. And some of the requests have been downright charming.

There was the steely-nerved five-year-old girl who jumped up on my lap and blurted, "I want a computer that talks back to me when I talk to it and a goat named Sparkly," and dashed away. There was the little boy who stood in front of me trembling violently, held my hand, and despite his trepidation, was determined to recite his Christmas list. There was the little girl who wanted only a doll for her sister; the little boy who just wanted cough drops. Then there was the young lady who, after telling me her long list of very specific Christmas needs, told me, "We don't celebrate Christmas too much at my house." When I asked why, she said, "Because I'm Jewish."

There was the three-year-old girl who brought me a picture of herself and some play money to help defray the cost of my trips back and forth from the North Pole. There was the boy with cerebral palsy who slapped me five and just stood in front of me on crutches, saying "Santa Claus," over and over. . . . There was the huge group of Hmong kids who didn't understand a word I said but gave me big hugs anyway. . . .

Today Howard, a ten-year Santa veteran who learned his craft while attending Santa school at Macy's in New York City, told me that masquerading as Santa "gets in your blood." I know the feeling. Right now, I'm starting to feel like one of those Elvis or Marilyn impersonators who starts believing they're the real thing because so many people believe in them and give them that god-like power. Bob, another vet, says he does it because of the healing hugs he gets from the kids. I know what he means, too. I've got a few days left on this job, and I'm not sure, but if you were to ask me [who] I am at this time next year, the answer might well be the same.

I'm Santa Claus.

ABOVE: Animated display of Cinderella in the Dayton's window, 1962. *Minnesota Historical Society Collections.* RIGHT: A worker at Animated Display Creators in Minneapolis working on a life-size animated Santa Claus for a display for Brett's Department Store on Mankato's Main Street, 1952. Star Tribune *photo by Duff Johnston, Minnesota Historical Society Collections.*

Donaldson's also began an annual tradition in the mid-1940s of placing a hand-carved crèche in the Seventh Street corner window the week of Christmas.

E. R. Dean created Dayton's first mechanical displays in 1922. That show included a life-size elephant in the Eighth Street corner that "breathed, wagged its tail and rolled its trunk." Dean was display manager at the store until retiring in 1951 after three decades of bringing enchantment to Nicollet Avenue.[2]

PINK SLIPS FOR SANTA

Two Santas were axed from the St. Paul Dayton's store in December 1972 for trying to talk kids out of wanting toy guns for Christmas.

Darrel Baird and William Devine, both twenty-four, lost their $2.40-an-hour seasonal jobs for not following the store's protocol of "not expressing a philosophy." Both admitted that when a child asked for a toy gun, they would suggest a different toy, such as a toy truck.

Minneapolis Star columnist Jim Klobuchar reported that one of the ousted Santas said a child asked him for a gun so he could "blast the reindeer." "What was the Santa Claus supposed to do," Klobuchar wrote, "ask the kid whether he wanted a telescopic sight?"

John Pellegrene, vice president of sales promotion for Dayton's, said he didn't think Dayton's even sold toy guns, but that the Santas were there to listen. Parents were the decision makers.[3]

Dayton's Christmas catalog, circa 1950. *Hennepin County Library.*

Sometime later, Tommy Rowland, a Staten Island, New York, woman, stepped in to provide the papier-mâché figures in the windows and later in the eighth-floor auditorium shows. Rowland, whom *Minneapolis Star* columnist Barbara Flanagan described as a four-foot, eleven-inch sprite, continued in the role into the 1970s.

Rowland was interviewed in 1966 while working on "Dickens' London Towne" for the Dayton's auditorium Christmas show. When *Minneapolis Tribune* columnist George Grim asked her how she got into this line of work, she described herself as a "one-shot actress" who began making cork angels at home to give as Christmas presents during the Depression. People liked the angels, and she soon found customers who wanted to buy them. She moved on to "shredded paper figures that are marketable, happily." Rowland and her husband began making props for TV shows, from *The Victor Borge Show* to soap operas, and displays in Minnesota that extended past Dayton's eighth-floor shows. In 1960, she

(continued on page 164)

In December 1955, the Maurice L. Rothschild Young-Quinlan Company ran an advertisement in local papers celebrating the Christmas spirit along Minneapolis's Nicollet Avenue. The ad was titled "A Few Remarks about Christmas on Nicollet Avenue" and was printed almost in poetry form.

Nicollet Avenue is all a-glitter. It is just as if the Chief of all the Chief Fairies had touched it with her very best wand and brought Fairyland to the heart of the Northwest—not just any old Fairyland, but the best of all Fairylands—especially the home of the good old Santa Claus. You actually have to rub your eyes to be sure you are not plumb in the center of the North Pole. Christmas trees glisten—red bells sway beneath bowers of evergreens . . . Nicollet Avenue is a mile long Christmas fantasy . . . a beaconing blaze of Christmas light at night. Angels fly here and there—and you almost bump into reindeer (some folks did not so long ago—right next door to us, too, remember!). And the treasure house of the world opens before your gladdened eyes.

Dayton's, so famous for their Christmas settings, is lavishly decorated with a magnificent candelabra bewreathed and beribboned in literally a forest of lights—almost a block long and six stories high. And Dayton's famous windows that almost everyone has stared and gaped at as a child, just like your youngster is doing today. You, too, flattened your nose against those famous windows to get a better look at that special train you yearned so much to have.

But now we will leave Dayton's. We are boastful enough to feel that Maurice L. Rothschild Young-Quinlan Co. windows are famous too. These windows, like Dayton's, contain a treasure house also. Not all the toys perhaps, but the beauty of far-flung lands to make everyone's Christmas a bit more glamorous than ever before. French imports to gladden the heart of every woman; bags, perfumes, gloves, handkerchiefs, jewelry, scarfs and umbrellas. Gorgeous things she'll drool over; and you can do as much for him with Cashmere sweaters to melt under his very touch, robes, shirts, ties and jackets to thrill him over and over again.

And the greatest of all our pleasures is our sales force. They have courtesy bred in their innermost bones, and each and every one gets as much fun out of helping you as you will in selecting and buying.

Come in. Christmas is a joyous time at Maurice L. Rothschild Young-Quinlan Co., and we invite you to share this joy with us.

Maurice L. Rothschild
Young-Quinlan Co.

ABOVE: Dayton's on Nicollet Avenue, 1931. *Hennepin County Library.* OPPOSITE, TOP: Christmastime on Nicollet Avenue at night, 1940s. BOTTOM: Young-Quinlan lit up for Christmas, 1963. *Both Minnesota Historical Society Collections.*

LDS
POWERS
STOP

Choate's department store's Santa House in downtown Winona, circa 1960s. *Lynne Hartert.*

created a series of figures modeled after the wives of Minnesota governors, which were displayed in the River Room in the St. Paul Dayton's store, and in 1961, she helped with the Dayton's float in the Aquatennial night parade. She continued her work in Minnesota well into the 1970s, including a patriotic display for a show that opened in the IDS tower in August 1975 to commemorate the upcoming US bicentennial.

At its St. Paul store, Dayton's used just as many resources in its display windows. Its fifth floor, while not an immersive auditorium like the one across the river, was turned into a winter wonderland. "It was like walking outdoors on a snowy day, even chilly," said Norene Stovall, who worked at Dayton's as a sales clerk in the late 1960s. "Santa was there for kids to sit on his lap and the décor changed every year."

Donaldson's created its own walk-through display in 1967 with Disney Village, featuring more than 150 animated Disney characters on the Minneapolis store's sixth floor. The

twelve-thousand-square-foot display was the largest in the store's history and included "Winterland in the Park" with thirty figures participating in winter sports; "Christmas at Daisy Duck's"; and "Jungle Walk-Through," featuring animated figures from the 1967 Disney movie *The Jungle Book.*

ABOVE: Christmas shopping in downtown St. Paul, 1946. St. Paul Dispatch *photo, Minnesota Historical Society Collections.* LEFT: This figure of Sarah Sibley, wife of Minnesota's first governor, Henry H. Sibley, in her 1858 inaugural gown was created by Tommy Rowland in 1960 and displayed in the River Room restaurant at Dayton's in St. Paul. *Minnesota Historical Society Collections.*

LIGHTING THE TOWN

What was a big-city downtown to do when the largest shopping mall in the world moved in down the road, complete with roller coasters, dozens of restaurants, stores galore, and Snoopy?

They had a parade.

Minneapolis merchants were rightfully nervous about the Mall of America's impact on holiday sales when it opened in 1992. The Minneapolis City Council wanted a validated parking program from the merchants, and in exchange for that, the council would pony up some funds for a holiday event that would bring crowds downtown.

Stewart Widdess, marketing director at Dayton's at the time, was asked by the Minneapolis Downtown Council to "come up with an event and sell it to the city." He hosted a brainstorming meeting that included many of the people who worked on the store's eighth-floor shows. "We kicked around a lot of ideas," including a laser show on Nicollet Mall, but the idea of a multinight lighted parade, similar to one at Disneyworld, rose to the surface. Widdess sent a crew to Orlando, Florida, to find out more.

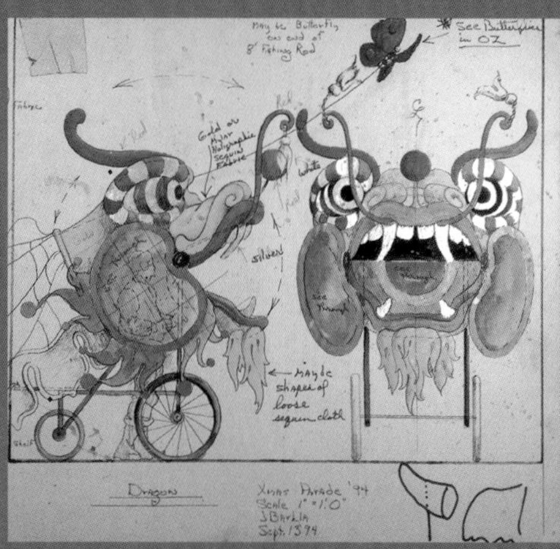

"We trekked out to Disney," said Todd Knaeble, then the special events manager at Dayton's. "There wasn't much time [to plan]. It was June."

"Disney said, 'We can do that for you,' but it would take three years and cost $300,000 a float," Widdess said. "We had to have something in November."

Widdess describes another meeting in Minneapolis: "Everyone's hanging their heads and commiserating on what to do, and someone said, 'Let's do it ourselves.'"

"And we did it," Knaeble said. "We certainly did it. [Disney] has special vehicles, tracks for their parade. We did it with old school buses, plywood, and scenery on top of them."

It wasn't Dayton's project, but Dayton's put a lot of money into it, Widdess said. And the eighth-floor group was a big part

of it: Knaeble; designer Jack Barkla; Michael Murname, who did lights; and Michael Gansmo, who did sound. Dan Witkowski—a consultant, illusionist, and president of MagicCom Inc.—came up with the name: Holidazzle. Widdess also pulled in Myron Johnson and his Ballet of the Dolls dance troupe, which performed at Dayton's fashion shows under Widdess's direction.

Then, after just a few months of preparation, on the Friday after Thanksgiving, November 27, 1992, seven lighted floats with nursery-rhyme and fairytale themes rolled down Nicollet Mall joined by bands, choirs, and local celebrities. And the parade continued for twenty more nights.

Widdess left Dayton's shortly after Holidazzle was launched, but the holiday spectacle continued until 2013, when the last glittering parade of characters marched down Nicollet for just eight nights.

OPPOSITE, TOP: Jack Barkla's design sketch for a float in the 1992 parade. BOTTOM: Jack Barkla's design sketch for a dragon float in the 1994 parade. *Both Jack Barkla.* THIS PAGE: Poster for the Holidazzle parade, 1994. *Minnesota Historical Society Collections.*

CLAN OF THE CHRISTMAS BEAR

After the Dayton Hudson Corporation's highly successful introduction of Santabear in 1985, John Pellegrene, the company's senior vice president of marketing, wasn't surprised to see other retailers come out with their own versions of the hot new collectible.

Ohio's Lazarus stores introduced Lazzie Bear in 1986, while Kmart brought out Our Christmas Bear, and Marshall Field's came up with Mistletoe Bear.

Dayton Hudson was ready for the competition. The company launched a nationwide promotion that placed Santabear on the back of General Mills' Cinnamon Toast Crunch cereal box and in a children's TV special. The company also published a Santabear book, and dozens of other related products were put on sale through mail order and in the company's stores.

Just days after Santabear was first offered in the 1985 Christmas catalog for $10 with every $50 purchase, or $25 without a purchase, the four-hundred-thousand-plus bears sold out. TV commercials featuring the toy were pulled, and bear seekers jammed the phone lines at the stores.

A new version was introduced each holiday over the next two decades. In 1987, Miss Bear was introduced. That same year, an Orrefors crystal Santabear, worth about $6,000, went missing from its case outside Dayton's eighth-floor auditorium show, the theme of which was "Santabear's High-Flying Adventures." The eleven-inch, thirty-pound crystal Santabear was found nearly a month later at Gillette Children's Hospital in St. Paul. Police received a telephone call from a priest who said one of his parishioners knew of the bear's whereabouts.

Bully Bear joined the family in 1989, and Santabear and Miss Bear were married in 2000. The bears' creator, Paul Starkey, died in January 2000. The company held a special event to commemorate Starkey's passing in December at the Citadel, a community center and day care in St. Paul run by the Salvation Army. The company donated one thousand specially made bears to the organization.

Macy's retired the bear in 2007 and took advantage of one last marketing opportunity: collector editions of the Santabear, Miss Bear, their two children, and a memory book went on sale for $175 at Macy's stores.

ABOVE: Promotional for Santabear merchandise, 1987. *Hennepin County Library.*

9
Shoppers' Delights: Department Store Dining

One of the last meals Rae MacDonough served at Macy's twelfth-floor Oak Grill was to three adolescents and their mom, who had pulled her children out of school that day to eat one last time in the beloved downtown Minneapolis restaurant whose doors would shut forever on January 27, 2017.

When Macy's announced the closing of the Minneapolis store earlier that month, diners flocked to its top-floor restaurants, the Oak Grill and the Sky Room, for weeks. Faithful customers who came in regularly for the chicken potpie, the Mandarin chicken salad, the wild rice soup, couldn't get in. And the phone rang and rang, but no one could answer to take a reservation. The restaurant and the halls outside of it were packed.

It was the end of an era: dining in a downtown Twin Cities department store was over.

The closing of the Oak Grill and the Sky Room came just four years after Macy's River Room restaurant in downtown St. Paul served its last popover in January 2013. A downtown destination for businesspeople and shoppers since 1947, the River Room closed along with the store, which, just like its counterpart at 700 Nicollet Avenue in Minneapolis, had transitioned from Dayton's to Marshall Field's and finally to Macy's in 2006.

The River Room was named for the large-scale murals of Mississippi River scenes that decorated the restaurant when it first opened in Schuneman's Department Store in 1947. After Dayton's bought Schuneman's in 1959 and moved the store across the street four years later, the River Room moved with it.

With pink booths, crystal chandeliers, and a salad bar added in the eighties, the River Room was the place to catch a fashion show in the sixties, enjoy children's matinees and puppet breakfasts in the seventies, or have a meal inspired by whatever Broadway musical was being performed at the Ordway Center for the Performing Arts after it opened just four blocks away in 1985. When *Show Boat* came to town in 1995, Ordway patrons could enjoy a Mississippi River–themed dinner of crawfish fettuccine, grits, and mustard greens at the River Room before attending the show.

The restaurant went through several renovations while a part of the Dayton's stores. In 1982, the Waterford chandeliers from Dayton's Sky Room in Minneapolis were brought in. That's about the same time River Room manager Robert Johnston introduced the legendary popover recipe to Dayton's restaurants. Johnston brought the recipe from a Rochester, Minnesota, restaurant, and it quickly became a staple in all of Dayton's eateries.

OPPOSITE: Dayton's Sky Room, circa 1949. THIS PAGE: Sign for Dayton's Oak Grill. *Both Minnesota Historical Society Collections.*

Aside from the free popovers, the Oak Grill in Minneapolis "had amazing dishes," said MacDonough, who started working there in 1998. It was affordable, it was easy to park (and free, as the restaurant validated parking in the store's ramp), and it was elegant. A customer once described it as "a private club where you aren't paying dues," she said.

Indeed, it was a semi-private club when it opened as the Men's Oak Grill in 1948. With its oak paneling, white table linens, and a fireplace salvaged from a British manor after World War II, the restaurant was off-limits to women—unless they had a male escort. (In the 1960s, women began bringing their young sons into the Oak Grill for lunch, as they qualified as "male escorts," MacDonough said.) Down the hall, the swanky Sky Room catered to women with fashion shows, breakfasts with Santa and the Easter Bunny, and charity dances. By 1969, the Oak Grill had dropped its male-only rule, and by 1987, the elegant Sky Room was remodeled to include the quick-service counters and a forty-foot salad bar that served lunch during the week right up to its closing in 2017.

The Golden Rule in St. Paul had a "men-only" room, the Men's Grill, at its Capitol Room restaurant. Norene Stovall worked in the Capitol Room in the early 1960s. The men's restaurant

OPPOSITE, TOP: Postcard view of Schuneman's River Room, circa 1940. BOTTOM: Dayton's Sky Room, circa 1949. *Both Minnesota Historical Society Collections.* THIS PAGE, RIGHT: Dayton's twelfth-floor Tiffin restaurant, circa 1960. *Hennepin History Museum.* BELOW: Luncheon and fashion show at Dayton's Sky Room, 1962. *Minnesota Historical Society Collections.*

CHEERS!

Donaldson's–Golden Rule was the first department store to be granted a liquor license in Minneapolis. In 1964, it began serving wine and cocktails at its North Shore Grill. With the new liquor license and Daylight Saving Time, Minneapolitans could have a "big swinging night out on the town before the sun even goes down," *Minneapolis Tribune* columnist Will Jones wrote in his July 9, 1964, column.

So he tried it: he headed to the North Shore Grill for some planked lake trout with a glass of white wine and a snifter of cognac to go with his maple frango and coffee for dessert. "You have to make it early because even with a liquor license they close the place at 8:30," he said. Dayton's liquor license came later. In 1968, *Minneapolis Star* columnist Jim Klobuchar welcomed the new amenity at Dayton's restaurants: "Dayton's thus becomes one of the few general stores in the territory that can sell screwdrivers not only from its eighth-floor hardware department but also from its twelfth-floor kitchen."

Donaldson's North Shore Grill, 1948. *Minnesota Historical Society Collections.*

featured curved booths with dark wood and red upholstery. The main room, which was open to women and men, had lime-green upholstery. There were four restaurants in the Golden Rule at the time Stovall was hired. At age sixteen, she began as a waitress at the store snack bar and sometimes worked at a coffee shop in the basement (where she had to wear a hairnet, much to her dismay). She was promoted to the Capitol Room but was never assigned to the Men's Grill. That was reserved for more seasoned waitresses. The Capitol Room remained with the store after it merged with Donaldson's in 1961.

Field-Schlick had its tearooms in its early days, and according to a 1906 newspaper advertisement, they were "immensely popular": "Newspapers and individuals alike are paying glowing tributes to these magnificent tea rooms. . . . Not only do women enjoy the dainty lunches as served, but men are coming here for their noonday lunches. The patronage has been so big that hereafter the tea rooms will be open until 5:30 instead of 5:00 and the English room will be reserved for men during the noon hour." In the store's later

TOP: The Capitol Room restaurant at the Golden Rule in St. Paul, 1951. ABOVE: The Golden Rule's first-floor lunch counter, 1951. *Both Minnesota Historical Society Collections.*

decades, Field-Schlick shoppers who stopped for a bite to eat in the little diner tucked between the children's and lingerie departments were eating at the Q Restaurant, a separate business. When Field-Schlick closed in the late 1970s, the building was gutted to create an office and retail mall, but the Q continued to operate in the building, under several different owners, until 2012.

When Minnesotans reminisce about the department stores that anchored downtowns throughout the state, that favorite lunch spot and the food it served frequently come into the conversation.

For Marisa Bear Krishef, who spent Saturdays with her mom, grandmother, and older sister, Lisa London, shopping at the Glass Block in Duluth in the 1970s, it was the grilled cheese

sandwich, the chocolate milk, and the smell of the just-out-of-the-oven orange sweet rolls coming from the bakery next door. For London, it was the Jell-O salad with fruit cocktail and a dollop of mayonnaise.

The chicken salad in the fourth-floor Fountain Room at Young-Quinlan made a trip downtown for a doctor's appointment special for Mary Scanlon, who raised seven children in Minneapolis and made many visits to the Medical Arts Building nearby. "The tearoom was one of everybody's favorites," said Scanlon. "You'd go downtown for your obstetrician appointment, then the tearoom for lunch. It was magical. The elevator operators wearing white gloves—everything was just so right."

OPPOSITE: "The Café" at Donaldson's, 1910. THIS PAGE: Donaldson's restaurant and Silver Gray Room, 1910. *All Minnesota Historical Society Collections.*

Donaldson's had its Tea Room, Garden Room, Minnesota Room, and North Shore Grill, the latter a seafood restaurant at the downtown Minneapolis store that in 1964 offered seventy-five varieties of fish on its menu. The grill had been noted for seafood since the turn of the twentieth century and for its maple frango dessert, which, according to *Minneapolis Star* columnist Will Jones, was introduced to Minnesota at Donaldson's. "The late L. S. Donaldson found the recipe in Oregon," Jones wrote on July 9, 1964. Chef Steve Wetoska told Jones that the dessert was of French origin and he "thinks the name *frango* is a corruption of *Franco.*"

When a remodeled North Shore Grill and Tea Room opened in 1948, the restaurants offered fresh baby orchids to "every feminine guest, young or old, who steps within the portals of either of these sparkling new restaurants during the dinner hour starting at five" and boasted dollar dinners for families and children's dinners for just fifty cents. Minnesotans who remember Donaldson's probably recall the Minnesota Room restaurants at the Brookdale, Rosedale,

"TWELVE HEPATITIS CASES LINKED TO POWERS"

The headline on the front page of the April 23, 1974, *Minneapolis Star* sounded the alarm: an outbreak of infectious hepatitis — a serious liver disease — had been traced to the restaurants in the downtown Minneapolis Powers Department Store. Eight of the people diagnosed were Powers employees, and two were roommates of employees.

Employees and shoppers who had eaten at the store's restaurants between mid-February and the time this was reported were urged to get a shot of gamma globulin, a substance that contains antibodies that can reduce the likelihood that a person will develop the illness.

Powers had closed its restaurants the day before the news went out, but as the week wore on, more cases were reported. By April 27, fifty-three cases were reported, along with one death, that of seventy-three-year-old Cora E. Golberg, who had been admitted to Fairview Hospital just nine days before.

In the end, 105 men and women had developed hepatitis after eating at Powers between mid-February and April 21, including an inmate at the St. Cloud Reformatory. Apparently, the prisoner had eaten at a Powers restaurant in mid-March while in Minneapolis standing trial. Twenty-eight of the store's five hundred employees developed the disease.

Based on interviews with the hepatitis patients, it appeared that most if not all of them ate at Powers on March 15 (a Friday), 16 (a Saturday), or 18 (a Monday), and most had eaten cold sandwiches, tossed salads, and, in a few cases, hot roast beef sandwiches in the downstairs restaurant and the adjoining employees' restaurant. According to Minneapolis health commissioner Dr. C. A. Smith, at least twenty thousand people were given protective shots of gamma globulin at the Minneapolis Health Department or from private physicians.

By May 3, the store opened its main-floor restaurant, and "the old regulars are coming back in," server Rachael Maros told the *Minneapolis Tribune*. The store's business dropped quite a bit because of the outbreak. A week after the restaurants reopened, Dr. Smith and epidemiologist Dr. Barry Levy held a press-conference lunch at the Powers main-floor restaurant to emphasize that the restaurants were good to go.

and Southdale stores, all of which closed in 1988. In the late 1960s, you could catch a children's Christmas play in the downtown Minneapolis Garden Room, a breakfast and magic show at the Capitol Room in St. Paul, meet WCCO personality Clancy the Cop at the Minnesota Room in Brookdale, or enjoy a puppet show at the Minnesota Room at Southdale.[1]

Powers was the first to offer sidewalk dining on the Nicollet Mall in the 1970s, something *Minneapolis Star* columnist Barbara Flanagan plugged often, even suggesting "a sidewalk café war" to Dayton's and Donaldson's in a 1976 column. The café, the Bowl and Roll, offered a wide selection of international breads for sandwiches, cinnamon rolls, and good people watching.

St. Paul's Emporium, at Seventh and Robert, had a tearoom that served the lunch crowd. It closed in 1968, but in the 1960s, a kid could stop in after a little shopping and be treated to an upside-down ice-cream cone decorated to look like a clown.

OPPOSITE: Young-Quinlan Fountain Room menu cover. *Hennepin County Library.* THIS PAGE: Emporium Tea Room, 1937. *Minnesota Historical Society Collections.*

Donaldson's Tea Room

Chicken Broth with Rice 15
Oyster Stew 40

Split Pea Soup 15
Oyster Cream Stew 60

VEGETABLES

Grilled Tomatoes 20
Candied Sweet Potatoes 20

Buttered New Spinach 15
Baked Squash 15

LUNCHEON — 75c

Fruit Cocktail or
Cream of Tomato Soup

Choice of:-
Fresh Lobster Patty

Broiled Lamb Chops, Mint Jelly

Long Branch Potatoes

Waldorf Salad
Rolls

Cocoanut Cream Pie or
Chocolate Sundae

Tea, Coffee or Milk

LUNCHEON — 65c.

Split Pea Soup

Choice of:-
Baked Lake Superior Whitefish
Tartar Sauce
Long Branch Potatoes or
Ham en Casserole, Baked Potato
Pineapple Salad or
Prime Ribs of Beef, Pan Gravy
Browned Potatoes

Fruit Jello or
Maple Caramel Sundae

Rolls
Tea, Coffee or Milk

LUNCHEON — 55c

Choice of:-
Broiled Fresh Mackerel
Baked Chicken Loaf
Country Steak

A LA CARTE SUGGESTIONS

No. 1 French Pancakes with Currant Jelly and Little Pig Sausage, Pot of Coffee 50

No. 2 Vegetable Plate with Cottage Cheese Center 50

No. 3 Chicken Broth with Rice, Toasted 3 Decker, Tomato, Cheese and Bacon Sandwich 55

(Rolls Served with Above Orders)

SHOPPER'S LUNCHEON — 50c

Chopped Vegetable Salad,
Chiffonade Dressing

Baked Veal Sandwich

Orange Pine Ice Cream

Tea, Coffee or Milk

SALAD COMBINATIONS

No. 4 Apricot, Marshmallow and Fig Salad, Rolls, Pot of Coffee 50

No. 5 Grape Fruit and Orange

Classic Recipes from the Department Store Restaurants and Cafés

DONALDSON'S MINNESOTA ROOM POTATO SALAD

2 quarts (8 cups) cubed cooked red potatoes
5 hard-boiled eggs, diced
1 cup chopped celery
½ cup chopped sweet pickles
⅓ cup finely chopped onion
½ cup finely chopped radishes
⅓ teaspoon white pepper
2 teaspoons salt
3 tablespoons sugar
1 teaspoon prepared mustard
1 ⅓ cups mayonnaise

Combine ingredients and chill for at least 2 hours. Serves 12 to 16.

DONALDSON'S MAPLE FRANGO

2 cups maple syrup
3 egg yolks
1 teaspoon maple flavoring
1 ½ quarts (6 cups) heavy cream

Heat syrup to nearly boiling. Beat egg yolks until creamy. Pour hot syrup over egg yolks, stirring continuously. Cook mixture until thick, stirring constantly. Add flavoring and strain. Cool. Whip cream to soft peaks, then fold into syrup and egg mixture. Whip together until thickened. Freeze. Serve on chilled dessert plates. Serves 10 to 12.

DONALDSON'S PECAN CRUNCH CAKE WITH LEMON SAUCE

1 package white or yellow cake mix
1 cup packed brown sugar
1 cup chopped pecans
4 tablespoons butter, melted
whipped cream
Lemon Sauce (recipe follows)

Heat oven to 325 degrees. Prepare cake mix according to package directions. Line a 9x13-inch pan with waxed paper and grease the waxed paper. Mix brown sugar, pecans, and melted butter and press mixture into pan. Pour cake batter over nut mixture. Place pan on a baking sheet and bake for 40 to 60 minutes, until a wooden pick inserted in the center comes out clean. Serve with whipped cream and Lemon Sauce. Serves 15.

LEMON SAUCE

3 cups water
juice of 3 lemons (4 ½ tablespoons), plus 1 teaspoon lemon zest
1 ¼ cups sugar
3 tablespoons cornstarch
4 tablespoons (¼ cup) butter

Combine water and lemon juice and bring to a boil. Mix sugar and cornstarch and add to the lemon-water mixture, blending well. Cook until clear and thick. Remove from heat. Stir in butter and lemon zest. Makes 3 cups.

DONALDSON'S NORTH SHORE GRILL SOUR CREAM RAISIN MERINGUE PIE

2 ¼ cups raisins
¾ cup sour cream
¾ cup buttermilk
3 tablespoons cornstarch
¾ teaspoon salt
¾ cup plus 6 tablespoons granulated sugar
1 ½ teaspoons cinnamon
¾ teaspoon nutmeg
3 eggs, separated
½ cup milk
1 (9-inch) prebaked pie shell
¼ teaspoon cream of tartar
½ teaspoon vanilla

Heat oven to 400 degrees. Combine raisins with sour cream, buttermilk, cornstarch, salt, ¾ cup sugar, cinnamon, and nutmeg in a saucepan. Stir until well blended. Bring the mixture to a boil and cook until thick, 2 to 3 minutes. Remove from heat. Beat the egg yolks and milk, then add to the hot mixture and stir briskly. Return to heat and cook, stirring, until thickened, about 2 minutes. Pour into baked pie shell.

Beat egg whites and cream of tartar until foamy. Beat in remaining 6 tablespoons sugar, 1 tablespoon at a time; continue beating until stiff and glossy. Beat in vanilla. Spread meringue over pie filling. Bake about 10 minutes, until light brown. Serves 8.

Power's Downtown 338-7679

Appetizers

Fresh Fruit Festival Cocktail 1.65
Choice of Chilled Orange, Grapefruit or Tomato Juice .85
Iced Melon and Fresh Ginger 1.75;
with Prosciutto Ham 2.95

Soups . . . Homemade, Of Course

A Crock of French Onion Soup Baked with Greyere 1.85
This Day's Soup, Cup .85; Crock 1.45

Soup and Combinations

SOUP AND SANDWICH
Cup of This Day's Soup (Crock of Onion Soup .75 Extra)
Chicken-Pecan or Chunky Tuna Salad, Sliced Roast Beef, Swiss Cheese or White Meat Turkey 4.35
SOUP AND QUICHE
Cup of This Day's Soup (Crock of Onion Soup .75 Extra)
Quiche Lorraine or Today's Special Quiche 4.35
THE DEMI LUNCH
Cup of This Day's Soup (Crock of Onion Soup .75 Extra)
A Wedge of Quiche Lorraine or Today's Quiche
Three Green Salad
Fresh Fruit Festival Cocktail
Coffee or Tea 4.65

The Cold Pantry

Italian Salad, Garbanzo Beans, Romaine Lettuce, Pimento and Tomato Topped with Julienne of Salami and Grated Parmesan Cheese, Chianti Dressing 4.45
Avocado Pear Stuffed with Chicken-Pecan or Chunky Tuna Salad 4.35
Chef's Salad Bowl of Meats, Cheese and Greens 4.35

Our Famous Quiche

Quiche Lorraine, The Classic Cheese and Bacon Pie 4.15
Today's Special Quiche 4.15
Quiche Sampler — A Delicious Taste Teaser of Quiche Lorraine and Today's Quiche 4.15
Served with Three Green Salad, Vinaigrette Dressing

Cheese Lovers' Treat

Three Cheese Board — Swiss, Gouda and Brie — with Seasonal Fresh Fruit and a Glass of Wine 4.75
Butter Croissant and Choice of Brie, Swiss, American or Cheddar Cheese 2.95

Coffee, Tea, Etc.

Café 429 Coffee, Hot or Iced .45
Breakfast Tea, Hot or Iced .45
Freshly Brewed Decaffeinated Coffee .45
Perrier and Lime 1.25
Diet Pepsi, Pepsi Cola, Seven Up or Dr. Pepper .55
Milk — Half Pint .55

Breakfast 'til 11

Butter Croissant, Marmalade or Jam, Coffee or Breakfast Tea 1.25
Chilled Orange, Grapefruit or Tomato Juice .85
Iced Florida Grapefruit Sections 1.25
Butter Croissant .85
Fruit-Filled, Almond or Chocolate Croissant 1.05
Toasted English Muffin .65
White, Buttered Toast .45
French Bread and Sweet Butter .65
Café 429 Coffee or Breakfast Tea .45

Some Good Sandwiches

JULIENNE OF IMPORTED HAM AND SWISS CHEESE on Butter Croissant 3.95
CHICKEN-PECAN OR CHUNKY TUNA SALAD on French Bread or Butter Croissant 3.95
ROAST BEEF with Choice of Bread 4.25
WHITE MEAT TURKEY on Toast, French Bread or Butter Croissant 3.75
CAFÉ 429 CLUB, White Meat Turkey, Bacon, Sliced Fresh Mushrooms, Tomato and Romaine Lettuce 4.25
VEGETARIAN DELIGHT, Sliced Avocado, Tomato and Cucumber, Topped with Bean Sprouts and Herb Dressing on Butter Croissant 3.65
BACON, LETTUCE AND TOMATO — California Style — with Sliced Avocado 3.25
GRILLED AMERICAN CHEESE and Tomato 2.65; with Bacon 2.95; with Ham 3.15
Served with a Potpourri of Mustards and Relishes

Dessert . . . At Last

French Double Chocolate-Mocca Cream 1.45
Strawberries and Real Whipped Cream 2.65
Apple Walnut Upside Down Pie, Cinnamon Whipped Cream 1.75
Fruit Filled, Almond or Chocolate Croissant 1.05
Tipsy Sherry-Raspberry Trifle 1.55
Carrot Cake 1.55
Today's Layer Cake 1.55

The Survival Kit

YES . . . You can Take It with You!
All menu items are available for take-out.
Call ahead — the number is 338-7679 — and the order will be waiting for you to be picked up.

Wine and Beer

Red, White or Rose Wine, Glass 1.65; 1/2 Carafe 3.65
Spritzer, White Wine and Soda 1.95
Miller or Miller Lite 1.10 Lowenbrau 1.30

PINEAPPLE COCONUT MOUSSE WITH PISTACHIOS A LA AL BOYCE AND DONALDSON'S

1 ½ cups canned pineapple in light syrup
½ cup grated coconut
7 ounces (¾ cup plus 2 tablespoons) coconut milk
¼ cup honey
2 envelopes powdered unflavored gelatin
½ cup chilled heavy cream
5 tablespoons chopped pistachios

Drain pineapple, reserving juice. Puree pineapple, coconut, coconut milk, and honey in a blender. Set aside. Sprinkle gelatin over ¼ cup pineapple juice and let sit for 10 minutes. Heat remaining reserved pineapple juice and stir in the gelatin-juice mixture until the gelatin is completely dissolved. Fold the gelatin mixture into the pureed pineapple-coconut mixture. Beat chilled cream until it forms soft peaks. Fold into the pineapple-coconut-gelatin mixture. Pour into a gelatin mold, cover, and refrigerate for 2 to 3 hours. Serve sprinkled with pistachios. Serves 4.

POWERS CAFÉ 429 APPLE WALNUT UPSIDE-DOWN PIE

1 (10-inch) apple pie (use your own recipe or buy a ready-made pie)
scant ½ cup brown sugar
⅔ cup butter or margarine, softened
1 tablespoon flour
pinch salt
1 tablespoon maple syrup
1 cup chopped walnuts
ground cinnamon
whipped cream

Bake pie until nearly done. Meanwhile, make caramel topping: mix together brown sugar, butter, flour, salt, and maple syrup. Remove baked pie from its tin by placing a plate over the top of the pie and carefully turning it upside down. Remove pie tin. Spread 1 cup caramel topping inside the pie tin. Spread chopped walnuts over the caramel. Replace pie tin with caramel and nuts on overturned baked pie. Turn it back over and remove the plate.

Return pie to oven and bake for 20 minutes. Remove pie from its tin by placing a plate over the top of the baked pie and carefully turning it upside down. Remove pie tin and set pie aside to cool. Stir cinnamon into whipped cream and serve with pie. Serves 8.

POWERS LUNCHEONETTE CAULIFLOWER CHEESE SOUP

16 tablespoons (2 sticks) butter
2 cups all-purpose flour
2 ½ quarts (10 cups) milk
2 cups water
1 ½ cups shredded cheddar cheese
2 tablespoons chicken base
½ cup chopped onions, sauteed
3 tablespoons white wine
2 cups frozen cauliflower, blanched
salt to taste

Melt butter in a large saucepan over low heat. Whisk in flour and simmer for 10 minutes. Add milk and water; cook over medium-low heat until cream sauce thickens. Stir in cheese, chicken base, onions, wine, cauliflower, and salt. Simmer slowly for 30 minutes. Do not boil. Serves 8 to 10.

POWERS BOWL AND ROLL CHICKEN, MUSHROOM, AND NOODLE CASSEROLE

1 (4–5 pound) chicken
1 (16-ounce) package egg noodles
4 tablespoons butter
¼ cup all-purpose flour
2 cups frozen carrots and peas
1 cup chopped mushrooms

Heat oven to 350 degrees. Simmer chicken in water to cover until interior temperature reaches 165 degrees. Remove chicken from broth and let cool; remove meat from skin and bones. Dice meat. Cook egg noodles according to package instructions. Rinse in cold water. Melt butter in saucepan. Whisk in flour until smooth. Gradually whisk in 3 cups chicken broth; cook, stirring, until sauce thickens. Stir together diced chicken, carrots and peas, mushrooms, and noodles; stir in chicken gravy, pour into 9x13-inch casserole, and bake until golden brown, about 25 minutes. Serves 6.

FOUNTAIN ROOM CHICKEN MOUSSE

1 tablespoon butter
1 tablespoon flour
1 teaspoon salt
1 cup milk
2 eggs, separated
½ cup chopped cooked chicken breast
1 cup heavy cream, whipped

Heat oven to 325 degrees. Melt butter in a saucepan. Stir in flour and salt, then slowly add milk, stirring constantly. Cook, stirring, until thick. Combine a small amount of the white sauce with egg yolks. Stir egg yolk mixture into remaining white sauce. Cool. Grind chicken in a food processor to make a smooth paste. Slowly add egg whites. Combine egg-chicken mixture with cooled white sauce. Chill for 30 minutes. Fold in whipped cream. Pour mixture into a 1-quart casserole. Place casserole in a pan of hot water and bake for 45 minutes. Serves 4.

FOUNTAIN ROOM RHUBARB CHIFFON CRUNCH PIE

1 cup oats
½ cup packed brown sugar
⅓ cup butter, melted
½ cup shredded coconut
2 ½ cups chopped rhubarb
¾ cup granulated sugar
1 (3-ounce) package strawberry gelatin
1 cup heavy cream, whipped

Heat oven to 375 degrees. Place oats in a shallow pan and bake for 5 to 6 minutes. Mix oats with brown sugar, butter, and coconut. Pack firmly into the bottom and sides of a 9-inch pie plate. Place in freezer and chill until firm.

Combine rhubarb, ⅓ cup water, and granulated sugar in a saucepan and simmer over low heat until tender, about 20 minutes. Cool. Dissolve gelatin in 1 cup boiling water, then add ¼ cup cold water. Chill until partially set. Whip the gelatin until fluffy. Fold in rhubarb and whipped cream. Chill until the mixture holds shape. Spread it into the pie shell and chill until firm. Serves 8.

FOUNTAIN ROOM POTATO CHIP COOKIES

12 tablespoons (1 ½ sticks) butter, softened
¾ cup sugar
1 egg yolk
1 teaspoon vanilla
1 ½ cups sifted all-purpose flour
¾ cup crushed potato chips
½ cup chopped nuts

Heat oven to 350 degrees. Beat butter and sugar until creamy. Blend in remaining ingredients, mixing well. Roll dough into 1-inch balls and place on ungreased baking sheet. Flatten cookies with a fork. Bake for 12 minutes. Makes 3 dozen cookies.

RIVER ROOM POPOVERS

5 eggs (about 1 cup)
1 ⅔ cups whole milk
5 tablespoons unsalted butter, melted
1 ⅔ cups flour
½ teaspoon salt

Heat oven to 400 degrees. Lightly coat popover pans or deep muffin tins with nonstick cooking spray and preheat pans in oven for at least 15 minutes (cover pans with aluminum foil to keep cooking spray from spattering). In a medium bowl, using an electric mixer on medium-high speed, beat eggs until frothy. Add milk and butter and mix well. Reduce speed to low and add flour and salt, mixing until just combined. Let batter rest for 15 to 30 minutes.

Divide batter among preheated pans, filling each cup just under half full (fill empty cups halfway with water). Bake for 30 to 40 minutes—do not open the oven door—until popovers are puffy and well browned. Remove from oven, transfer pans to a wire rack, and cool 2 minutes. Popovers should pull away from the pan easily; if not, use a dull-bladed knife to nudge them from the pan. Serve warm. Makes 12 popovers.

RIVER ROOM CHICKEN AND STRAWBERRY SALAD

7 strawberries
1 tablespoon olive oil
1 tablespoon butter
½ cup chicken breast strips
¼ cup Honey-Soy Dressing (recipe follows)
¾ cup mixed greens
2 tablespoons chopped walnuts
parsley for garnish

Hull 6 strawberries, then slice in half. Leave 1 strawberry whole. Heat oil and melt butter in a skillet over low heat. Add chicken strips and cook, stirring, until brown on all sides. Add dressing and simmer 1 minute. Add halved strawberries and heat slightly. Pour chicken and strawberries over mixed greens. Sprinkle with walnuts. Garnish with parsley and the whole strawberry. Serves 1.

HONEY-SOY DRESSING

½ cup red wine vinegar
½ cup honey
2 tablespoons soy sauce
2 teaspoons chopped garlic
2 teaspoons chopped fresh ginger
¼ teaspoon pepper

Blend together all ingredients. Makes 5 servings.

Dayton's Sky Room
Fashion Review Luncheon
(No. 4)
Turkey a la King — $1.50
Long Branch Potato
White Cake, Marshmallow Icing
Ice Cream
Apple Pie
Coffee, Tea or

APPETIZERS

JUICES:- Tomato Juice Cocktail 15
Pineapple Juice
Grape Juice 20
Half Grapefruit 20
Fruit Cocktail 35
Wine Herring
Cottage Cheese with Chives 20
French Onion Soup 20
Oyster Milk

DAYTON'S BOUNDARY WATERS WILD RICE SOUP

6 tablespoons butter
1 small yellow onion, chopped
½ cup all-purpose flour
4 cups chicken broth
1 cup heavy cream
⅓ cup dry sherry
1 ½ cups cooked wild rice
½ teaspoon white pepper
salt to taste

Melt butter in a medium saucepan. Add onions and cook until soft, about 5 minutes. Stir in flour and cook 1 minute, stirring often. Whisk in broth until smooth. Stir in cream and sherry and heat to a simmer. Add rice, pepper, and salt. Simmer gently 5 minutes, until heated through and slightly thickened. Serve hot. Serves 6.

DAYTON'S MARKET PLACE MARCO POLO SALAD

1 (16-ounce) package pasta
¾ cup olive oil, divided
2 cloves garlic, crushed
½ cup chopped fresh parsley
1–1 ½ tablespoons chopped fresh basil
1 tablespoon chopped fresh oregano
2 teaspoons salt
1 teaspoon coarsely ground pepper
½ cup half-and-half
1 green bell pepper, cut in strips
1 red bell pepper, cut in strips
⅔ pound Jarlsberg cheese, cut in strips
½ cup chopped pecans
¾ cup freshly grated Parmesan

Cook pasta until al dente. Drain and toss with 2 tablespoons olive oil. Stir together remaining olive oil, garlic, parsley, basil, oregano, salt, and pepper. Pour in half-and-half, whisk, and then toss with the pasta. Stir in peppers, cheese, and pecans. Sprinkle with Parmesan. Serve at room temperature. Serves 4 as a main or 6 to 8 as a side.

DAYTON'S KEY LIME PIE

4 large eggs
½ cup plus 2 tablespoons fresh lime juice
1 (14-ounce) can sweetened condensed milk
1 (9- or 10-inch) prebaked pie shell
1 cup heavy cream

Heat oven to 400 degrees. Beat eggs until frothy. Stir in lime juice, then milk, mixing well. Pour into pie shell. Bake until slightly warm, about 7 minutes. Cool to room temperature, then refrigerate several hours before serving. Beat cream until it holds soft peaks. Spread over the top of the pie. Serves 8.

OYSTER STEW A LA GOLDEN RULE

2 cups whole milk
½ cup heavy cream
4 tablespoons butter
1 pint fresh oysters with their liquor (juice)
1 teaspoon salt
freshly ground pepper
butter
oyster crackers

In a saucepan, heat milk and cream until they just start to simmer. In another saucepan, melt butter. Add oysters and their liquor and cook just until the edges begin to curl. Add oysters to the hot milk mixture and heat through, but do not boil. Stir in salt and pepper. To each portion, add a pat of butter. Serve with oyster crackers. Serves 6.

Menus courtesy of the Hennepin County Library.

Grill Dinners Served Monday Evenings Only —
Dayton's Oak Grill
PPETIZERS and RELISHES
ktail 15
Pineapple Juice 15
Fresh Orange Juice 30
Apple Juice 15
lf Grapefruit 20
Wine Herring 25
Stuffed Celery 35
Celery Hearts 35
FRESH SHRIMP COCKTAIL 50

QualiCraft Shoes
Baker's
QualiCraft Shoes
Buttreys
FLAGG BROS.
F. W. WOOLWORTH

10

A Pleasure Dome with Parking: Southdale

It was conceived as an air-conditioned public square, a place where the outdoors were brought inside and merchants could extend Minnesota's "126 ideal shopping days a year."[1]

Seven and a half months before Dayton's president Donald Dayton and Donaldson's president Kenneth Iverson turned the first earth with ceremonial golden shovels at the groundbreaking of the country's first enclosed shopping center, Southdale's architect, Victor Gruen, introduced the project at the opening of the Walker Art Center exhibit "Shopping Centers of Tomorrow" in March 1954. Southdale was meant to be more than a center of shops with a big parking lot, he explained. It was a planned community.

"Southdale is the first center to have a blight-proof community planned around it," Gruen said in an interview with the *Minneapolis Tribune* on March 14. "Park-like buffers" would separate the shopping center from a planned residential area complete with schools and a medical center. "When our cities were built, we didn't plan for cars," Gruen said. "Then cars made possible the mass migration from the city to the suburbs. Now our cars begin to get in our way. We can't park them, we get penalized because of them, we get exasperated."

The best solution, he thought, was to build outlying shopping centers "designed to take advantage of our new mobility" but also to serve as an indoor city center.

Judy Dayton, wife of Ken Dayton, couldn't quite envision that when she attended the groundbreaking ceremony on October 29 that year. It was a cold, windy afternoon, and she could barely hear her brother-in-law Bruce Dayton give the opening remarks. "The wind was blowing and the paper was fluttering. It was hard to hear what Bruce was saying," she said in a 2013 interview. "It was a field as far as the eye could see, and I was standing there thinking, 'I can't imagine shopping here.'"

Yet two years later, when the grand opening festivities were held, some seventy-five thousand

OPPOSITE: Interior of Southdale mall, 1964. *Minnesota Historical Society Collections.* THIS PAGE: Southdale architects Victor Gruen, R. L. Baumfield, and Herman Guttman. *Edina Historical Society.*

DOING THE NUMBERS

Dayton's Southdale Center issued the following stats after its grand opening in October 1956:

$20 Million
The cost of Southdale's construction, outside and inside

$1.25 Million
The cost of road improvements around the shopping center

2,000+
The number of men and women who will be employed at Southdale

800,000
The square footage of the mall in 1956

195,023
The square footage of Dayton's Southdale store

140,000
The square footage of Donaldson's Southdale store

7,000
The number of parking spaces available at the mall

40,000
The cubic yards of concrete poured at Southdale

1 Million
The cubic yards of dirt moved to build the center

visitors came. The event was covered by *Life, Fortune, Time, Women's Wear Daily,* the *New York Times, Business Week,* and *Newsweek. Time* called the mall a "pleasure-dome with parking."

The mall opened with fifty stores, and within the first year, seventy-two spots were filled, including a thirty-thousand-square-foot Red Owl grocery store.

The Dayton brothers began exploring the company's expansion to the suburbs shortly after Northgate shopping mall opened outside of Seattle in 1950. They hired Seattle real estate consultant Lawrence P. Smith, who was working with Austrian architect Victor Gruen on J. L. Hudson's Northland shopping center near Detroit. After several months of market analysis, Smith convinced the Daytons they should develop in the suburbs. For a location, he recommended a cornfield in the area of what is now Sixty-Sixth Street and France Avenue in Edina, which was being eyed for development by a number of concerns. The Daytons bought five hundred acres and hired Gruen and Associates to plan the new project. Gruen convinced them that an enclosed climate-controlled shopping mall would be a better way to draw customers.[2]

In July 1952, the Dayton Company announced its plans for the first indoor shopping mall.

The new mall was meant to be a high-end experience when it opened on October 8, 1956. The Garden Court of Perpetual Spring was a large open space in the center that featured a goldfish pond, an aviary, sculptures and art, a sidewalk

OPPOSITE, TOP: Aerial view of Southdale during construction. *Edina Historical Society.* BOTTOM: Aerial view of the new Southdale shopping center in Edina, August 1956. Minneapolis Star Journal Tribune *photo, Minnesota Historical Society Collections.* THIS PAGE, TOP: Southdale parking lot, 1956. LEFT: Dayton's and Red Owl at Southdale, 1964. *Both Minnesota Historical Society Collections.*

Postcard view of the Southdale interior. *Minnesota Historical Society Collections.*

café, and a performance stage. Balls, banquets, fine art exhibits, and antique shows were held there. The mall catered to families by including play areas, a small zoo in the basement, and a child-care area where parents could drop off their children while they shopped.

Seven well-known contemporary artists were commissioned to create pieces for the new shopping center. Italian-born Harry Bertoia, a renowned abstract sculptor, created the mall's centerpiece, a forty-five-foot steel sculpture titled *Golden Trees.* California artist Joseph Young created two curved mosaic murals of Byzantine glass for the exterior walls of a Garden Court kiosk. New York sculptor Louise Kruger created a laminated walnut carving of two two-and-a-half-foot boys on eight-foot stilts and placed them in a planter in the lower level of the center court.

The rest of the sculptures were made by Minneapolis artists. Dorothy Berge created *Unicycle,* a twelve-foot sculpture of copper and bronze depicting three clowns on a unicycle. Daniel Solerlin's nonobjective copper-and-bronze sculpture was fastened to the retaining wall at the entrance to Dayton's. Bernard Arnest painted a five-foot-by-ten-foot mural for the Southdale branch of the First National Bank. Dayton's restaurant, which was called Valley View Room at the time, held the six-by-forty-one-foot mural by John Anderson.

Southdale's first anniversary was celebrated in the *Minneapolis Sunday Tribune* with a special

section on October 13, 1957. "Thriving Southdale Plans for Future on First Birthday," read a headline. More stores opened that first year, including a knit shop, a cafeteria, an airline ticket office, an electronics store, and a shoe repair shop. Southdale management reported that the primary trade area for the mall had far exceeded the five-mile-radius defined by market analysts the year before.

"Over five million people have passed through the center during its first year of operation," Southdale president Bruce Dayton reported in the *Tribune*. "One of the center's restaurants started a guest register and within a month collected signatures from 34 states, Washington, D.C., three Canadian provinces, Hawaii, Alaska, England and Formosa."

Southdale was not only the first climate-controlled indoor mall, it was also the first mall in which the owners brought in a chief competitor, in this case Donaldson's, as one of its anchor stores. "Our studies indicated clearly that a successful shopping center must include a strong community of competing business neighbors," said Bruce Dayton in the *Minneapolis Tribune* on Sunday, October 6, 1956. "This increases the drawing power greatly and allows comparative shopping."

ABOVE LEFT: Sculptor Dorothy Berge, one of seven artists who created work for the new mall, working on her *Unicycle* piece. ABOVE: Aviary in the Garden Court of Perpetual Spring. *Both Edina Historical Society.*

Gruen was involved in the design of the Daytons' subsequent suburban shopping centers—Brookdale in Brooklyn Center (1966), Rosedale in Roseville (1969), and Ridgedale in Minnetonka (1974)—as well as the new downtown St. Paul store in 1963.

The success of Southdale and other malls designed by Gruen launched a wave of covered malls in the country. More than eight thousand new shopping malls opened in the United States between 1960 and 1970. Initially, Gruen thought he had found the formula for conquering urban sprawl, but in the end, he found he'd contributed to it, according to Thomas Fisher, director of the Minnesota Design Center and Dayton Hudson Chair in Urban Design at the University of Minnesota.[3]

ABOVE: Postcard view of Southdale's sidewalk café. OPPOSITE, CLOCKWISE FROM TOP LEFT: Donaldson's shoppers on Southdale's opening day, October 1956. TV and radio department at Dayton's in Southdale, 1958. J. B. Hudson store at Southdale, 1957. *All Minnesota Historical Society Collections.* View of the garden court. *Edina Historical Society.*

The architect envisioned shopping centers as the core of more vibrant communities with houses, apartments, schools, and offices surrounding them. He was disappointed that his ideas weren't fully embraced, and in 1964, he refocused his architectural practice on revitalizing downtowns through the creation of pedestrian malls.

By the end of the 1970s, Dayton's had left the mall business. In 1978, the company sold Southdale and eight other malls to the Equitable Life Assurance Society of the United States for $305 million. By then, JCPenney and Sears had become the third and fourth anchor tenants at Southdale.

The mall's new owners launched an expansion and updating project in 1988, and in 1990 the Dayton's store was gutted and a new 358,000-square-foot Dayton's opened. One year later, fifty new specialty stores and a food court opened in the former Dayton's space. Carson Pirie Scott (in the former Donaldson's space) and JCPenney held grand openings of their newly remodeled stores as well. Carson Pirie Scott remained at the mall for four years, until Mervyn's of California took its place in one of the anchor spots.

Southdale took a major hit in 1992, when the Mall of America opened in Bloomington, just a ten-minute drive to the east. Concordia Properties bought the Southdale mall in 1997, and by 2000, management was making changes to attract younger shoppers, such as adding clothing stores like Abercrombie & Fitch and home-décor stores like Crate & Barrel. The mall's efforts to bring in more restaurants were helped when Edina voters passed an ordinance that year to allow mall restaurants to serve alcohol. Still, by 2007, the old Mervyn's space remained vacant, as did several spaces in the food court and other storefronts.

TV·RADIOS
TV·RADIOS
RECORDS
261-055

J.B. Hudson Co.

TOP, LEFT TO RIGHT: Boat show at Southdale, 1963. Rocket display at Southdale, 1960s. Donaldson's at Southdale, 1974. *All Edina Historical Society.* RIGHT: Architect's sketch of Brookdale mall, 1964. *Minnesota Historical Society Collections.*

Simon Property Group purchased Southdale in 2011 with the goal of giving the fading mall a turnaround. Herberger's moved in as an anchor tenant that year. The mall celebrated its sixtieth anniversary in 2016. A year later, JCPenney moved out, and in 2018 Herberger's closed.

Americans' move to online shopping in the new millennium brought tough times for many malls throughout the country. Some mall owners have added attractions such as indoor ice skating rinks or bowling alleys to bring people back into the shopping centers. In 2018, Simon Property Group listed more than 120 specialty stores as tenants at Southdale, along with an AMC theater complex, several restaurants, a Hennepin County service center, and a dance studio. Plans were in the works for the construction of a hotel, a fitness center in the former JCPenney space, apartments, and more.

You can still catch a small taste of Southdale's beginnings in the center court of the mall: Bertoia's *Golden Trees* is the one sculpture still on display from the opening of the first indoor mall in America in 1956.

Buttreys
SPACE SHIP
ROUND TRIP to THE MOON

BROOKDALE SHOPPING CENTER
MINNEAPOLIS, MINNESOTA

BLAME IT ON THE ARCHITECTS

Just weeks after Southdale opened to national fanfare and praise, renowned architect Frank Lloyd Wright shared some sharp criticisms of the mall and of the city. During his talk to a gathering of 2,500 at the annual meeting of the Citizens League of Minneapolis and Hennepin County on November 27, 1957, the eighty-seven-year-old champion of American modernist architecture offered his thoughts on Minneapolis ("a frantic jungle of incongruity"), the new Prudential Insurance building overlooking Brownie Lake in the city's Bryn Mawr neighborhood ("an insurance company that will go into a park and deliberately desecrate it"), the automobile ("what a selfish, immobile thing"), and Southdale. Wright described the new mall as a "flight from Egypt"—an attempt to liberate shoppers from the congestion of downtown, but "planned just the way it is downtown." He was quoted in the *Minneapolis Tribune:* "Is that moral? I don't think it is." The blame for all this, he said, lies with architects.

Wright had his own critics following his remarks. "He insulted our intelligence," Ralph Rapson, dean of the University of Minnesota School of Architecture, told the *Tribune*. "We can all stand criticism, but I maintain we're doing a much better job in the schools than he is at Taliesin, Ariz. I think he's full of hot air."

William Dahl, a representative for Victor Gruen and Associates, the designers of Southdale, had this to say: "No comment."

Twelve years later, Rapson, who was serving as vice chairman of the Minneapolis Committee on Urban Environment in 1969, had a new perspective on suburban design. The Minneapolis suburban area was "a cancerous growth that goes on and on because some farmer or developer decides he can get more money," he told *Minneapolis Star* reporter Betty Wilson in a December 25 article titled "Arts Leaders Say Area Is a Mess." The suburban scene at that time was full of "cruddy architecture" and "chaos, confusion and bastardization of our natural resources," Rapson said.[4]

Southdale had deteriorated into "a conglomerate of stuff," and Rapson was advocating for a strong metropolitan planning agency with power to decide on and enforce good integrated planning. "Dayton's doesn't put up shopping centers foolishly," Rapson said, "but they put them up from a Dayton's point of view, not a total community point of view and I don't think they should be allowed to do this."

Insisting that good design doesn't cost any more money than bad design, Rapson said, "I wish I could get everybody mad about our environment. What we have done here is just nothing short of catastrophic."

A few years later, Rapson got his wish when the Minnesota Legislature passed the Metropolitan Land Planning Act of 1976, which directed the Metropolitan Council—an agency founded in 1967 to deal with area wastewater and transportation issues—to prepare a long-range development plan for the region every ten years. The law also requires all local governments to adopt their own comprehensive plans consistent with the regional plans.

Frank Lloyd Wright visits Southdale, November 27, 1956. Star Tribune *photo, Minnesota Historical Society Collections.*

EPILOGUE

The End, or Maybe Not

Dolores DeFore has seen the retail landscape around the country undergo many changes since she began working at the Dayton's hat counter in the 1940s. At the time, downtown Minneapolis was full of department stores, dime stores, small shops, and restaurants. It was a lively retail scene.

Now, nearly seventy years later and many years into retirement, DeFore lives in a condominium just over a mile from Nicollet Avenue, where she spent her retail career, first at Dayton's and then as president and co-owner of Harold. If she wants to shop, she drives to a suburban mall to do it, or goes online, because there are no department stores and few women's clothing shops downtown.

"Shopping is entirely different today," DeFore said. "There are no salespeople in the large suburban stores. Years ago, if you saw somebody even pick up a dress, you would say, 'Can I put you in a fitting room?' We all wanted to sell. Now, [the clerks] are all behind the cash register. They don't look at the clothes. They don't know if it's the right size, if the colors match, if there's a tear in it. The service is totally gone." And for many city centers and suburban malls, so are the stores.

The golden age of shopping at landmark department stores has passed, and now the suburban shopping malls that rose up in the 1950s and 1960s are having their own existential crises as national chains move out and storefronts stand empty.

What does a brick-and-mortar retail business need to survive?

Service is key, said Barbara Armajani, who worked under DeFore early in her career at Dayton's and, like DeFore, was promoted into management positions that, for Armajani, led her to serve as CEO of J. B. Hudson Jewelers and Powers before starting her own businesses.

A successful retail business today is upscale, forward-looking, highly serviced by people who know what they are selling, and mindful of how to compete with the internet, she said.

Armajani opened her gift and home décor store, Ampersand, in the Edina shopping district at Fiftieth Street and France Avenue in 1995 and then in 2004 moved to the Galleria, the upscale Edina shopping mall across the street from Southdale. In addition to its brick-and-mortar location, Ampersand has a thriving online bridal registry. "We couldn't have that registry if not for the internet," she said.

In 1981, while serving as president and CEO of Powers department stores, Armajani predicted that retailing would become a mix of budget stores and high-end specialty stores. What she didn't put into that equation nearly forty years ago was the internet.

OPPOSITE: Ladies' hats at Dayton's, circa 1949. *Minnesota Historical Society Collections.*

Thank You

Thank You

Thank You

ACKNOWLEDGMENTS

Writing this book has been one big shopping trip, and I have a long list of helpful people who guided me along the way. Thanks to everyone who shared their stories of working, shopping, and playing at these Minnesota department stores.

I am especially grateful to Dolores DeFore for taking so much time to talk with me and to write about the start of her career at the Dayton's hat bar in the late 1940s. Dolores also introduced me to her longtime friend and colleague Barbara Armajani, who spent a Saturday morning talking with me about her retail career. Thanks, Barbara, for sharing your insights.

The folks who worked on the eighth-floor shows at Dayton's (and Marshall Field's and Macy's) deserve standing ovations for all they brought to Minnesota. Thanks, Jack Barkla, for letting me into your world (and putting me up to this), and thanks to Dan Mackerman, Todd Knaeble, Stewart Widdess, Lyle Jackson, Dale Bachman, Sue Hartley, and all the artists, craftspeople, and idea people I didn't talk to, for sharing your work in this book and with everyone who walked through that storied auditorium for more than half a century. To all of you who worked there, thank you!

Thanks to Sarah Massey, Attila Ray Dabasi, Richard Stryker, Mary Scanlon, Jim Crego, Vanessa Green, Catherine Dehdashti, Rae MacDonough, sisters Norene Stovall and Jill Kyvig, Sarah Gorham, Mary Liebelt Jensen, Mike Barich, Al Boyce Sr. and Al Boyce Jr., Nita Anderson, and Christine Johnson for your anecdotes, photos, and ephemera from your days growing up, shopping, and working in the Twin Cities stores. Thanks to writer Jim Walsh for giving us a glimpse of a week in the life of a Dayton's Santa Claus. To Valerie Atkinson, thank you for sharing your work and your story about being an artist in the advertising department at Powers in the 1960s.

Thanks to Lynne Hartert, who opened a back room at the former Choate's in Winona on a blustery winter morning and allowed me to spend a couple of hours going through a few piles of photos. To Bill and Judy Morgan, Peter Fandel, Jett Heckler, and Jeanne Malley, it was a pleasure meeting you and learning about Fandel's in St. Cloud (and thanks for lunch, Peter).

If you haven't visited the fourth floor of the downtown Minneapolis branch of the Hennepin County Library, do it. The librarians in the Minneapolis History Collection and Special Collections can find almost anything you want to know about Minneapolis's past. They found many things for me and got to know me well. (Thank you, Bailey Diers and company!) Thank you Eunice Haugen and Ellen Skoro at the Goldstein Museum of Design.

To the folks at the Minnesota Historical Society's Gale Family Library and the Minnesota Historical Society Press, thank you, too. I am grateful for the guidance and patience of my editor, Josh Leventhal; for the sharp eyes of managing editor Shannon Pennefeather; for the delightful layouts of designer Adam Demers; and for the expert hand of copyeditor Betty Christiansen, who saved me from a few blunders. Copyeditors are often the unsung heroes in the book-publishing world. You are my hero, Betty.

Last, thanks to my neighbor Alice Wagner-Hemstad for showing up with Girl Scout cookies at just the right time, and to Don Stryker for bringing home all that takeout food over the year it took me to complete this project.

NOTES

INTRODUCTION

1. Hy Berman, quoted in an interview on Twin Cities Public Television's *Almanac*, October 22, 1999, mnvideovault.org.

CHAPTER 1

1. Larry Batson, *Minneapolis Star and Tribune,* July 15, 1982, 1C.
2. "The Story of a Store," *Minneapolis Sunday Tribune,* December 31, 1911, 5.
3. "New Donaldson Open Today," *Minneapolis Star,* November 10, 1924, 5.
4. Ben Cohen, "Departure of Carson's Isn't Leaving Twin Cities Shoppers Speechless," *Star Tribune,* January 13, 1995, 2D.

CHAPTER 2

1. Charles McFadden, "Powers May Stay No. 3, but It Plans to Grow," *Minneapolis Tribune,* June 18, 1972, 11C.

CHAPTER 3

1. Agnes Taaffe, "Elizabeth Quinlan Honored by Women Leaders at Luncheon," *Minneapolis Star,* December 17, 1940.
2. Taaffe, "Elizabeth Quinlan Honored."
3. "Thousands Fill New Store of Young-Quinlan," *Minneapolis Morning Tribune,* June 15, 1926, 1.
4. Hope Ridings Miller, "Elizabeth Quinlan's Career Stirs Admiration in the East," *Washington Post,* March 14, 1937.

CHAPTER 4

1. Bruce B. Dayton with Ellen B. Green, *George Draper Dayton: A Man of Parts* (Minneapolis: privately printed, 1997), 58.
2. Dayton with Green, *George Draper Dayton,* 67.
3. Barbara Flanagan, "Life Is Dedicated to Fashion," *Minneapolis Sunday Tribune,* March 1, 1964, 72.
4. Martin Merrick, "Dayton's Aide Tells Retailers to 'Swing Well With the Young,'" *Minneapolis Star,* October 11, 1966, 51.
5. Jim Klobuchar, "One of His Illusions Crashes at Dayton's," *Minneapolis Star,* January 31, 1979, 17.

CHAPTER 5

1. Advertisement, *Minneapolis Sunday Tribune,* November 24, 1963, 29.
2. "Problems Bloom Along with Exotic Blossoms," *Minneapolis Morning Tribune,* March 11, 1960, 12.

CHAPTER 6

1. Timothy Blodgett, "Store Had Start to 70 Years Ago," *Minneapolis Star,* November 28, 1958, 10A.
2. "Jacob Dittenhofer, Golden Rule Founder, Returns from Annual 3-Month Southern Vacation Sojourn," *Pioneer Press,* April 18, 1926.
3. "Golden Rule Completes Store Modernizing Plan," *St. Paul Dispatch,* March 26, 1938.
4. "St. Paul's Big New Store," *Minneapolis Journal,* February 27, 1902, 7.
5. Advertisement, *Minneapolis Journal,* October 1, 1902, 10.

CHAPTER 7

1. "H. Choate & Co. Success From Very Start in '61," *Winona Daily News,* September 19, 1955, 18.
2. "Downtown Malls Sprucing Up Cities, Business Prospects, Too," *Minneapolis Tribune,* January 14, 1973, 13C.
3. "Brainerd Buildings and Parks," Crow Wing County Historical Society, www.crowwinghistory.org/buildings.html#OBRIENDEPARTMENTSTORE.

CHAPTER 8

1. Advertisement, *Sunday Tribune,* December 11, 1892, 9.
2. Herb Paul, "Granddaddy of Dayton Toy Windows Retires," *Minneapolis Star,* February 3, 1951, 3.
3. Jim Shoop, "2 Santas Who Tried to Discourage Toy Guns Lose Jobs in St. Paul," *Minneapolis Star,* December 15, 1972, 1.

CHAPTER 9

1. Advertisement, *Minneapolis Tribune,* November 7, 1948, 9.

CHAPTER 10

1. Sterling Soderlind, "Architect Says Southdale Planned as 'Cultural Center' for Its Patrons," *Minneapolis Sunday Tribune,* March 14, 1954, 29.
2. Bruce B. Dayton with Ellen B. Green, *The Birth of Target* (Minneapolis, MN: privately printed, 2008), 30.
3. Kristal Leebrick, *Dayton's: A Twin Cities Institution* (Charleston, SC: History Press, 2013), 75.
4. Betty Wilson, "Arts Leaders Say Area Is a Mess," *Minneapolis Star,* December 25, 1969, 25.

BIBLIOGRAPHY

Bergerson, Roger. *Winging It at a Country Crossroads: The Ups and Downs of Minnesota's First Real Airport: Snelling and Larpenteur, Rose Township 1919–1930.* St. Paul, MN: Bergerson & Cunningham, 2008.

Bon, Leila Fraser. *The First Fifty Years, 1894–1944.* Minneapolis: The Young-Quinlan Company, 1944.

Dayton, Bruce B., with Ellen B. Green. *The Birth of Target.* Minneapolis: Privately printed, 2008.

———. *George Draper Dayton, A Man of Parts.* Minneapolis: Privately printed, 1997.

Dayton Hudson Corporation. *Someone's in the Kitchen with Dayton's Marshall Field's Hudson's.* Minneapolis: Dayton Hudson Corporation, 1992.

Firestone, Mary. *Dayton's Department Store.* Chicago: Arcadia Publishing, 2007.

Gladwell, Malcolm. "The Terrazzo Jungle." *The New Yorker* (March 2004).

"The Goldstein Presents: Fashion Lives, Fashion Lives." *Minneapolis St. Paul Magazine* (August 2000).

Gray, James. *You Can Get It At Dayton's.* Minneapolis: Privately published, 1962.

Koutsky, Kathryn Strand, and Linda Koutsky. *Minnesota Eats Out: An Illustrated History.* St. Paul: Minnesota Historical Society Press, 2003.

Leebrick, Kristal. *Dayton's: A Twin Cities Institution.* Charleston, SC: The History Press, 2013.

Marling, Karal Ann. *Merry Christmas! Celebrating America's Greatest Holiday.* Cambridge, MA: Harvard University Press, 2001.

Millett, Larry. *Lost Twin Cities.* St. Paul: Minnesota Historical Society Press, 1992.

Pitrone, Jean Maddern. *Hudson's: Hub of America's Heartland.* West Bloomfield, MI: Altwerger and Mandel Publishing Company, 1991.

Rowley, Laura. *On Target: How the World's Hottest Retailer Hit a Bull's-Eye.* Hoboken, NJ: John Wiley & Sons Inc., 2003.

Twyman, Robert W. *History of Marshall Field & Co., 1852–1906.* Philadelphia: University of Pennsylvania Press, 1954.

Whitaker, Jan. *Service and Style: How the American Department Store Fashioned the Middle Class.* New York: St. Martin's Press, 2006.

INDEX